Fat-Tailed and Skewed Asset Return Distributions

THE FRANK J. FABOZZI SERIES

Fat-Tailed and Skewed Asset Return Distributions

Implications for Risk Management, Portfolio Selection, and Option Pricing

SVETLOZAR T. RACHEV

CHRISTIAN MENN

FRANK J. FABOZZI

WILEY

John Wiley & Sons, Inc.

Copyright © 2005 by John Wiley & Sons, Inc. All rights reserved

Published by John Wiley & Sons, Inc., Hoboken, New Jersey
Published simultaneously in Canada

No part of this publication may be reproduced, stored in a retrieval system, or transmitted in any form or by any means, electronic, mechanical, photocopying, recording, scanning, or otherwise, except as permitted under Section 107 or 108 of the 1976 United States Copyright Act, without either the prior written permission of the Publisher, or authorization through payment of the appropriate per-copy fee to the Copyright Clearance Center, Inc., 222 Rosewood Drive, Danvers, MA 01923, (978) 750-8400, fax (978) 750-4470, or on the web at www.copyright.com. Requests to the Publisher for permission should be addressed to the Permissions Department, John Wiley & Sons, Inc., 111 River Street, Hoboken, NJ 07030, (201) 748-6011, fax (201) 748-6008, or online at http://www.wiley.com/go/permissions.

Limit of Liability/Disclaimer of Warranty: While the publisher and author have used their best efforts in preparing this book, they make no representations or warranties with respect to the accuracy or completeness of the contents of this book and specifically disclaim any implied warranties of merchantability or fitness for a particular purpose. No warranty may be created or extended by sales representatives or written sales materials. The advice and strategies contained herein may not be suitable for your situation. You should consult with a professional where appropriate. Neither the publisher nor author shall be liable for any loss of profit or any other commercial damages, including but not limited to special, incidental, consequential, or other damages.

For general information on our other products and services or for technical support, please contact our Customer Care Department within the United States at (800) 762-2974, outside the United States at (317) 572-3993 or fax (317) 572-4002.

Wiley also publishes its books in a variety of electronic formats. Some content that appears in print may not be available in electronic books. For more information about Wiley products, visit our web site at www.wiley.com.

ISBN-13 978-0-471-71886-4
ISBN-10 0-471-71886-6

10 9 8 7 6 5 4 3 2 1

Contents

Preface

The theory and practice of finance draws heavily on probability theory. All MBA programs prepare finance majors for their career in the profession by requiring one generalist course in probability theory and statistics attended by all business majors. While several probability distributions are covered in the course, the primary focus is on the normal or Gaussian distribution.

Students find it easy to understand and apply the normal distribution: Give them the expected value and standard deviation and probability statements about outcomes can be easily made. Moreover, even if a random variable of interest is not normally distribution, students are told that a theorem in statistics called the *Central Limit Theorem* proves that under certain conditions the sum of independent random variables will be asymptotically normally distributed. Loosely speaking, this means that as the number of random variables are summed, the sum will approach a normal distribution.

Armed with this rudimentary knowledge of probability theory, finance students march into their elective courses in finance that introduce them to the quantitative measures of risk (the standard deviation) and the quantitative inputs needed to implement modern portfolio theory (the expected value or mean and the standard deviation). In listing assumptions for most theories of finance, the first assumption on the list is often: "Assume asset returns are normally distributed." The problem, however, is that empirical evidence does not support the assumption that many important variables in finance follow a normal distribution. The application of the Central Limit Theorem to such instances is often inappropriate because the conditions necessary for its application are not satisfied.

And this brings us to the purpose of this book. Our purpose is fourfold. First, we explain alternative probability distributions to the normal distributions for describing asset returns as well as defaults. We focus on the stable Paretian (or alpha stable) distribution because of the strong support for that distribution that dates back four decades to the seminal work of Benoit Mandelbrot. Second, we explain how to estimate distributions. Third, we present empirical evidence rejecting the hypothesis that returns for stocks and bonds are normally distributed and instead show that they exhibit fat tails and skewness. Finally, we explain the implications of fat tails and skewness to portfolio selection, risk management, and option pricing.

We must admit that our intent at the outset was to provide a "non-technical" treatment of the topic. However, we could not do so. Rather, we believe that we have provided a less technical treatment than is provided in the many excellent books and scholarly articles that deal with probability and statistics applied to finance and risk management. The book is not simple reading. It must be studied to appreciate the pitfalls that result from the application of the normal distribution to real-world financial problems.

Acknowledgments

We thank the following individuals with whom we have worked with on research papers for allowing us to use portions of that research in various writings in this book:

Almira Biglova
Anna Chernobai
Dylan D'Souza
Michael Grebeck
Teo Jašić
Irina Khindanova
Douglas Martin
Stefan Mittnik
Sergio Ortobelli
Borjana Racheva-Iotova
Gennady Samorodnitsky
Eduardo Schwartz
Stoyan Stoyanov
Yesim Tokat

Svetlozar Rachev's research was supported by grants from Division of Mathematical, Life and Physical Sciences, College of Letters and Science, University of California, Santa Barbara and the Deutschen Forschungsgemeinschaft.

Christian Menn gratefully acknowledges research support received by the German Academic Exchange Service (Deutsche Akademische Austausch Dienst, DAAD).

Frank Fabozzi received various forms of assistance from the International Center for Finance at Yale University

We thank Megan Orem for her skillful typesetting of this book.

Svetlozar T. Rachev
Christian Menn
Frank J. Fabozzi

About the Authors

Professor Dr. Svetlozar T. (Zari) Rachev is Chair-Professor at the University of Karlsruhe in the School of Economics and Business Engineering and Professor Emeritus at the University of California, Santa Barbara in the Department of Statistics and Applied Probability. He completed his PhD. in 1979 from Moscow State University and his Doctor of Science Degree in 1986 from the Steklov Mathematical Institute in Moscow. He has published six monographs and more than 250 research articles. His research areas include mathematical and empirical finance, econometrics, probability, and statistics. He is a Fellow of the Institute of Mathematical Statistics, Elected Member of the International Statistical Institute, Foreign Member of the Russian Academy of Natural Science, and holds an honorary doctorate degree from St. Petersburg Technical University. Professor Rachev is cofounder of Bravo Risk Management Group, specializing in financial risk-management software. Bravo Group was recently acquired by FinAnalytica for which he currently serves as Chief-Scientist.

Dr. Christian Menn is Hochschulassistent at the Chair of Statistics, Econometrics and Mathematical Finance at the University of Karlsruhe. Currently, he is Visiting Scientist at the School of Operations Research and Industrial Engineering at Cornell University as a post-doctorate fellow. In 1998, he received a degree in mathematics (Maîtrise des mathématiques) from the University J. Fourier in Grenoble, France and in 2000 a degree in mathematics (Diplom in Wirtschaftsmathematik) from the University of Karlsruhe, Germany. Recently, Christian earned his doctorate in economics at the University of Karlsruhe, Germany.

Dr. Frank J. Fabozzi, CFA, CPA is the Frederick Frank Adjunct Professor of Finance in the School of Management at Yale University. Prior to joining the Yale faculty, he was a Visiting Professor of Finance in the Sloan School at MIT. Professor Fabozzi is a Fellow of the International Center for Finance at Yale University and the editor of the *Journal of Portfolio Management*. He earned a doctorate in economics from the City University of New York in 1972. In 1994 he received an honorary doctorate of Humane Letters from Nova Southeastern University and in 2002 was inducted into the Fixed Income Analysts Society's Hall of Fame.

CHAPTER 1

Introduction

Most of the concepts in theoretical and empirical finance that have been developed over the last 50 years rest upon the assumption that the return or price distribution for financial assets follows a normal distribution. Yet, with rare exception, studies that have investigated the validity of this assumption since the 1960s fail to find support for the normal distribution—or *Gaussian* distribution as it is also called. Moreover, there is ample empirical evidence that many, if not most, financial return series are heavy-tailed and possibly skewed.

The "tails" of the distribution are where the extreme values occur. Empirical distributions for stock prices and returns have found that the extreme values are more likely than would be predicted by the normal distribution. This means that, between periods where the market exhibits relatively modest changes in prices and returns, there will be periods where there are changes that, are much higher (i.e., crashes and booms) than predicted by the normal distribution. This is not only of concern to financial theorists, but also to practitioners who are, in view of the frequency of sharp market down turns in the equity markets, troubled by the "... compelling evidence that something is rotten in the foundation of the statistical edifice ..." used, for example, to produce probability estimates for financial risk assessment.[1] Heavy or fat tails can help explain larger price fluctuations for stocks over short time periods than can be explained by changes in fundamental economic variables as observed by Robert Shiller (1981).

Mathematical models of the stock market developed through the joint efforts of economists and physicists have provided support for price and return distributions with heavy tails. This has been done by

---

[1] Hope 1999, p. 16.

modeling the interaction of market agents.[2] While these mathematical models by their nature are a gross simplification of real-world financial markets, they provide sufficient structure to analyze return distributions. Computer simulations of these models have been found to generate fat tails and other statistical characteristics that have been observed in real-world financial markets.

The first fundamental attack on the assumption that price or return distribution are not normally distributed was in the 1960s by Benoit Mandelbrot (1963). He strongly rejected normality as a distributional model for asset returns. Examining various time series on commodity returns and interest rates, Mandlebrot conjectured that financial returns are more appropriately described by a nonnormal stable distribution. To distinguish between Gaussian and non-Gaussian stable distributions, the latter are often referred to as "stable Paretian" distributions[3] or "Lévy stable" distributions.[4] His early investigations on asset returns were carried further by Eugene Fama (1965a, 1965b), among others, and led to a consolidation of the hypothesis that asset returns can be better described as a stable Paretian distribution.

There was obviously considerable concern in the finance profession by the findings of Mandelbrot and Fama. Shortly after the publication of the Mandelbrot paper, Paul Cootner (1964) expressed his concern regarding the implications of those findings for the statistical tests that had been published in prominent scholarly journals in economics and finance. He warned that:

> Almost without exception, past econometric work is meaningless. Surely, before consigning centuries of work to the ash pile, we should like to have some assurance that all our work is truly useless. If we have permitted ourselves to be fooled for as long as this

---

[2] Probably the most well-known model is the Santa Fe Stock Market Model (see Arthur et al., 1997). There are others. Bak, Paczuski, and Shubik (1996) and Lux (1999) analyze the interaction between two categories of market agents: "rational investors" and "noise traders." Rational agents act on fundamental information in order to analyze risk-return opportunities and then act to optimize their utility function. "Noise" traders are market agents whose behavior is governed only by their analysis of market dynamics. Their choice at which to transact (buy or sell) may imitate the choice of other market agents. Cont and Bouchaud (2000) develop a model based on herding or crowd behavior that has been observed in financial markets.

[3] The reason for this name is to emphasize the fact that the tails of the non-Gaussian stable distribution have Pareto power-type decay.

[4] This name honors Paul Lévy for his seminal work introducing and characterizing the class of non-Gaussian stable distributions.

into believing that the Gaussian assumption is a workable one, is it not possible that the Paretian revolution is similarly illusory? (Cootner 1964, 337)

While that evidence has been supplied in numerous studies, the "normality" assumption remains the cornerstone of many leading theories used in finance.

There was also concern at a theoretical level because one feature of the stable Paretian distribution is that there is an *infinite* variance. The variance of a return distribution for a highly diversified portfolio was just beginning to be accepted as the appropriate measure of risk in finance. It was one of the only two parameters needed in the theory of portfolio selection that had been developed by Harry Markowitz (1952, 1959). Moreover, the key feature of the framework developed by Markowitz, commonly referred to as "mean-variance analysis," is the notion of how to diversification benefits investors. The underlying principle is that the risk (as measured by the variance) of a portfolio of returns consisting of stocks whose returns did not have perfect positive correlation would be less than the weighted average of the risk of the individual stocks comprising the portfolio. This quantification of diversification became known as "Markowitz diversification."

Fama (1965c) revisited the notion of diversification if stock returns followed a stable Paretian distribution rather than a normal distribution. As we will see in Chapter 7, there are four parameters that describe a stable Paretian distribution. One of those parameters, the characteristic exponent of the distribution (also called the "tail index"), is critical in analyzing the benefits of diversification—reducing the dispersion of stock returns as the number of holdings increases. Fama derived the boundaries for the parameter so that an increase in the number of holdings in a portfolio provides the benefit of diversification. However, if the parameter was not within the narrow range he derived, increasing holdings could result in a greater dispersion of stock returns![5]

As one would expect in the development of ideas in any field, defendants of the prevailing theories went on the offensive. One attack on the stable Paretian distribution was that there is no closed-form solution to obtain the necessary information about the distribution—probability density, distribution functions, and quantile, concepts of a probability distribution that we will describe in Chapter 3. While this may have been a valid criticism at one time, advances in computational finance make it fairly straightforward to fit observed returns to determine the parameters of a stable Paretian distribution. Thus, this criticism is no longer valid.

---

[5] For a more general derivation, see Chapter 9 in Rachev and Mittnik (2000).

The major attack in the 1970s and 1980s centered around the claim that while the empirical evidence does not support the normal distribution, it is also not consistent with the stable Paretian distribution. For example, it was observed that asset return distributions are not as heavy tailed as the stable Paretian distribution would predict and furthermore they did not remain constant under temporal aggregation.[6] That is, while there was no disagreement that the distribution of returns for assets were found to have heavier tails relative to the normal distribution, it was thinner than a stable Paretian distribution. Studies that came to such conclusions were typically based on a statistical test of the tail of the empirical distributions.[7] However, the test that has been typically used to estimate the tails is highly unreliable for testing whether a distribution follows a stable Paretian distribution because sample sizes in excess of 100,000 are required to obtain reasonably accurate estimates. In other words, even if we were generating a small sample of a true stable Paretian distribution and then estimate the tail thickness with the estimator that has been used, we would most probably generate tail thickness estimates which contradict the stable assumption. There are other technical problems with these studies.[8]

Partly in response to these empirical "inconsistencies," various alternatives to the stable Paretian distribution that had a finite variance were proposed in the literature. One alternative is the Student-t distribution, a distribution that under certain conditions not only has a finite variance[9] but also allows for tails with more observations than the normal distribution. Battberg and Gonedes (1974) presented evidence supporting the Student t-distribution. Yet another distribution that has been proposed is a finite mixture of normal distributions. Kon (1984) found that this alternative explains daily returns for stocks better than the Student-t distribution.

A major drawback of all these alternative models is their lack of stability. As has been stressed by Mandelbrot and argued by Rachev and Mittnik (2000), among others, the stability property is highly desirable for asset returns. This is particularly evident in the context of portfolio analysis and risk management. Only for stable (which includes the Gaussian as a special case) distributed returns of independent assets does one obtain the property that the linear combination of the returns (portfolio returns) follow again a stable distribution. The independence assumption

---

[6] See Officer (1972), Akgiray and Booth (1988), and Akgiray and Lamoureux (1989).
[7] The procedure for estimating the tail that has been used is the Hill estimator.
[8] See Rachev and Mittnik (2000).
[9] Specifically, the degrees of freedom must be greater than 2. With 2 degrees of freedom or less, a Student-t distribution has infinite variance as well.

of the returns can be replaced by assuming that the returns are jointly stable distributed (similar to the multivariate Gaussian case). Then again any portfolio return has a stable distribution, while the returns of the assets in the portfolios are jointly dependent with multivariate stable distribution. While the Gaussian distribution shares this feature, it is only one particular member of a large and flexible class of distributions, which also allows for skewness and heavy-tailedness.

This stability feature of the stable Paretian distribution that is not shared by other non-Gaussian distributions allows the generalization of the cornerstone normal-based financial theories and, thus, to build a coherent and more general framework for financial modeling. The generalizations are only possible because of specific probabilistic properties that are unique to stable (Gaussian and non-Gaussian) distributions, namely, the stability property, the Central Limit Theorem, and the Invariance Principle that we will describe in Chapter 7.

ORGANIZATION OF THE BOOK

The book is divided into five parts. Part One of the book includes six chapters that provide an introduction to the essential elements of probability theory and statistics for understanding the analysis of financial times series, risk management, and option pricing. In Chapters 2, 3, and 4 we explain how a probability distribution is used to describe the potential outcomes of a random variable, the general properties of probability distributions (including statistical moments), and the different types of probability distributions. In Chapter 3 we look at the normal probability distribution and its appeal.

In Chapter 5 we move from the probability distribution of a single random variable to that of multiple random variables, introducing the concept of a joint probability distribution, marginal probability distribution, and correlation and covariance that is commonly used to measure how random variables move together. We also discuss the multivariate normal distribution and a special class of distributions, the elliptical distribution. The limitations of correlation as a measure of the dependence between two random variables and how that limitation can be overcome by using copulas is provided in Chapter 6.

The stable distribution is the focus of Chapter 7. We explain the properties of stable distributions and considerations in the application of the distribution. We conclude the chapter with a brief introduction to smoothly truncated stable distributions that have been suggested for various applications in finance. In Chapter 8, we explain methodologies for testing whether the probability distribution for a time series of returns for a particular asset follows a specific distribution and then present methodologies to fit a stable distribution from an empirical distribution.

The two chapters in Part Two of the book cover stochastic processes. The theory of stochastic processes in *discrete time* is an important tool when examining the characteristics of financial time series data. An introduction to this tool is provided in Chapter 9. One of the simplest time series models is provided by the linear models of the *autoregressive moving average* (ARMA). However, when the focus is on modeling financial return data, it is sometimes necessary to incorporate time-varying conditional volatility. Statistical models for doing so are the *autoregressive conditional heteroskedasticity* (ARCH) model and *generalized ARCH* (GARCH) model and they are described in the chapter. Our approach in Chapter 9 is to motivate the reader as to why an understanding of this theory is important, rather than set forth a rigorous analytical presentation.

In some applications it might be more useful if we had the opportunity to model stochastic phenomena on a continuous-time scale rather than in discrete time. An example is the valuation of options (Black-Scholes option pricing model). The tool used in this case is continuous-time stochastic processes. In Chapter 10, we describe this tool and the most prominent representatives of the class of continuous-time stochastic processes: Brownian motion, Geometric Brownian motion, and the Poisson process.

Part Three provides the first of the three applications to finance. Application to portfolio selection is covered in this part, beginning in Chapter 11 with a description of recent empirical evidence on the return distribution for common stock and bonds that supports the stable Paretian hypothesis and clearly refutes the normal (Gaussian) hypothesis. Some desirable features of investment risk measures, the limitations of using the most popular measure of risk in finance and risk management, the variance, and a discussion of alternative risk measures are covered in Chapter 12. Also in that chapter, we describe two disjointed categories of risk measures, dispersion measures and safety risk measures, and review some of the most well known of each along with their properties.

There are two basic approaches to the problem of portfolio selection under uncertainty—one based on utility theory and the other based on reward-risk analysis. The former approach offers a mathematically rigorous treatment of the portfolio selection problem but appears sometimes detached from the world because it requires that asset managers specify their utility function and choose a distributional assumption for the returns. The latter approach is one that is more practical to implement. According to this approach, portfolio choice is made with respect to two criteria—the expected portfolio return and portfolio risk—with the preferred portfolio being the one that has higher expected return and lower risk. The most popular reward-risk measure is the Sharpe ratio (see Sharpe 1966). In Chapter 13, we describe some new reward-risk measures that take into account the observed phenomena that assets returns distributions are fat tailed and skewed.

Applications to the management of market, credit, and operational risk are the subject of Part 4. Chapter 14 which covers market risk management begins with a review of the adoption of Value at Risk (VaR) by bank regulators for determining risk-based capital requirements and various methodologies for measuring VaR. We then discuss the stable VaR approach and present empirical evidence comparing VaR modeling based on the normal distribution with that of the stable Paretian distribution. We conclude with an explanation of an alternative market risk measure to VaR, Expected Tail Loss (or Conditional VaR) and the advantage of using this risk measure in portfolio optimization.

Credit risk management is the subject of Chapter 15, where we provide a description of credit risk (which consists of credit default risk, credit spread risk, and downgrade risk), an overview of the credit risk framework for banks as set forth in the Basel Accord II, credit risk models (structural models and reduced form models), and commercially available credit risk tools. We also present a framework for integrating market and credit risk management.

Our coverage of operational risk in Chapter 16 starts with a discussion of the distributions suggested by the Basel Committee for Regulatory Supervision for measuring exposure to operational risk. We then present evidence against the measure suggested by regulators for measuring exposure to operational risk by showing that the stable Paretian distribution may provide the best fit to the frequency and severity data.

Option pricing models depend on the assumption regarding the distribution of returns. In the three chapters in Part 5 we look at the most popular model for pricing options, the Black-Scholes model and how it can be extended. Chapter 17 covers the basic features of options, how options can be valued using the binomial model, and how one can obtain a continuous-time option pricing model by iteratively refining the binomial model. In Chapter 18 we then introduce the most popular continuous-time model for option valuation, the Black-Scholes model, looking at the assumptions and their importance. In Chapter 19 we look at several topics related to option pricing: the smile effect, continuous-time generalizations of the geometric Brownian motion for option pricing (stochastic volatility models and so-called "local volatility models"), models with jumps, models with heavy-tailed returns, and generalization of the discrete time model for pricing options.

REFERENCES

Akgiray, A., and G. G. Booth. 1988. "The Stable-Law Model of Stock Returns." *Journal of Business and Economic Statistics* 6: 51–57.

Akgiray, V. and C. G. Lamoureux. 1989. "Estimation of Stable-Law Parameters: A Comparative Study." *Journal of Business and Economic Statistics* 7: 85–93

Arthur, W. B., J. H. Hollan, B. LeBaron, R. Palmer, and P. Tayler. 1997. "Asset Pricing under Endogeneous Expectations in an Artificial Stock Market." In W.B. Arthur, S. Durlauf, and D. Lane (eds.), *The Economy as an Evolving Complex System, II, Vol. XXVII* of SFI Studies in the Sciences of Complexit. Redwood, CA: Addison-Wesley.

Bak, P., M. Paczuski, and M. Shubik. 1996. "Price Variations in a Stock Market with Many Agents." No 1132, Cowles Foundation Discussion Papers, Cowles Foundation, Yale University.

Blattberg, R. C. and N. J. Gonedes. 1974. "A Comparison of the Stable and Student Distributions as Statistical Models for Stock Prices." *Journal of Business* 47: 244–280.

Cont, R. and J.P. Bouchaud. 2000. "Herd Behavior and Aggregate Fluctuations in Financial Markets." *Macroeconomic Dynamics* 4: 170–196.

Cootner, P.H. 1964. *The Random Character of Stock Market Prices*. Cambridge, MA: The M.I.T. Press.

Fama, E. 1963a. *The Distribution of Daily Differences of Stock Prices: A Test of Mandelbrot's Stable Paretian Hypothesis*. Doctoral Dissertation, Graduate School of Business, University of Chicago.

Fama, E. F. 1963b. "Mandelbrot and the Stable Paretian Hypothesis." *Journal of Business* 36: 420–429.

Fama, E. F. 1965c. "Portfolio Analysis in a Stable Paretian Market." *Management Science* 11: 404–419.

Hoppe, R. 1999. "It's Time We Buried Value-at-Risk." *Risk Professional*, Issue 1/5, July/August: 16.

Kon, S., 1984. "Models of Stock Returns—A Comparison." *Journal of Finance* 39: 147–165.

Lux, T. 1998. "The Socio-Economic Dynamics of Speculative Markets." *Journal of Economic Behavior and Organization* 33: 143–165.

Mandelbrot, B. B. 1963. "The Variation of Certain Speculative Prices." *Journal of Business* 36: 394–419.

Markowitz, H. M. 1952. "Portfolio Selection." *Journal of Finance* 7: 77–91.

Markowitz, H. M. 1959. *Portfolio Selection: Efficient Diversification of Investment.* New York: John Wiley.

Officer, R. R. 1972. "The Distribution of Stock Returns." *Journal of the American Statistical Association* 76: 807–812.

Rachev, S. T., and S. Mittnik. 2000. *Stable Paretian Models in Finance.* John Wiley & Sons, Chichester.

Sharpe, W. F. 1966. "Mutual Funds Performance." *Journal of Business*, January: 119–138.

Shiller, R. 1981. "Do Stock Prices Move Too Much to be Justified by Subsequent Changes in Dividends." *American Economic Review* 71: 421–436.

Probability and Statistics

CHAPTER 2

Discrete Probability Distributions

Will Microsoft's stock return over the next year exceed 10%? Will the 1-month London Interbank Offered Rate (LIBOR) three months from now exceed 4%? Will Ford Motor Company default on its debt obligations sometime over the next five years? Microsoft's stock return over the next year, 1-month LIBOR three months from now, and the default of Ford Motor Company on its debt obligations are each variables that exhibit randomness. Hence these variables are referred to as *random variables.*[1] In the chapters in Part One, we will see how probability distributions are used to describe the potential outcomes of a random variable, the general properties of probability distributions, and the different types of probability distributions.[2] Random variables can be classified as either discrete or continuous. In this chapter, our focus is on discrete probability distributions.

---

[1] The precise mathematical definition is that a random variable is a measurable function from a probability space into the set of real numbers. In the following the reader will repeatedly be confronted with imprecise definitions. The authors have intentionally chosen this way for a better general understandability and for sake of an intuitive and illustrative description of the main concepts of probability theory. The reader already familiar with these concepts is invited to skip this and some of the following chapters. In order to inform about every occurrence of looseness and lack of mathematical rigor, we have furnished most imprecise definitions with a footnote giving a reference to the exact definition.

[2] For more detailed and/or complementary information, the reader is referred to the textbook by Larsen and Marx (1986) or Billingsley (1995).

BASIC CONCEPTS

An *outcome* for a random variable is the mutually exclusive potential result that can occur. A *sample space* is a set of all possible outcomes. An *event* is a subset of the sample space.[3] For example, consider Microsoft's stock return over the next year. The sample space contains outcomes ranging from –100% (all the funds invested in Microsoft's stock will be lost) to an extremely high positive return. The sample space can be partitioned into two subsets: outcomes where the return is less than or equal to 10% and a subset where the return exceeds 10%. Consequently, a return greater than 10% is an event since it is a subset of the sample space. Similarly, a 1-month LIBOR three months from now that exceeds 4% is an event.

DISCRETE PROBABILITY DISTRIBUTIONS DEFINED

As the name indicates, a *discrete random variable* limits the outcomes where the variable can only take on discrete values. For example, consider the default of a corporation on its debt obligations over the next five years. This random variable has only two possible outcomes: default or nondefault. Hence, it is a discrete random variable. Consider an option contract where, for an upfront payment (i.e., the option price) of $50,000, the buyer of the contract receives the following payment from the seller of the option depending on the return on the S&P 500 index:

If S&P 500 return is	Payment received by option buyer
Less than or equal to zero	$0
Greater than zero but less than 5%	$10,000
Greater than 5% but less than 10%	$20,000
Greater than or equal to 10%	$100,000

In this case, the random variable is a discrete random variable but on the limited number of outcomes.

The probabilistic treatment of discrete random variables is comparatively easy: Once a probability is assigned to all different outcomes, the probability of an arbitrary event can be calculated by simply adding the

---

[3] Precisely, only certain subsets of the sample space are called *events*. In the case that the sample space is represented by a subinterval of the real numbers, the events consist of the so-called "Borel sets." For all practical applications, we can think of Borel sets as containing all subsets of the sample space.

single probabilities. Imagine that in the previous example on the S&P 500 every different payment occurs with the same probability of 25%. Then the probability of losing money by having invested $50,000 to purchase the option is 75%, which is the sum of the probabilities of getting either $0, $10,000, or $20,000 back.

In the following sections we provide a short introduction to the most important discrete probability distributions: Bernoulli distribution, Binomial distribution, and Poisson distribution. A detailed description, together with an introduction to several other discrete probability distributions, can be found, for example, in the textbook by Johnson, Kotz, and Kemp (1993).

BERNOULLI DISTRIBUTION

We will start the exposition with the *Bernoulli distribution*. A random variable X is called *Bernoulli distributed* with parameter p if it has only two possible outcomes, usually encoded as "1" (which might represent "success" or "default") or "0" (which might represent "failure" or "survival") and if the probability for realizing "1" equals p and the probability for "0" equals $1 - p$.

One classical example for a Bernoulli-distributed random variable occurring in the field of finance is the default event of a company. We observe a company C in a specified time interval I, e.g., January 1, 2006, until December 31, 2006. We define

$$X = \begin{cases} 1 & \text{if } C \text{ defaults in } I \\ 0 & \text{else} \end{cases}$$

The parameter p in this case would be the annualized probability of default of company C.

BINOMIAL DISTRIBUTION

In practical applications, we usually do not consider only one single company but a whole basket $C_1,...C_n$ of companies. Assuming that all these n companies have the same annualized probability of default p, this leads to a natural generalization of the Bernoulli distribution, called *Binomial distribution*. A Binomial distributed random variable Y with parameters n and p is obtained as the sum of n independent[4] and identically Bernoulli-distributed random variables $X_1,...,X_n$. In our example, Y represents the total number of defaults occurring in the year 2006 observed for companies $C_1,...C_n$. Given the two parameters, the probability of observing k, $0 \le k \le n$ defaults can be explicitly calculated as follows:

$$P(Y = k) = \binom{n}{k} p^k (1-p)^{n-k}$$

The notation

$$\binom{n}{k}$$

means

$$\frac{n!}{(n-k)!k!}$$

Recall that the factorial of a positive integer n is denoted by $n!$ and is equal to $n(n-1)(n-2) \cdot ... \cdot 2 \cdot 1$. Exhibit 2.1 provides a graphical visualization of the Binomial probability distribution for several different parameter values.

POISSON DISTRIBUTION

The last distribution that we treat in this chapter is the *Poisson distribution*. The Poisson distribution depends upon only one parameter λ and can be interpreted as an approximation to the binomial distribution. A Poisson-distributed random variable is usually used to describe the random number of events occurring over a certain time interval. We used this previously in terms of the number of defaults. One main difference compared to the binomial distribution is that the number of events that might occur is unbounded—at least theoretically. The parameter λ indicates the rate of occurrence of the random events, that is, it tells us how many events occur on average per unit of time.

The probability distribution of a Poisson-distributed random variable N is described by the following equation:

$$P(N = k) = \frac{\lambda^k}{k!} \cdot e^{-\lambda}, \quad k = 0, 1, 2,...$$

---

[4] A definition of what independence means is provided in Chapter 5. The reader might think of independence as no-interference between the random variables.

EXHIBIT 2.1   Visualization of Binomial Probability Distribution for Different Values of p and $n = 10$

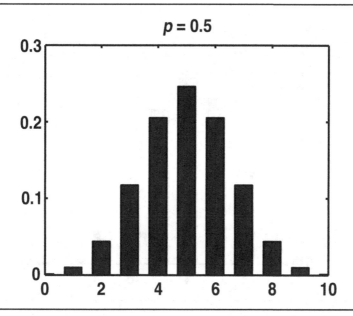

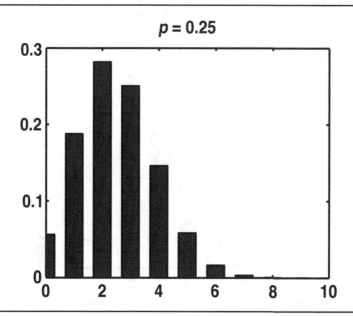

EXHIBIT 2.1   (Continued)

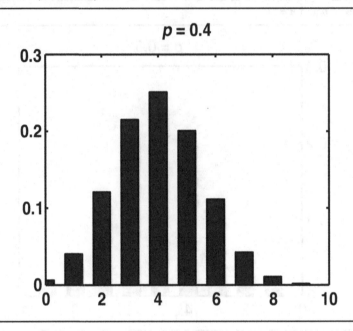

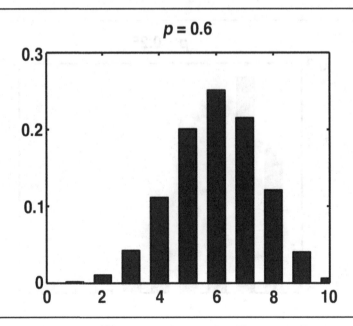

Again we provide a visualization of the distribution function. Exhibit 2.2 shows the Poisson probability distribution for several values of the parameter λ.

The Poisson distribution occurs in the context of finance as generic distribution of a stochastic process, called *Poisson process*, which is used to model the time of default in some credit risk models described in Chapter 10.

EXHIBIT 2.2 Visualization of the Poisson Probability Distribution for Different Values of λ

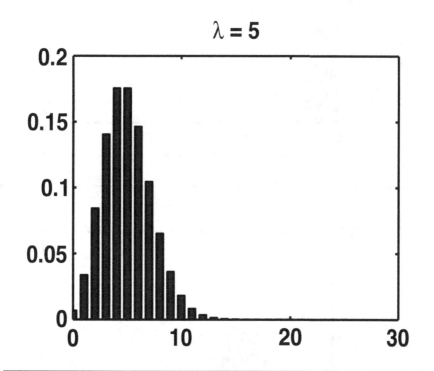

EXHIBIT 2.2   (Continued)

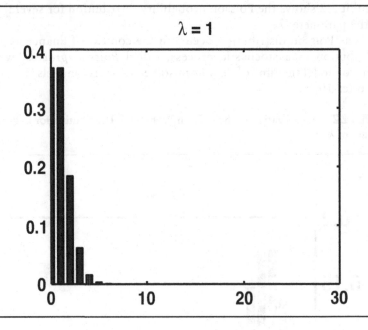

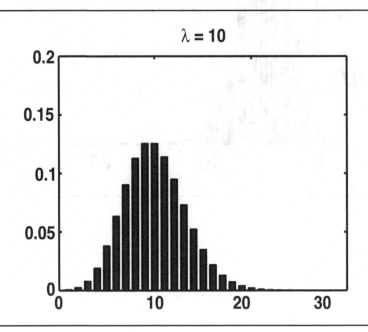

EXHIBIT 2.2   (Continued)

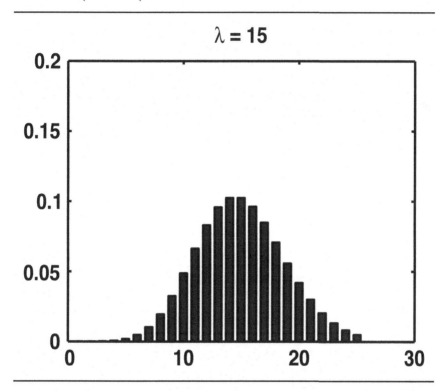

$$\lambda = 15$$

REFERENCES

Billingsley, P. 1995. *Probability and Measure: Third Edition.* New York: John Wiley & Sons.

Johnson, N. L., S. Kotz, and A. W. Kemp, 1993. *Univariate Discrete Distributions. Second Edition,* New York: John Wiley & Sons.

Larsen, R. J. and M. L. Marx. 1986. *An Introduction to Mathematical Statistics and its Applications.* Englewood Cliffs, NJ: Prentice Hall.

CHAPTER 3

Continuous Probability Distributions

I n this chapter, we define continuous probability distributions and describe the most popular ones. We look closely at the normal probability distribution, which is the mainstay of finance theory, risk measures, and performance measures—and its appeal, despite the preponderance of empirical evidence and theoretical arguments that many financial economic variables do not follow a normal distribution. We postpone until Chapter 7 a discussion of a class of continuous probability distributions, called stable *Paretian distributions*, which we show in later chapters are more appropriate in many applications in finance.

CONTINUOUS RANDOM VARIABLES AND PROBABILITY DISTRIBUTIONS

If the random variable can take on any possible value within the range of outcomes, then the probability distribution is said to be a *continuous random variable*.[1] When a random variable is either the price of or the return on a financial asset or an interest rate, the random variable is assumed to be continuous. This means that it is possible to obtain, for example, a price of 95.43231 or 109.34872 and any value in between. In practice, we know that financial assets are not quoted in such a way. Nevertheless, there is no loss in describing the random variable as continuous and in

---

[1] Precisely, not every random variable taking its values in a subinterval of the real numbers is continuous. The exact definition requires the existence of a density function such as the one that we use later in this chapter to calculate probabilities.

many times treating the return as a continuous random variable means substantial gain in mathematical tractability and convenience.

For a continuous random variable, the calculation of probabilities works substantially different from the discrete case. The reason is that if we want to derive the probability that the realization of the random variable lays within some range (i.e., over a subset or subinterval of the sample space), then we cannot proceed in a similar way as in the discrete case: The number of values in an interval is so large, that we cannot just add the probabilities of the single outcomes. The new concept needed will be explained in the next section.

Probability Distribution Function, Probability Density Function, and Cumulative Distribution Function

A *probability distribution function P* assigns a probability $P(A)$ for every event A, that is, of realizing a value for the random value in any specified subset A of the sample space. For example, a probability distribution function can assign a probability of realizing a monthly return that is negative or the probability of realizing a monthly return that is greater than 0.5% or the probability of realizing a monthly return that is between 0.4% and 1.0%.

To compute the probability, a mathematical function is needed to represent the probability distribution function. There are several possibilities of representing a probability distribution by means of a mathematical function. In the case of a continuous probability distribution, the most popular way is to provide the so-called *probability density function* or simply *density function*.

In general, we denote the density function for the random variable X as $f(x)$. Note that the lower case X is used. This is the convention adopted to denote a particular value for the random variable. The density function of a probability distribution is always nonnegative and as its name indicates: Large values for $f(x)$ of the density function at some point x imply a relatively high probability of realizing a value in the neighborhood of x, whereas $f(x) = 0$ for all x in some interval (a,b) implies that the probability for observing a realization in (a,b) is zero.

Exhibit 3.1 will aid in understanding a continuous probability distribution. The specific probability density shown in the exhibit corresponds to a normal probability distribution. The area between an interval on the horizontal axis and the curve is equal to the probability of getting an outcome laying in this specific interval. So, the area under the entire curve is equal to 1 (see panel a). In panel b, we see the probability of realizing a return that is less than A. The shaded area is the probability of realizing a return less than or equal to A. In panel c, the

EXHIBIT 3.1   Illustration of the Calculation of Probabilities by Means of a Probability Density

Panel a: The area between f and x-axis equals one

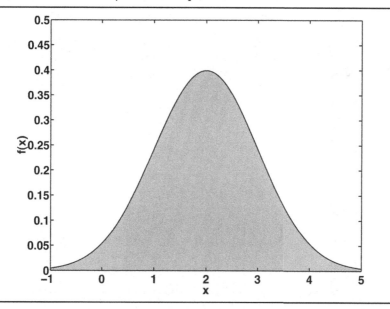

Panel b: $P(X \leq A)$

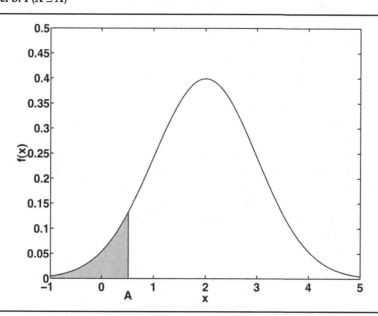

EXHIBIT 3.1   (Continued)

Panel c: $P(A < X \leq B)$

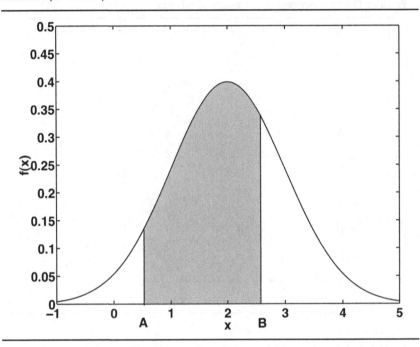

shaded area shows the probability of realizing a return between A and B. As probabilities are represented by areas under the density function, it follows that the probability for every single outcome of a continuous random variable always equals zero.

While the shaded areas in Exhibit 3.1 represent the probabilities associated with realizing a return within the specified range, how does one compute the probability? This is where the tools of calculus are applied. Calculus involves differentiation and integration of a mathematical function. The latter tool is called *integral calculus* and involves computing the area under a curve. Hence, it should not be surprising that integral calculus is used to compute the probability.

For example, a typical density function is the density of the normal or Gaussian distribution:

$$f(x) = \frac{1}{\sqrt{2\pi}\sigma} \cdot e^{-\frac{(x-\mu)^2}{2\sigma^2}} \qquad (3.1)$$

In equation (3.1), π is approximately 3.141593 and e is approximately equal to 2.718282. The parameters μ and σ determine which concrete normal distribution we consider; their meaning will be explained later. For example, suppose that we want to know the value of the normal probability density function assuming the following values:

$$\mu = 7.0\% \quad x = 0\% \quad \sigma = 2.6\%$$

Substituting these values into equation (3.1), we would get $f(0\%)$ = 0.0041.[2] The result of this calculation is only the ordinate for the probability density function (see Exhibit 3.2). It is not the probability of getting a realization of less than or equal to 0%. The probability is obtained by integrating the density function from minus infinity to x equal to zero. Fortunately, this need not be calculated (and by the way cannot be calculated analytically as there is no analytical expression for

EXHIBIT 3.2   Illustration of the Density Function for the Normal Distribution

Panel a: Density of a Normal Distribution with $\mu = 7.0\%$, $\sigma = 2.6\%$

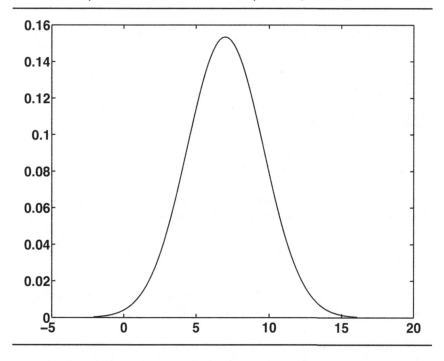

---

[2] The value can be obtained using, for example, Microsoft Excel, which has a built in function that provides this value for the normal distribution.

EXHIBIT 3.2   (Continued)

Panel b: Determination of the Ordinate and the Probability

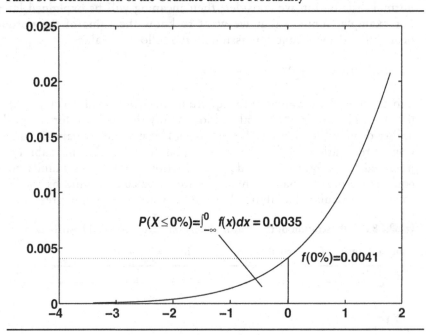

the cumulative distribution function of a normal distribution) because electronic spreadsheets preprogram this feature. In our illustration the obtained probability equals 0.0035.

The mathematical function that provides the cumulative probability of a probability distribution, that is, the function that assigns to every real value x the probability of getting an outcome less than or equal to x, is called the *cumulative distribution function*—or *cumulative probability function* or simply *cumulative distribution*—and is denoted mathematically by $F(x)$. A cumulative distribution function is always nonnegative, nondecreasing, and, as it represents probabilities, it takes only values between zero and one.[3]

The mathematical connection between a probability density function f, a probability distribution P, and a cumulative distribution function F of some random variable X is given by the following formula:

---

[3] Negative values would imply negative probabilities. If F decreased, that is, for some $x < y$ we have $F(x) > F(y)$, it would create a contradiction because the probability of getting a value less than or equal to x must be smaller or equal to the probability of getting a value less than or equal to y.

$$P(X \le t) = F(t) = \int_{-\infty}^{t} f(x)dx$$

The cumulative distribution function is another way to uniquely characterize an arbitrary probability distribution on the set of real numbers and in Chapter 7 we learn a third possibility, the so-called *characteristic function*.

THE NORMAL DISTRIBUTION

The class of normal distributions is certainly one of the most important probability distributions in statistics and, due to some of its appealing properties, the class that is used in most applications in finance. Here we introduce some of its basic properties.

Panel a of Exhibit 3.3 shows the density function of a normal distribution with $\mu = 0$ and $\sigma = 1$. A normal distribution with these parameter values is called a *standard normal distribution*. Notice the following

EXHIBIT 3.3   Density Function of a Normal Distribution
Panel a: Standard Normal Distribution ($\mu = 0$, $\sigma = 1$)

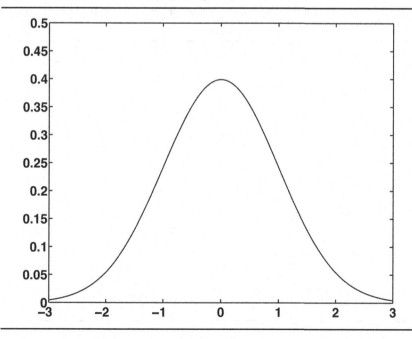

EXHIBIT 3.3   (Continued)
Panel b: Two Normal Distributions with $\sigma = 1$ but Different Location Parameters
($\mu = 0$ and $\mu = 0.5$)

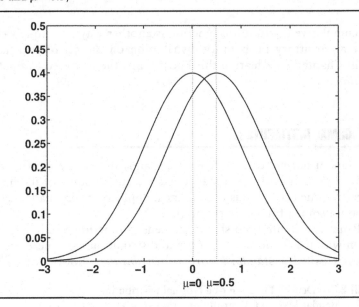

Panel c: Three Normal Distributions with $\mu = 0$ but Different Shape Parameters ($\sigma^2 = 1$, $\sigma^2 = 2$, and $\sigma^2 = 0.5$)

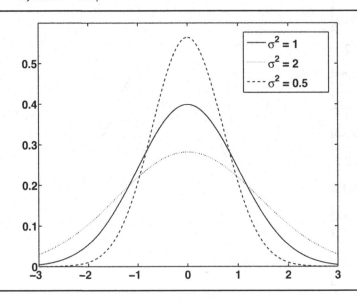

characteristics of the normal distribution. First, the middle of the distribution equals μ. Second, the distribution is symmetric around μ. This second characteristic justifies the name *location parameter* for μ. In panel b, we show two normal distributions with $\sigma = 1$, but with $\mu = 0$ for one distribution and $\mu = 0.5$ for the other. Notice that the shape of the two distributions is the same but the location as specified by the location parameter μ has changed. Panel c shows the effect of the second parameter σ on the normal distribution. For small values of σ, the density function becomes more narrow and peaked, whereas for larger values of σ the shape of the density widens. These observations lead to the name *shape* or *dispersion parameter* for σ.

Having discussed the influence of the two parameters on the distribution, we continue with presenting some of the most prominent properties of normal distributions. One important properties is the so-called *location-scale invariance* of the normal distribution. What does this mean? Imagine that you have random variable X, which is normally distributed with the parameters μ and σ. Now we consider the random variable Y, which is obtained as $Y = aX + b$. In general, the distribution of Y might substantially differ from the distribution of X, but in the case where X is normally distributed, the random variable Y is again normally distributed with parameters $\tilde{\mu} = a\mu + b$ and $\tilde{\sigma} = a\sigma$. Thus, we do not leave the class of normal distributions if we multiply the random variable by a factor or shift the random variable. This fact can be used if we change the scale where a random variable is measured: Imagine that X measures the temperature at the top of the Empire State Building on January 1, 2006, at 6 A.M. in degrees Celsius. Then $Y = \%X + 32$ will give the temperature in degrees Fahrenheit, and if X is normally distributed then Y will be too.

Another interesting and important property of normal distributions is their *summation stability*. If you take the sum of several independent[4] random variables, which are all normally distributed with mean μ_i and standard deviation σ_i, then the sum will be normally distributed again. The two parameters of the resulting distribution are obtained as

$$\mu = \mu_1 + \mu_2 + \ldots + \mu_n$$

$$\sigma = \sqrt{\sigma_1^2 + \sigma_2^2 + \ldots + \sigma_n^2}$$

Why is the summation stability property important for financial applications? Imagine that the daily returns of the S&P 500 are inde-

---

[4] A definition of what *independent* means is provided in Chapter 5. The reader might think of independence as no-interference between the random variables.

pendently normally distributed with $\mu = 0.05\%$ and $\sigma = 1.6\%$. Then the monthly returns again are normally distributed with parameters $\mu = 1.05\%$ and $\sigma = 7.33\%$ (assuming 21 trading days per month) and the yearly return is normally distributed with parameters $\mu = 12.6\%$ and $\sigma = 25.40\%$ (assuming 252 trading days per year). This means that the S&P 500 monthly return fluctuates randomly around 1.05% and the yearly return around 12.6%.

The last important property that is often misinterpreted to justify the nearly exclusive use of normal distributions in financial modeling is the fact that the normal distribution possesses a *domain of attraction*. A mathematical result called the *central limit theorem* states that—under certain technical conditions—the distribution of a large sum of random variables behaves necessarily like a normal distribution. In the eyes of many, the normal distribution is the unique class of probability distributions having this property. This is wrong and actually it is the class of stable distributions (containing the normal distributions), which is unique in the sense that a large sum of random variables can only converge to a stable distribution. We discuss the stable distribution in Chapter 7.

OTHER POPULAR DISTRIBUTIONS

In the remainder of this chapter, we provide a brief introduction to some popular distributions that are of interest for financial applications and which might be used later in this book. We start our discussion with the exponential distribution and explain the concept of *hazard rate*. this leads to the class of Weibull distributions, which can be interpreted as generalized exponential distributions. Together with the subsequently introduced class of Chi square distributions, the Weibull distributions belong to the more general class of Gamma distributions. We continue our exposition with the Beta distribution, which can be of particular interest for credit risk modelling and the *t* distribution. The log-normal distribution is the classical and most popular distribution when modeling stock price movements. Subsequently, we introduce the logistic and extreme value distribution. The latter has become popular in the field of operational risk analysis and is contained in the class of generalized extreme value distributions. We conclude the chapter with a short discussion of the generalized Pareto and the skewed normal distribution and the definition of a mixed distribution.[5]

---

[5] For a thorough treatment of all mentioned distributions, the reader is referred to the standard reference Johnson, Kotz, and Balakrishnan (1994 and 1995).

Exponential Distribution

The *exponential distribution* is popular, for example, in queuing theory when we want to model the time we have to wait until a certain event takes place. Examples include the time until the next client enters the store, the time until a certain company defaults or the time until some machine has a defect.

As it is used to model waiting times, the exponential distribution is concentrated on the positive real numbers and the density function f and the cumulative distribution function F possess the following form:

$$f(x) = \frac{1}{\beta} \cdot e^{-\frac{x}{\beta}} \quad , x > 0$$

$$F(x) = 1 - e^{-\frac{x}{\beta}} \quad , x > 0$$

where $\beta > 0$ represents a positive real parameter, whose meaning will be explained below.

Exhibit 3.4 visualizes the exponential probability density for different choices of the distribution parameter beta.

EXHIBIT 3.4   Visualization of the Exponential Distribution

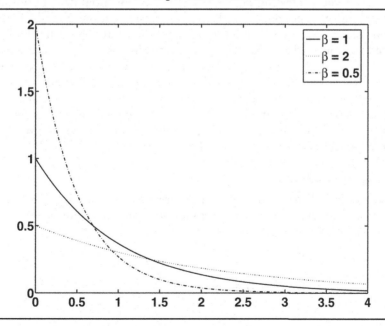

In credit risk modeling, the parameter $\lambda = 1/\beta$ has a natural interpretation as *hazard rate* or *default intensity*. Let τ denote an exponential distributed random variable, e.g., the random time (counted in days and started on January 1, 2006) we have to wait until Ford Motor Company defaults. Now, consider the following expression:

$$\lambda(\Delta t) = \frac{P(\tau \in (t, t + \Delta t] \mid \tau > t)}{\Delta t} = \frac{P(\tau \in (t, t + \Delta t])}{\Delta t \cdot P(\tau > t)}$$

where Δt denotes a small period of time. The symbol $\in$ means belongs to.

What is the interpretation of this expression? $\lambda(\Delta t)$ represents a ratio of a probability and the quantity Δt. The probability in the numerator represents the probability that default occurs in the time interval $(t, t + \Delta t]$ conditional upon the fact that Ford Motor Company survives until time t.

Now the ratio of this probability and the length of the considered time interval can be denoted as a default rate or default intensity. In applications different from credit risk we also use the expressions hazard or failure rate.

Now, letting Δt tend to zero we finally obtain after some calculus the desired relation $\lambda = 1/\beta$. What we can see is that in the case of an exponentially distributed time of default, we are faced with a constant rate of default which is independent of the current point in time t. The class of probability distributions presented in the next section will generalize this fact.

Another interesting fact linked to the exponential distribution is the following connection with the Poisson distribution described earlier. Consider a sequence of independent and identical exponentially distributed random variables τ_1, τ_2, ... We can think of τ_1, for example, as the time we have to wait until a firm in the Dow Jones Industrial Average defaults. τ_2 will then represent the time between the first and the second default and so on. These waiting times are sometimes called interarrival times. Now, let N_t denote the number of defaults which have occurred until time $t \geq 0$. One important probabilistic result states that the random variable N_t is Poisson distributed with parameter $\lambda = t/\beta$.

Weibull Distribution

The *Weibull distribution* can be interpreted as a generalized exponential distribution where the density function f and distribution function F possess the following form:

$$f(x) = \frac{\alpha x^{\alpha-1}}{\beta^{\alpha}} \cdot e^{-\left(\frac{x}{\beta}\right)^{\alpha}}, x > 0$$

$$F(x) = 1 - e^{-\left(\frac{x}{\beta}\right)^{\alpha}} \quad , x > 0$$

where α and β denote two positive real parameters. Like for the exponential distributio,n we can calculate the default intensity λ for some Weibull distributed random default time τ and obtain

$$\lambda(t) = \lim_{\Delta t \to 0} \lambda(\Delta t) = \frac{P(\tau \in (t, t + \Delta t] \mid \tau > t)}{\Delta t} = \frac{\alpha}{\beta} \cdot \left(\frac{t}{\beta}\right)^{\alpha - 1}$$

The main difference to the case of an exponential distribution is the fact that the default intensity depends upon the point in time t under consideration. For $\alpha > 1$—also called the "light-tailed" case—the default intensity is monotonically increasing with increasing time, which is useful for modeling the "aging effect" as it happens for machines: The default intensity of a 20-year old machine is higher than the one of a 2-year old machine. For $\alpha < 1$—the "heavy-tailed" case—the default intensity decreases with increasing time. That means we have the effect of "teething troubles," a figurative explanation for the effect that after some trouble at the beginning things work well, as it is known from new cars. The credit spread on noninvestment-grade corporate bonds provides a good example: Credit spreads usually decline with maturity. The credit spread reflects the default intensity and, thus, we have the effect of "teething troubles." If the company survives the next two years, it will survive for a longer time as well, which explains the decreasing credit spread. For $\alpha = 1$, the Weibull distribution reduces to an exponential distribution with parameter β.

Exhibit 3.5 visualizes Weibull density functions for different choices of α and β.

Chi-Square Distribution

Consider n independent standard normal random variables $X_1, ..., X_n$ and define a random variable Y via

$$Y = \sum_{i=1}^{n} X_i^2$$

By definition, the random variable follows a *Chi-square distribution* with n degrees of freedom. (The Chi-square distribution is denoted by $\chi^2(n)$.) This distribution occurs, for example, when we estimate the parameter σ^2 of a normal distribution. The density function of a Chi-square distribution possesses the following form:

EXHIBIT 3.5   Visualization of the Weibull Distribution

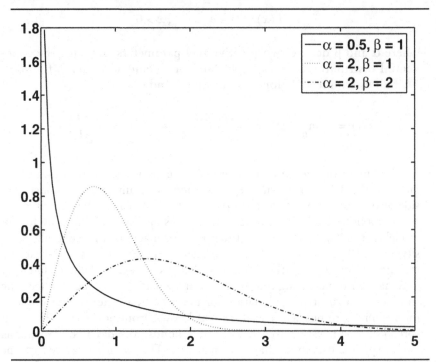

$$f(x) = \frac{1}{2^{k/2} \cdot \Gamma(k/2)} \cdot e^{-x/2} \cdot x^{k/2-1} \quad , x > 0$$

where Γ denotes the gamma function. The *gamma function* is defined to be an extension of the factorial and it has no explicit representation; but the gamma function is implemented in all mathematical and statistical software packages. Exhibit 3.6 contains some density function plots for different values of n.

The class of exponential distributions as well as the class of Chi-square distributions is a special representative of a more general class of probability distributions called *Gamma distributions*.

Gamma Distribution

The family of Gamma distributions forms a two parameter probability distribution family with the following density function[6]:

---

[6] There are different possible parametrizations of the Gamma distribution.

EXHIBIT 3.6 Density Function of the Chi-Square Distribution for Different Degrees of Freedom n

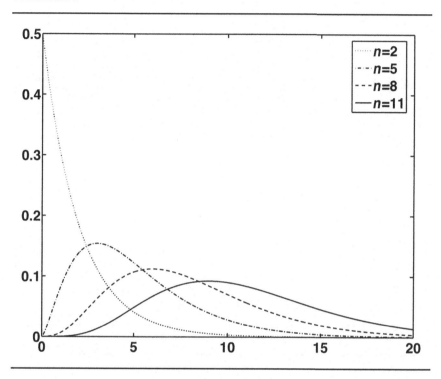

$$f(x) = \frac{1}{\beta \cdot \Gamma(\alpha)} \cdot e^{-x/\beta} \cdot \left(\frac{x}{\beta}\right)^{\alpha-1} \quad , x > 0$$

Exhibit 3.7 contains some density function plots for different values of α and β. For $\alpha = 1$ we obtain the exponential distribution and for $\alpha = k/2$ and $\beta = 2$ we have the Chi-square distribution.

Beta Distribution

The *Beta distribution* is a probability distribution whose mass is concentrated on the interval (0,1). This justifies its use for generating "random probabilities." We will see two applications of the Beta distribution when we discuss credit risk modeling in Chapter 15. The Beta distribution can be used in credit risk models to model the unknown default probabilities for the companies whose debt an analyst seeks to value. In some credit risk models, the probability of companies migrating from

EXHIBIT 3.7   Different Density Functions of the Gamma Distribution

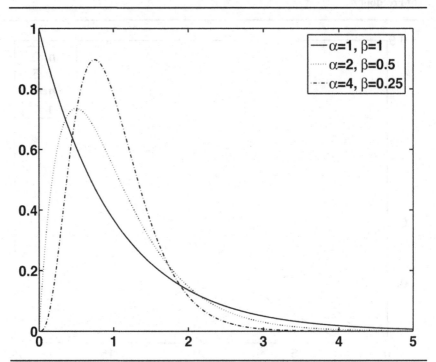

one credit rating to another must be estimated. The Beta distribution can be used to model the unknown probability of migration.

The density function of the Beta distribution is given by the following equation:

$$f(x) = \frac{1}{B(\alpha_1, \alpha_2)} \cdot x^{\alpha_1 - 1} \cdot (1 - x)^{\alpha_2 - 1}$$

$$= \frac{\Gamma(\alpha_1 + \alpha_2)}{\Gamma(\alpha_1) \cdot \Gamma(\alpha_2)} \cdot x^{\alpha_1 - 1} \cdot (1 - x)^{\alpha_2 - 1} \quad , \quad 0 < x < 1$$

Exhibit 3.8 contains some density function plots for different values of α_1 and α_2.

t-Distribution

The t-*distribution* (also known as the *Student* t-*distribution*) occurs again as a function of other random variables, namely the normal and

EXHIBIT 3.8 Different Representatives of the Beta Distribution

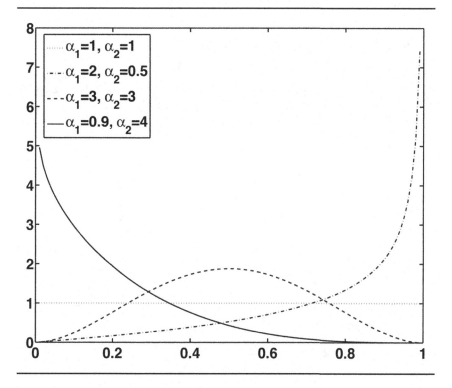

the Chi-square distribution. If X is a standard normal random variable and Z a Chi-square distributed random variable with n degrees of freedom which is independent of X, then by definition the distribution of the random variable Y defined as

$$Y = \frac{X}{\sqrt{Z/n}}$$

possesses a t-distribution with n degrees of freedom. The density function of the t-distribution is given by the following equation:

$$f(x) = \frac{1}{\sqrt{\pi \cdot n}} \cdot \frac{\Gamma((n+1)/2)}{\Gamma(n/2)} \cdot \left(1 + \frac{x^2}{n}\right)^{-\frac{n+1}{2}}$$

EXHIBIT 3.9   Different Density Functions of the *t*-Distribution and its Approximation to the Standard Normal Distribution

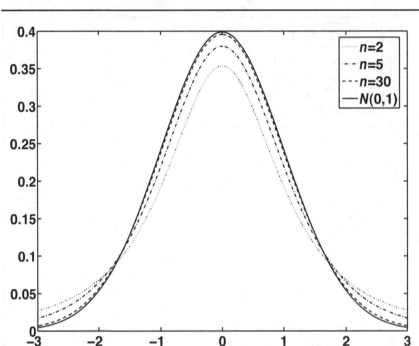

For large values of *n* the *t*-distribution does not significantly differ from a standard normal distribution. Usually, for values *n* > 30 the *t*-distribution is considered as equal to the standard normal distribution (see Exhibit 3.9).

The *t*-distribution belongs to a larger class of probability distributions, the so-called "scale mixtures of normals." These distributions are constructed by multiplying a normal random variable X with zero mean with an independent and positively distributed random variable Z. Other examples include, for example, the so-called sub-Gaussian stable distributions.

Lognormal Distribution

The *lognormal distribution* is obtained when considering the exponential of a normal random variable. More concrete, if X denotes a normal random variable with mean μ and standard deviation σ, then $Y = e^X$ follows a lognormal distribution with parameters μ and σ.

EXHIBIT 3.10   Visualization of the Lognormal Distribution

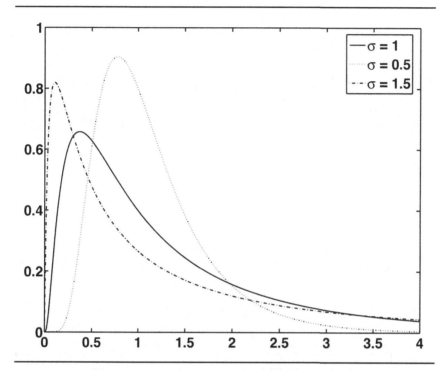

The lognormal distribution can serve as a model for the value of a financial asset if the continuously compounded asset return is modeled by a normal distribution. The density function of a lognormal distribution has the following form:

$$f(x) = \frac{1}{x\sigma\sqrt{2\pi}} \cdot e^{-\frac{(\ln x - \mu)^2}{2\sigma^2}} \quad , \quad x > 0$$

The total mass of a lognormal distribution is concentrated on the positive real line. The distribution is skewed to right and possesses a heavy right tail. Exhibit 3.10 visualizes the lognormal probability density for different choices of the distribution parameters.

Logistic Distribution

The class of logistic distributions forms a location scale family which is characterized by the following density function f and distribution F:

EXHIBIT 3.11   Density Functions of the Logistic Distribution for Different Choices of Parameters α and β (Density function of the standard normal distribution provided for comparison purposes)

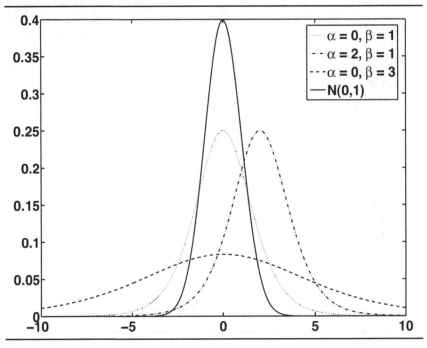

$$f(x) = \frac{e^{-(x-\alpha)/\beta}}{\beta(1 + e^{-(x-\alpha)/\beta})^2}$$

$$F(x) = \frac{1}{(1 + e^{-(x-\alpha)/\beta})^2}$$

where α denotes the location parameter and $\beta > 0$ denotes the scale parameter. The distribution function possesses the form of a logistic growth function (bounded growth) which explains the name of the distribution. Exhibit 3.11 visualizes logistic density functions for different choices of α and β.

Extreme Value Distribution

The *extreme value distribution*—sometimes also denoted as *Gumbel-type extreme value distribution*—occurs as the limit distribution of the (appropriately standardized) largest observation in a sample of increasing size. This fact explains its popularity in operational risk applications where we are concerned about a large or the largest possible loss. (Operational risk is discussed in Chapter 16.) Its density function f and distribution function F respectively is given by the following equations:

$$f(x) = \frac{1}{b} \cdot e^{-\frac{x-a}{b} - e^{-\frac{x-a}{b}}}$$

$$F(x) = e^{-e^{-\frac{x-a}{b}}}$$

where a denotes a real location parameter and $b > 0$ a positive real shape parameter. The class of extreme value distributions forms a location-scale family. Exhibit 3.12 visualizes extreme value density functions for different choices of α and β.

EXHIBIT 3.12 Density Functions of the Extreme Value Distribution for Different Choices of the Parameters α and β (Density function of the standard normal distribution provided for comparison purposes)

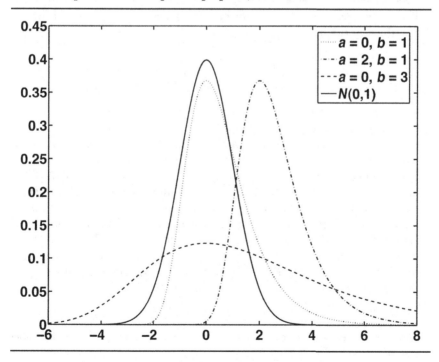

Generalized Extreme Value Distribution[7]

Besides the previously mentioned (Gumbel type) extreme value distribution, there are two other types of distributions which can occur as the limiting distribution of appropriately standardized sample maxima. One class is denoted as the *Weibull-type extreme value distribution* and has a similar representation as the Weibull distribution. The third type is also referred to as the *Fréchet-type extreme value distribution*. All three can be represented as a three parameter distribution family referred to as a *generalized extreme value distribution* with the following cumulative distribution function:

$$F(x) = e^{-\left(1 + \xi \cdot \frac{x - \mu}{\sigma}\right)^{-1/\xi}} \quad, \quad 1 + \xi \cdot \frac{x - \mu}{\sigma} > 0$$

where ξ and μ are real and σ is a positive real parameter. If ξ tends to zero, we obtain the extreme value distribution discussed above. For positive values of ξ the distribution is called Fréchet-type and for negative values of ξ Weibull-type extreme value distribution.

Generalized Pareto Distribution

The *generalized Pareto distribution* is characterized by the following distribution function:

$$F(x) = 1 - \left(1 + \frac{\xi x}{\sigma}\right)^{-1/\xi} \quad, \quad x > 0 \text{ and } 1 + \frac{\xi x}{\sigma} > 0$$

where σ is a positive real parameter and ξ a real parameter.

The generalized Pareto distribution occurs in a natural way as the distribution of so-called "peaks over threshold." Let us assume we have a sequence of independent and identically distributed random variables X_1, X_2, ... where the distribution of the single X_i is given by the distribution function F and we assume that the maximum of the random variables converges in distribution to a generalized extreme value distribution with parameter ξ. Now consider a large enough threshold u, and consider the distribution of $X - u$ conditional on X being greater than u. It can be shown that the limit of this conditional distribution will be a member of the class of generalized Pareto distributions. Possible applications are in the field of operational risks (see Chapter 16), where one is only concerned about losses above a certain threshold.

---

[7] An excellent reference for this and the following section is Embrechts, Klueppelberg, and Mikosch (1997).

Skewed Normal Distribution

The *skewed normal distribution* was introduced to allow for modeling skewness within the Gaussian framework. Its density function *f* is given by the following expression (φ denotes the density and Φ the cumulative distribution function of a standard normal random variable):

$$f(x) = \frac{2}{\sigma} \cdot \varphi\left(\frac{x-\mu}{\sigma}\right) \cdot \Phi\left(\alpha\frac{x-\mu}{\sigma}\right)$$

where μ and $\sigma > 0$ play the same role as in the classical normal setting whereas α is a skewness parameter. The effect of α on the density is visualized in Exhibit 3.13.

Mixtures of Distributions

As a last example, we present a rather general method of how one can generate new distributions from known ones. Take *n* probability density

EXHIBIT 3.13   Density Functions of the Skewed Normal Distribution for Different Choices of Parameters α (Parameters $\mu = 0$ and $\sigma = 1$ kept constant as their influence already visualized in Exhibit 2.5)

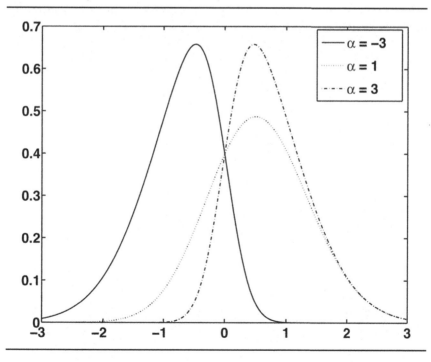

functions $f_1,...f_n$ and n positive real numbers $\alpha_1,...\alpha_n$ with the property $\Sigma\alpha_i = 1$ and define a new probability density f via

$$f(x) = \sum_{i=1}^{n} \alpha_i f_i(x)$$

The so defined mixed distributions are often used when no well-known distribution family seems appropriate to explain the specific observed phenomenon.

REFERENCES

Embrechts, P., C. Klueppelberg, and T. Mikosch. 1997. *Modelling Extremal Events for Insurance and Finance*, vol. 33 of *Applications of Mathematics*. Berlin: Springer-Verlag.

Johnson, N. L., S. Kotz, and N. Balakrishnan. 1994. *Continuous Univariate Distribution, Volume 1, 2nd ed.* New York: John Wiley & Sons.

Johnson, N. L., S. Kotz, and N. Balakrishnan. 1995. *Continuous Univariate Distribution, Volume 2, 2nd ed.* New York: John Wiley & Sons.

CHAPTER 4

Describing a Probability Distribution Function: Statistical Moments and Quantiles

In describing a probability distribution function, it is common to summarize it by using various measures. The five most commonly used measures are:

- Location
- Dispersion
- Asymmetry
- Concentration in tails
- Quantiles

In this chapter we describe these measures and present the formula for computing them for the probability distributions described in the previous two chapters.

LOCATION

The first way to describe a probability distribution function is by some measure of *central value* or *location*. The various measures that can be used are the mean or average value, the median, or the mode. The relationship among these three measures of location depends on the skewness of a probability distribution function that we will describe later. The most commonly used measure of location is the *mean* and is denoted by μ or EX or $E(X)$.

DISPERSION

Another measure that can help us to describe a probability distribution function is the dispersion or how spread out the values of the random variable can realize. Various measures of dispersion are the range, variance, and mean absolute deviation. The most commonly used measure is the *variance*. It measures the dispersion of the values that the random variable can realize relative to the mean. It is the average of the squared deviations from the mean. The variance is in squared units. Taking the square root of the variance one obtains the *standard deviation*. In contrast to the variance, the *mean absolute deviation* takes the average of the absolute deviations from the mean.[1] In practice, the variance is used and is denoted by σ^2 or VX or $V(X)$ and the standard deviation by σ or $\sqrt{VX}$.

ASYMMETRY

A probability distribution may be symmetric or asymmetric around its mean. A popular measure for the asymmetry of a distribution is called its *skewness*. A negative skewness measure indicates that the distribution is skewed to the left; that is, compared to the right tail, the left tail is elongated (see panel a of Exhibit 4.1). A positive skewness measure indicates that the distribution is skewed to the right; that is, compared to the left tail, the right tail is elongated (see panel b of Exhibit 4.1).

CONCENTRATION IN TAILS

Additional information about a probability distribution function is provided by measuring the concentration (mass) of potential outcomes in its tails. The tails of a probability distribution function contain the extreme values. In financial applications, it is these tails that provide information about the potential for a financial fiasco or financial ruin. As we will see, the fatness of the tails of the distribution is related to the peakedness of the distribution around its mean or center. The joint measure of peakedness and tail fatness is called *kurtosis*.

---

[1] It is also common to define the mean absolute deviation from the median because it minimizes the average absolute distance from an arbitrary point x.

EXHIBIT 4.1   Skewed Distributions

Panel a: Distribution Skewed to the Left

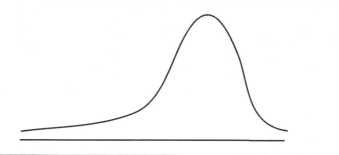

Panel b: Distribution Skewed to the Right

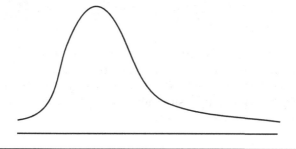

STATISTICAL MOMENTS

In the parlance of the statistician, the four measures described previously are called *statistical moments* or simply *moments*. The mean is the *first moment* and is also referred to as the *expected value*. The variance is the *second central moment*, skewness is a rescaled *third central moment*, and kurtosis is a rescaled *fourth central moment*. The general mathematical formula for the calculation of the four parameters is shown in Exhibit 4.2.

Exhibit 4.3 shows the mean, variance, and skewness for several probability distribution functions that have been used in financial modeling and risk management.

The definition of skewness and kurtosis is not as unified as for the mean and the variance. The skewness measure reported in Exhibit 4.2 is the so-called *Fishers' skewness*. Another possible way to define the mea-

EXHIBIT 4.2   General Formula for Parameters

Parameter	Discrete Probability Distribution	Continuous Probability Distribution
Mean	$EX = \sum_i x_i P(X = x_i)$	$EX = \int_{-\infty}^{\infty} x \cdot f(x)dx$
Variance	$VX = \sum_i (x_i - EX)^2 P(X = x_i)$	$VX = \int_{-\infty}^{\infty} (x - EX)^2 f(x)dx$
Skewness	$\varsigma = \dfrac{E(X - EX)^3}{(VX)^{\frac{3}{2}}}$	$\varsigma = \dfrac{E(X - EX)^3}{(VX)^{\frac{3}{2}}}$
Kurtosis	$\kappa = \dfrac{E(X - EX)^4}{(VX)^2}$	$\kappa = \dfrac{E(X - EX)^4}{(VX)^2}$

sure is the *Pearson's skewness* which equals the square of the Fisher's skewness. The same holds true for the kurtosis, where we have reported the *Pearson's kurtosis. Fishers' kurtosis* (sometimes denoted as excess kurtosis) can be obtained by subtracting three from Pearson's kurtosis.

QUANTILES

Sometimes not only are the four statistical moments described above used to summarize a probability distribution but a concept called α-quantile. The α-*quantile* gives us information where the first α% of the distribution are located. Given an arbitrary observation of the considered probability distribution, this observation will be smaller than the α-quantile q_α in α% of the cases and larger in $(100 - \alpha)$% of the cases.[2] For example, earlier we found that for the normal distribution with mean 7% and standard deviation 2.6%, the value 0% represents the 0.35% quantile.

Some quantiles have special names. The 25%, 50%, and 75% quantile are referred to as the *first quartile, second quartile,* and *third quartile,* respectively. The 1%, 2%, ..., 98%, 99% quantiles are called *percentiles.* As

---

[2] Formally, the α-quantile for a continuous probability distribution P with strictly increasing cumulative distribution function F is obtained as $q_\alpha = F^{-1}(\alpha)$.

EXHIBIT 4.3 Distributions and their Mean, Variance, and Skewness

Panel a. Distribution Descriptions

	Density Function	Parameters	Mean	Variance
Normal	$f(x) = \dfrac{1}{\sqrt{2\pi}\sigma} e^{-\frac{1}{2}\left(\frac{x-\mu}{\sigma}\right)^2}$	μ location σ scale $\sigma > 0$	μ	σ^2
Beta	$f(x) = \dfrac{x^{\alpha_1 - 1}(1-x)^{\alpha_2 - 1}}{B(\alpha_1, \alpha_2)}$	α_1 shape $\alpha_1 > 0$ α_2 shape $\alpha_2 > 0$	$\dfrac{\alpha_1}{\alpha_1 + \alpha_2}$	$\dfrac{\alpha_1 \alpha_2}{(\alpha_1 + \alpha_2)^2 (\alpha_1 + \alpha_2 + 1)}$
Exponential	$f(x) = \dfrac{e^{-x/\beta}}{\beta}$	β scale $\beta > 0$	β	β^2
Extreme Value	$f(x) = \dfrac{1}{b}\left(\dfrac{1}{e^{\frac{(x-a)}{b} + \exp\left(\frac{a-x}{b}\right)}}\right)$	a location b scale $b > 0$	$a + 0.577b$	$\dfrac{\pi^2 b^2}{6}$
Gamma	$f(x) = \dfrac{1}{\beta\Gamma(\alpha)}\left(\dfrac{x}{\beta}\right)^{\alpha - 1} e^{-x/\beta}$	α location β scale $\beta > 0$	$\beta\alpha$	$\beta^2\alpha$

EXHIBIT 4.3 Panel a. Continued

	Density Function	Parameters	Mean	Variance
Logistic	$f(x) = \dfrac{e^{-(x-\alpha)/\beta}}{\beta\left(1+e^{-(x-\alpha)/\beta}\right)^2}$	α location β scale $\beta > 0$	α	$\dfrac{\pi^2\beta^2}{3}$
Lognormal	$f(X) = \dfrac{1}{x\sqrt{2\pi}\sigma}\, e^{-\frac{1}{2}\left(\frac{\ln x - \mu}{\sigma}\right)^2}$	$\mu > 0$ $\sigma > 0$	$e^{\mu + \frac{\sigma^2}{2}}$	$e^{2\mu}e^{\sigma^2}\left(e^{\sigma^2}-1\right)$
Student-t	$f(x) = \dfrac{1}{\sqrt{\pi\cdot n}}\cdot\dfrac{\Gamma((n+1)/2)}{\Gamma(n/2)}\cdot\left(1+\dfrac{x^2}{n}\right)^{-\frac{n+1}{2}}$	n degrees of freedom	0	$\dfrac{n}{n-2}$
Skewed Normal	$f(x) = \dfrac{2}{\sigma}\cdot\varphi\left(\dfrac{x-\mu}{\sigma}\right)\cdot\Phi\left(\alpha\dfrac{x-\mu}{\sigma}\right)$	μ location σ scale α shape	μ	σ^2
Weibull	$f(x) = \dfrac{\alpha x^{\alpha-1}}{\beta^\alpha}\, e^{-(x/\beta)^\alpha}$	α shape $\alpha > 0$ β scale $\beta > 0$	$\beta\Gamma\left(1+\dfrac{1}{\alpha}\right)$	$\beta^2\left[\Gamma\left(1+\dfrac{2}{\alpha}\right)-\Gamma^2\left(1+\dfrac{1}{\alpha}\right)\right]$

EXHIBIT 4.3   (Continued)
Panel b. Domain and Symmetry

	Domain	Skewness
Normal	$-\infty < x < +\infty$	0
Beta	$0 < x < 1$	$2\dfrac{\alpha_2 - \alpha_1}{\alpha_1 + \alpha_2 + 2}\sqrt{\dfrac{\alpha_1 + \alpha_2 + 1}{\alpha_1 \alpha_2}}$
Exponential	$0 < x < +\infty$	2
Extreme Value	$-\infty < x < +\infty$	1.139547
Gamma	$0 < x < +\infty$	$\dfrac{2}{\sqrt{\alpha}}$
Logistic	$-\infty < x < +\infty$	0
Lognormal	$0 < x < +\infty$	$(w + 2)\sqrt{(w - 1)}$ where $w = e^{\alpha^2}$
Student-t	$-\infty < x < +\infty$	0
Skewed Normal	$-\infty < x < +\infty$	a
Weibull	$0 < x < +\infty$	$\dfrac{\Gamma\left(1 + \dfrac{3}{\alpha}\right) + 3\Gamma\left(1 + \dfrac{2}{\alpha}\right)\Gamma\left(1 + \dfrac{1}{\alpha}\right) + 2\Gamma^3\left(1 + \dfrac{1}{\alpha}\right)}{\left[\Gamma\left(1 + \dfrac{2}{\alpha}\right) - \Gamma^2\left(1 + \dfrac{1}{\alpha}\right)\right]^{3/2}}$

Source: Adapted from Exhibit 1 in Levy and Duchin (2004, pp. 50–51). For the sake of exposition and consistency we have sometimes used a slightly different notation and omitted some entries.

we will see in later chapters, the α-quantile is closely related with the Value-at-Risk measure (VaR_α) commonly used in risk management.

SAMPLE MOMENTS

The previous section has introduced the four statistical moments mean, variance, skewness, and kurtosis. Given a probability density function f or a probability distribution P we are able to calculate these statistical moments according to the formulae given in Exhibit 4.2. In practical applications however, we are faced with the situation that we observe realizations of a probability distribution (e.g., the daily return of the S&P 500 index over the last two years), but we do not know the distribution which generates these returns. Consequently we are not able to apply our knowledge about the calculation of statistical moments. But, having the observations x_1, ..., x_n, we can try to estimate the "true moments" out of the sample. The estimates are sometimes called *sample moments* to stress the fact that they are obtained out of a sample of observations.

The idea is quite simple: The empirical analogue for the mean of a random variable is the average of the observations:

$$EX \approx \frac{1}{n} \sum_{i=1}^{n} x_i$$

For large n it is reasonable to expect that the average of the observations will not be far from the mean of the probability distribution. Now, we observe that all theoretical formulae for the calculation of the four statistical moments are expressed as "means of something." This insight leads to the expression for the sample moments, summarized in Exhibit 4.4.[3]

EXHIBIT 4.4   Calculation of Sample Moments

Moment	Sample Moment
Mean EX	$\bar{x} = \dfrac{1}{n} \sum_{i=1}^{n} x_i$
Variance VX	$s^2 = \dfrac{1}{n} \sum_{i=1}^{n} (x_i - \bar{x})^2$
Skewness	$\hat{\varsigma} = \dfrac{\dfrac{1}{n} \sum_{i=1}^{n} (x_i - \bar{x})^3}{(s^2)^{\frac{3}{2}}}$
Kurtosis	$\hat{\kappa} = \dfrac{\dfrac{1}{n} \sum_{i=1}^{n} (x_i - \bar{x})^4}{(s^2)^2}$

---

[3] A "hat" on a parameter (like $\hat{\kappa}$) symbolizes the fact that the true parameter (in this case the kurtosis κ) is estimated.

NORMAL DISTRIBUTION REVISITED

Let us look again at the normal distribution, especially at the four statistical moments for the normal distribution. The previously called location parameter μ actually equals the mean of the normal distribution; the parameter σ represents the standard deviation and consequently the variance coincides with the value of σ^2. This is consistent with our observations that the density is located and symmetric around μ and that the variation of the distribution increases with increasing values of σ. Because a normal distribution is symmetric, its skewness measure is zero. The kurtosis measure of all normal distributions is 3.

Exhibit 4.5 shows a normal distribution and a symmetric nonnormal distribution with a mean of zero. The symmetric nonnormal distribution has a higher peak at the mean (zero) than the normal distribution. A distribution that has this characteristic is said to be a *leptokurtic distribution* with the same mean of zero. Look at the result of the greater

EXHIBIT 4.5   Illustration of Kurtosis: Difference Between a Standard Normal Distribution and a Distribution with High Excess Kurtosis

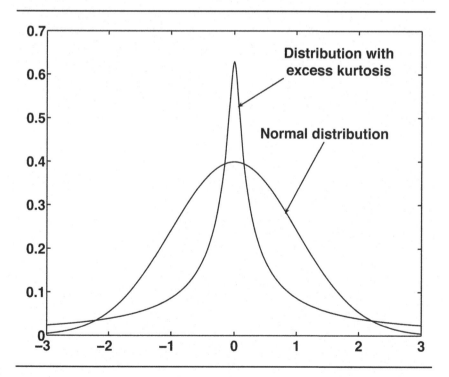

peakedness. The tails of the symmetric nonnormal distribution are "thicker" or "heavier" than the normal distribution. A probability distribution with this characteristics is said to be a "heavy-tailed distribution" or "fat tailed." The kurtosis measure for such a heavy-tailed distribution will exceed 3. Statistical programs commonly report a measure called "excess kurtosis" or "Fisher's kurtosis." This is simply the kurtosis for the distribution minus 3 (the kurtosis for the normal distribution) and will be a positive value for a heavy-tailed distribution. When a distribution is less peaked than the normal distribution, it is said to be *platykurtic*. This distribution is characterized by less probability in the tails than the normal distribution. It will have a kurtosis that is less than 3 or, equivalently, an excess kurtosis that is negative.

REFERENCES

Levy, H. and R. Duchin. 2004. "Asset Return Distributions and the Investment Horizon Explaining Contradictions." *Journal of Portfolio Management*, Summer: 47–62.

CHAPTER 5

Joint Probability Distributions

In the previous three chapters we explained the properties of a probability distribution of a single random variable; that is, the properties of a univariate distribution. An understanding of univariate distributions allows us to analyze the time series characteristics of individual assets. In this chapter we move from the probability distribution of a single random variable (univariate distribution) to that of multiple random variables (multivariate distribution). Understanding multivariate distributions is important because financial theories such as portfolio selection theory and asset-pricing theory involve distributional properties of sets of investment opportunities (i.e., multiple random variables). For example, Markowitz portfolio theory covered in Part Two of this book assumes that returns of alternative investments have a joint multivariate distribution whose relevant properties are described by certain parameters.

To do so, we first introduce the concept of a joint probability distribution, marginal probability distribution, and correlation and covariance. We also discuss the multivariate normal distribution and a special class of distributions that have been used in the theory of finance, the family of elliptical distributions.

JOINT PROBABILITY DISTRIBUTIONS DEFINED

A portfolio or a trading position consists of a collection of financial assets. Thus, portfolio managers and traders are interested in the return on a portfolio or a trading position. Consequently, in real-world applications, the interest is in the *joint probability distribution* or *joint distri-*

bution of more than one random variable. For example, suppose that a portfolio consists of a position in two assets, asset 1 and asset 2. Then there will be a probability distribution for (1) asset 1, (2) asset 2, and (3) asset 1 and asset 2. The first two distributions are referred to as the *marginal probability distributions* or *marginal distributions*. The distribution for asset 1 and asset 2 is called the joint probability distribution.

Like in the univariate case, there is a mathematical connection between the probability distribution P, the cumulative distribution function F, and the density function f of a multivariate random variable $X = (X_1, ..., X_d)$. The formula looks similar to the equation that we presented in the previous chapter showing the mathematical connection between a probability density function, a probability distribution, and a cumulative distribution function of some random variable X:

$$P(X_1 \leq t_1, ..., X_d \leq t_d) = F(t_1, ..., t_d)$$

$$= \int_{-\infty}^{t_1} ... \int_{-\infty}^{t_d} f(x_1, ..., x_d) dx_1 ... dx_d$$

The formula can be interpreted as follows: The joint probability that the first random variable realizes a value less than or equal to t_1 and the second less than or equal to t_2 and so on is given by the cumulative distribution function F. The value can be obtained by calculating "the volume" under the density function f. Because there are d random variables, we have now d arguments for both functions: the density function and the cumulative distribution function.

MARGINAL DISTRIBUTIONS

Beside this joint distribution, we can consider the above mentioned marginal distributions, that is, the distribution of one single random variable X_i. The marginal density f_i of X_i is obtained by integrating the joint density over all variables which are not taken into consideration:

$$f_i(x) = \int_{-\infty}^{\infty} ... \int_{-\infty}^{\infty} f(x_1, ..., x_{i-1}, x, x_{i+1}, ..., x_d) dx_1 ... dx_{i-1} dx_{i+1} ... dx_d$$

DEPENDENCE OF RANDOM VARIABLES

Typically, when considering multivariate distributions, we are faced with inference between the distributions; that is, large values of one random variable imply large values of another random variable or small values of a third random variable. If we are considering, for example, X_1 as the height of a randomly chosen U.S. citizen and X_2 the weight of this citizen, then large values of X_1 tend to result in large values of X_2. This property is denoted as the *dependence of random variables* and it is a powerful concept to measure dependence that will be introduced in a later section on copulas.

The inverse case of no dependence is denoted as *stochastic independence*. More precisely, two random variables are *independently distributed* if and only if their joint distribution given in terms of the joint cumulative distribution function F or the joint density function f equals the product of their marginal distributions:

$$F(x_1, ..., x_d) = F_1(x_1) \cdots F_d(x_d)$$

or

$$f(x_1, ..., x_d) = f_1(x_1) \cdots f_d(x_d)$$

In the special case of $d = 2$, we can say that two random variables are said to be independently distributed, if knowing the value of one random variable does not provide any information about the other random variable.

Covariance and Correlation

There are two strongly related measures among many that are commonly used to measure how two random variables tend to move together, the covariance and the correlation. Letting

σ_X = standard deviation for X
σ_Y = standard deviation for Y
$\sigma_{X,Y}$ = covariance between X and Y
$\rho_{X,Y}$ = correlation between X and Y

The relationship between the correlation and covariance is as follows:

$$\rho_{X,Y} = \frac{\sigma_{X,Y}}{\sigma_X \cdot \sigma_Y}$$

or

$$\sigma_{X,Y} = \rho_{X,Y} \cdot \sigma_X \cdot \sigma_Y$$

Here the *covariance* is defined as the difference of the mean $\mu_{X,Y}$ of the product XY and the product of the means μ_X and μ_Y:

$$\sigma_{X,Y} = E(XY) - EX \cdot EY = \mu_{XY} - \mu_X \mu_Y$$

It can be shown that the correlation can only have values from −1 to +1. When the correlation is zero, the two random variables are said to be *uncorrelated*.

If we add two random variables, $X + Y$, the expected value (first central moment) is simply the sum of the expected value of the two random variables. That is,

$$\mu_{X+Y} = \mu_X + \mu_Y$$

The variance of the sum of two random variables, denoted by σ_{X+Y}, is

$$\sigma_{X+Y}^2 = \sigma_X^2 + \sigma_Y^2 + 2\sigma_{X,Y}$$

Here the last term accounts for the fact that there might be a dependence between X and Y measured through the covariance.

MULTIVARIATE NORMAL DISTRIBUTION

In finance, it is common to assume that the random variables are normally distributed. The joint distribution is then referred to as a *multivariate normal distribution*.[1] To get a first impression of multivariate distributions, Exhibit 5.1 shows a surface and a contour plot of a bivariate normal distribution with standard normal marginals and a positive correlation of $\rho = 0.8$. The next sections explain how such a distribution can be constructed from the univariate distribution and how an explicit expression for the density function can be obtained.

---

[1] Precisely, the joint distribution of a random vector $X = (X_1, ..., X_n)$ is called a multivariate normal distribution if any linear combination $a_1 X_1 + ... + a_n X_n$ of its components is normally distributed. Especially, it is not sufficient that only the marginals are normally distributed.

EXHIBIT 5.1   Visualization of Abivariate Normal Density with Standard Normal Marginals and a Correlation of $\rho = 0.8$

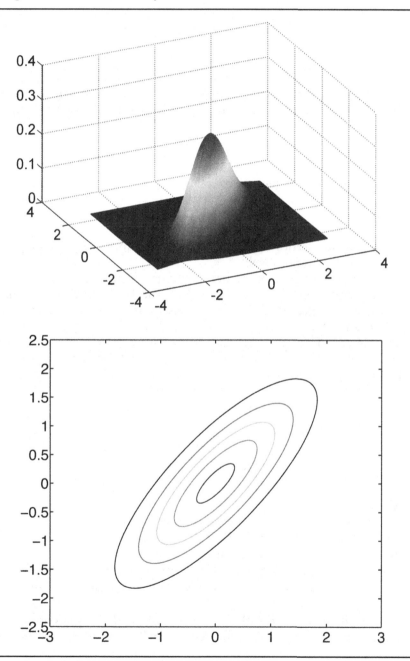

Two Important Properties of Multivariate Normal Distributions

There are important properties of the multivariate normal distribution. To explain them, we will discuss the special case where there are two random variables. This case is referred to as a *bivariate normal distribution.* The two properties are:

Property 1: If X and Y have a bivariate normal distribution, then $Z = w_X X + w_Y Y$ where w_X and w_Y are constants is normally distributed with an expected value equal to $\mu_Z = w_X \mu_X + w_Y \mu_Y$ and the variance is

$$\sigma_Z^2 = w_X^2 \sigma_X^2 + w_Y^2 \sigma_Y^2 + 2 w_X w_Y \sigma_{X,Y}$$

Property 2: If X and Y have a bivariate normal distributions and the covariance between the two variables is zero, then the two variable are independent.

These two properties apply in a generalized form to the multivariate normal distribution as well.

Why are these two properties important? Assume a two-asset portfolio that is comprised of two assets. Let X and Y denote the return on the two assets. Suppose that a portfolio consists of a relative portion w_X and w_Y of assets X and Y, respectively, where w_X and w_Y are less than 1 and $w_X + w_Y = 1$. The return on the portfolio, denoted by *Port*, is then *Port* = $w_X X + w_Y Y$. If X and Y have a bivariate normal distribution, then from Property 1, the portfolio's expected value (μ_{port}) and variance (σ_{port}^2) are

$$\mu_{port} = w_X \mu_X + w_Y \mu_Y$$

$$\begin{aligned}
\sigma_{port}^2 &= w_X^2 \sigma_X^2 + w_Y^2 \sigma_Y^2 + 2 w_X w_Y \sigma_{X,Y} \\
&= w_X^2 \sigma_X^2 + w_Y^2 \sigma_Y^2 + 2 w_X w_Y \rho_{X,Y} \sigma_X \sigma_Y
\end{aligned}$$

where

σ_X = standard deviation for asset X's return
σ_Y = standard deviation for asset Y's return
$\sigma_{X,Y}$ = covariance between asset X's return and asset Y's return
$\rho_{X,Y}$ = correlation between asset X's return and asset Y's return

For those familiar with mean-variance portfolio analysis (and for those who are not, it will be covered in Part Two of this book), these are the equations for the mean and variance of a two-asset portfolio. The extension to a multi-asset portfolio when the asset returns are multivariate normal is what is used in mean-variance analysis.

If we want to characterize the density function of a univariate normal distribution, we have to specify the mean μ and the variance σ^2. In the bivariate setting, we have to specify the two means μ_X and μ_Y of the returns X and Y and the two variances σ_X^2 and σ_Y^2. Additionally, we need the parameter $\sigma_{X,Y}$ which determines the dependence structure. In the general case of a d-dimensional multivariate normal distribution, we have to specify $d + d(d + 1)/2$ parameters.

Now consider Property 2. It is sometimes stated that if two random variables have a zero covariance, then this implies independence. However, this does *not* apply in general but in the special case where the asset returns have a multivariate normal distribution the implication is correct.

Density Function of a General Multivariate Normal Distribution

As we did in Chapter 3, we also provide an explicit representation of the density function of a general multivariate normal distribution. Consider first d, independent standard normal random variables $X_1, X_2, ..., X_d$. Their common density function can be written as the product of their individual density functions and so we obtain the following expression as the density function of the random vector $X = (X_1, X_2, ..., X_d)$:

$$f_X(x_1, ..., x_d) = \frac{1}{(\sqrt{2\pi})^d} \cdot e^{-\frac{\sum_{i=1}^{d} x_i^2}{2}}$$

$$= \frac{1}{(\sqrt{2\pi})^d} \cdot e^{-\frac{x' \cdot x}{2}}$$

Now consider d weight vectors $a^{(i)} = (a_1^{(i)}, ..., a_d^{(i)})$ and d constants $\mu_1, ..., \mu_d$ and define the d dimensional random variable $Y = (Y_1, ..., Y_d)$ through the following system of linear equations:

$$Y_1 = a_1^{(1)} \cdot X_1 + a_2^{(1)} \cdot X_2 + ... + a_d^{(1)} \cdot X_d + \mu_1$$
$$Y_2 = a_1^{(2)} \cdot X_1 + a_2^{(2)} \cdot X_2 + ... + a_d^{(2)} \cdot X_d + \mu_2$$
$$...$$
$$Y_1 = a_1^{(d)} \cdot X_1 + a_2^{(d)} \cdot X_2 + ... + a_d^{(d)} \cdot X_d + \mu_d$$

Using matrix notation, this can be written in the following more compact form:[2]

$$Y = AX + \mu$$

This is the most general form of generation of a multivariate normal random vector, that is, every multivariate normal random vector can be expressed in the above form with appropriately chosen weight vectors $a^{(i)}$ and shift vector μ. The density function of Y can now be expressed as[3]

$$f_Y(y_1, \ldots, y_d) = \frac{1}{(\pi\Delta)^{d/2}} \cdot e^{-\frac{\sum_{i=1}^{d}\sum_{j=1}^{d} s_{ij}(y_i - \mu_i)(y_j - \mu_j)}{2}}$$

$$= \frac{1}{(\pi|\Sigma|)^{d/2}} \cdot e^{-\frac{(y-\mu)'\Sigma^{-1}(y-\mu)}{2}}$$

where $\Delta = |\Sigma|$ denotes the determinant of the matrix Σ, and $\Sigma^{-1} = (s_{ij})_{i,j=1, \ldots, d}$ represents the inverse of Σ. The matrix $\Sigma = AA'$ is obtained from the weight vectors.

We illustrate the density function formula for the spacial case $d = 2$, that is, the bivariate normal distribution. Let us take two standard normal random variables X_1 and X_2 and choose $a^{(1)} = (0.5,1)$, $a^{(2)} = (1,1.5)$, and $\mu = (2,3)'$. So we obtain

$$Y_1 = 0.5X_1 + X_2 + 2$$

and

$$Y_2 = X_1 + 1.5X_2 + 3$$

We already know that a bivariate distribution is described through the two means, the two variances, and the covariance of the two random variables Y_1, Y_2. So we calculate:

$$EY_1 = 2 = \mu_1$$

---

[2] The ith row of the matrix A is given by the ith weight vector $a^{(i)}$.
[3] In order for the density function to exist, the joint distribution of Y must be nondegenerate (i.e., the matrix Σ must be positive definite).

and

$$EY_2 = 3 = \mu_2$$

and

$$\sigma_1^2 = V(Y_1) = 0.5^2 + 1 = 1.25$$

$$\sigma_2^2 = V(Y_2) = 1^2 + 1.5^2 = 3.25$$

$$\sigma_{1,2} = Cov(Y_1, Y_2) = 0.5 \cdot 1 + 1 \cdot 1.5 = 2$$

The matrix Σ and its determinant are given by the following equations:

$$\Sigma = \begin{bmatrix} \sigma_1^2 & \sigma_{1,2} \\ \sigma_{1,2} & \sigma_2^2 \end{bmatrix} = \begin{bmatrix} 1.25 & 2 \\ 2 & 3.25 \end{bmatrix}$$

$$\Delta = |\Sigma| = \sigma_1^2 \sigma_2^2 - 2\sigma_{1,2}$$
$$= 0.0625$$

The inverse Σ^{-1} of Σ has the following form:

$$\Sigma^{-1} = 16 \cdot \begin{bmatrix} 3.25 & -2 \\ -2 & 1.25 \end{bmatrix}$$

Now we obtain

$$f_Y(y) = \frac{16}{2\pi} \cdot e^{-\frac{3.25(y_1-2)^2 - 4(y_1-2)(y_2-3) + 1.25(y_2-3)^2}{2 \cdot 16}}$$

Exhibit 5.2 contains a visualization of this density function. We observe that due to the strong positive correlation of

$$\rho = 2/\sqrt{1.25 \cdot 3.25} \approx 0.99$$

the level curves are extremely stretched in the left-bottom to the right-top direction. Large values of Y_1 go very likely together with large values of Y_2 and vice versa. Most of the probability mass (i.e., most of the volume under the density function) is concentrated around the first axis of

EXHIBIT 5.2   Density of a Bivariate Normal Distribution with Contour Plot

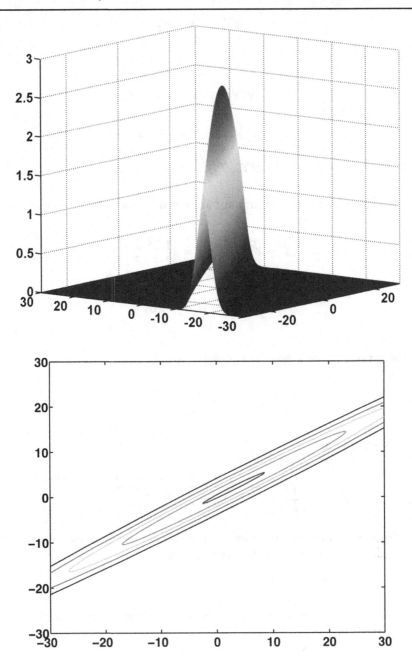

the elliptically form level curves shown in panel b of Exhibit 5.2. The observation that these level curves are elliptically contoured leads already to a generalization of the multivariate normal distribution which is covered in the next section.

ELLIPTICAL DISTRIBUTIONS

A generalization of the multivariate normal distribution is given by the class of elliptical distributions.[4] We discuss this class because elliptical distributions offer desirable properties in the context of portfolio selection theory, an issue which is treated in Part Three of this book. It will turn out that in fact it is the class of elliptical distributions where the correlation is the right dependence measure, and that for distributions which do not belong to this family, alternative concepts must be sought.

Simply speaking, a d-dimensional random vector X with density function f is called *spherically distributed* if all the level curves,[5] that is, the set of all points, where the density function f admits a certain value c, possesses the form of a sphere.[6] In the special case when $d = 2$, the density function can be plotted and the level curves look like circles. As an example, we consider Exhibit 5.3 where the density function of a 2-dimensional t-distribution is plotted. Analogously, a d-dimensional random vector X with density function f is called *elliptically distributed* if the form of all level curves equals the one of an ellipse.[7]

One can think of elliptical distributions as a special class of symmetric distributions which possess a number of desirable properties. Examples of elliptically distributed random variables include all multivariate normal distributions, multivariate t-distributions, logistic distributions, Lapace distributions, and a part of the multivariate stable distributions.[8] Elliptical distributions with existing density function can be

---

[4] This section provides only a brief review of elliptical distributions. Bradley and Taqqu (2003) provide a more complete introduction to elliptical distributions and their implications for portfolio selection.

[5] The reader interested in outdoor activities such as hiking or climbing as well as geographically interested people might know the concept of level curves from their hiking maps, where the mountains are visualized by there iso-level lines.

[6] The exact definition imposes a special structure on the characteristic function that we describe in Chapter 7, when we discuss stable distributions. The density must not necessarily exist for every spherically distributed random variable.

[7] Again, the general definition involves the characteristic function.

[8] For a thorough introduction into the class of ellipitcal distribution, see Fang, Kotz, and Ng (1990).

EXHIBIT 5.3 Illustration of the Density of a Multivariate t-Distribution with its Contour Lines

Panel a: 2-dimensional t-distribution with $n = 4$ degrees of freedom and zero correlation. This distribution belongs to the class of spherical distributions.

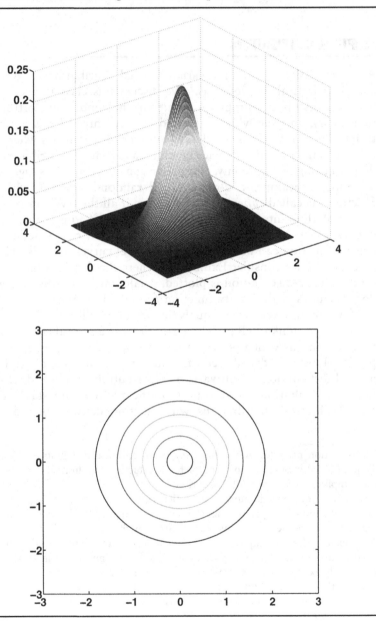

EXHIBIT 5.3   (Continued)
Panel b: 2-dimensional t-distribution with $n = 4$ degrees of freedom and strong positive correlation. This distribution belongs to the class of elliptical distributions.

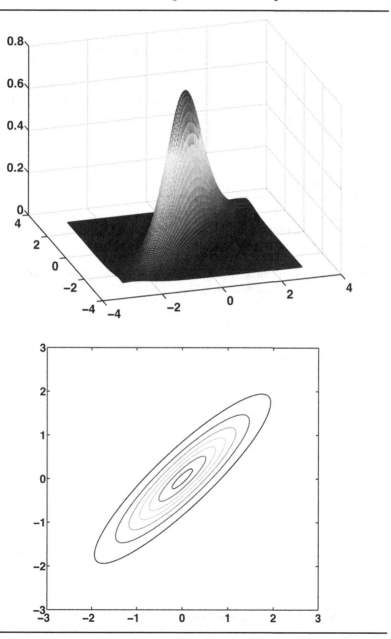

described by a triple (μ, Σ, g),[9] where μ and Σ play similar roles as the mean vector and the variance-covariance matrix in the multivariate normal setting. The function g is the so-called *density generator*. All three together define the density function of the distribution as

$$f(x) = \frac{c}{\sqrt{|\Sigma|}} g((x-\mu)'\Sigma^{-1}(x-\mu))$$

where c is a normalizing constant. The reader may compare the similarity between this expression and the density function of a multivariate normal distribution.

REFERENCES

Bradley, B., and M.S. Taqqu. 2003. "Financial Risk and Heavy Tails." In *Handbook of Heavy-Tailed Distributions in Finance*, ed. S. T. Rachev, 35–103. Amsterdam: Elsevir.

Fang, K-T., S. Kotz, and K-W. Ng. 1990. *Symmetric Multivariate and Related Distributions*. London: Chapman & Hall.

---

[9] A "triple" or a "3-tuple" is simply the notation used by mathematicians for a group of three elements.

CHAPTER 6

Copulas

Correlation is a widespread concept in modern finance and insurance and stands for a measure of dependence between random variables. However, this term is very often incorrectly used to mean any notion of dependence. Actually correlation is one particular measure of dependence among many. In the world of multivariate normal distribution and, more generally, in the world of spherical and elliptical distributions, it is the accepted measure. This follows from Property 2 of the multivariate normal distribution explained in the previous chapter. Because financial theories and risk management analysis rely crucially on the dependence structure of assets, we discuss the limitations of correlation as a measure of the dependence between two random variables and introduce an alternative measure to overcome these limitation, copulas.[1]

DRAWBACKS OF CORRELATION

In the general case, there are at least three major drawbacks of the correlation measure. Consider the case of two real-valued random variables X and Y. First, the variances of X and Y must be finite or the correlation is not defined. This assumption causes problems when working with heavy-tailed data as explained in the next chapter, where we cover stable distributions, because under certain circumstances the variances are infinite and, for that reason, the correlation between them is not defined.

Second, independence of two random variables implies correlation equal to zero; however, generally speaking the opposite is not correct—

---

[1] For a discussion of applications in finance and insurance, see Embrechts, McNeil, and Straumann (1999) and Patton (2003a, 2003b, 2004).

zero correlation does not imply independence.[2] Only in the case of elliptical distribution is uncorrelatedness and independence interchangeable notions. This statement is not valid if only the marginal distributions are elliptical and the joint distribution is nonelliptical.

Lastly, a more technical point. The correlation is not invariant under nonlinear strictly increasing transformations, a serious disadvantage. In general $corr(T(X),T(Y)) \neq corr(X,Y)$. One example that explains this technical requirement is the following: Assume that X and Y represent the continuous return (log-return) of two financial assets over the period $[0,t]$, where t denotes some point of time in the future. If you know the correlation of these two random variables, this does not imply that you know the dependence structure between the asset prices itself because the asset prices (P and Q for asset X and Y, respectively) are obtained by $P_t = P_0 \cdot \exp(X)$ and $Q_t = Q_0 \cdot \exp(Y)$. The asset prices are strictly increasing functions of the return but the correlation structure is not maintained by this transformation. This observation implies that the return could be uncorrelated whereas the prices are strongly correlated and vice versa.

OVERCOMING THE DRAWBACKS OF CORRELATION: COPULAS

A more prevalent approach, which overcomes this disadvantage, is to model dependency using copulas. As noted by Patton (2004, p. 3): "The word *copula* comes from Latin for a 'link' or 'bond', and was coined by Sklar (1959), who first proved the theorem that a collection of marginal distributions can be 'coupled' together via a copula to form a multivariate distribution." The idea is as follows. The description of the joint distribution of a random vector is divided into two parts:

1. The specification of the marginal distributions
2. The specification of the dependence structure by means of a special function, called *copula*.

The use of copulas offers the following advantages:

■ The nature of dependency that can be modeled is more general. In comparison, only linear dependence can be explained by the correlation.

---

[2] A simple example is the following: Let X be a standard normal distribution and $Y = X^2$. Because the third moment of the standard normal distribution is zero, the correlation between X and Y is zero despite the fact that Y is a function of X, which means that they are dependent.

■ Dependence of extreme events might be modeled.

■ Copulas are indifferent to continuously increasing transformations (not only linear as it is true for correlations).

Because of these advantages, in recent years there has been increased application of copulas in asset and option pricing, portfolio selection, and risk management.

MATHEMATICAL DEFINITION OF COPULAS

From a mathematical viewpoint, a copula function C is nothing more than a probability distribution function on the d-dimensional hypercube $I_d = [0,1] \times [0,1] \times \ldots \times [0,1]$:

$$C: I_d \to [0, 1]$$
$$(x_1, \ldots, x_d) \to C(x_1, \ldots, x_d)$$

It has been shown[3] that any multivariate probability distribution function F_Y of some random vector $Y = (Y_1, \ldots, Y_d)$ can be represented with the help of a copula function C in the following form:

$$F_Y(y_1, \ldots, y_d) = P(Y_1 \leq y_1, \ldots, Y_d \leq y_d) = C(P(Y_1 \leq y_1), \ldots, P(Y_d \leq y_d))$$
$$= C(F_{Y_1}(y_1), \ldots, F_{Y_d}(y_d))$$

where the F_{Y_i}, $i = 1, \ldots, d$ denote the marginal distribution functions of the random variables Y_i, $i = 1, \ldots, d$.

The copula function makes the bridge between the univariate distribution of the individual random variables and their joint probability distribution. This justifies the fact that the copula function creates uniquely the dependence, whereas the probability distribution of the involved random variables is provided by their marginal distribution.

As an example we consider the following three bivariate copula functions:

■ $C(x,y) = x \cdot y$
■ $C(x,y) = \min(x, y)$

---

[3] The importance of copulas in the modeling of the distribution of multivariate random variables is provided by Sklar's theorem. The derivation was provided in Sklar (1959).

$$C(x, y) = \int_{-\infty}^{\Phi^{-1}(x)} \int_{-\infty}^{\Phi^{-1}(y)} \frac{1}{2\pi(1-\rho^2)^{1/2}} \exp\left(-\frac{s^2 - 2\rho st + t^2}{2(1-\rho^2)}\right) ds\, dt$$

The first represents the independent case as the joint probability distribution equals the product of their marginals. The second example represents a case of extreme dependence whereas the third example represents the general Gaussian copula function for the bivariate case.

We illustrate the effect of the different copulas by applying them to two different marginal distributions, namely (1) the uniform distribution on the interval [0,1] and (2) the standard normal distribution. The results are presented in the Exhibits 6.1, 6.2, and 6.3.

REFERENCES

Embrechts, P., A. McNeil, and D. Straumann. 1999. "Correlation and Dependence Properties in Risk Management: Properties and Pitfalls." In *Risk Management: Value at Risk and Beyond*, ed. M. Dempster, 176–223. Cambridge: Cambridge University Press.

Patton, A.J. 2003a. "On the Importance of Skewness and Asymmetric Dependence for Asset Allocation." *Journal of Financial Econometrics* 2 (1): 130–168.

Patton, A. J. 2003b. "Estimation of Copula Models for Time Series of Possibly Different Lengths." Working paper. London School of Economics, September.

Patton, A.J. 2004. "Modelling Asymmetric Exchange Rate Dependence." Working paper. London School of Economics, September.

Sklar, A. 1959. "Fonctions de Répartition à n dimensions et Leurs Marges." *Publications de l'Institut de Statistique de l'Université de Paris* 8: 229–231.

EXHIBIT 6.1   Visualization of the Copula for Bivariate Independence
The graphs show the joint distribution function of a bivariate random vector for
two different marginal distributions. Each panel consists of a surface and a
corresponding contour plot.
Panel a: Uniform Marginal Distributions.

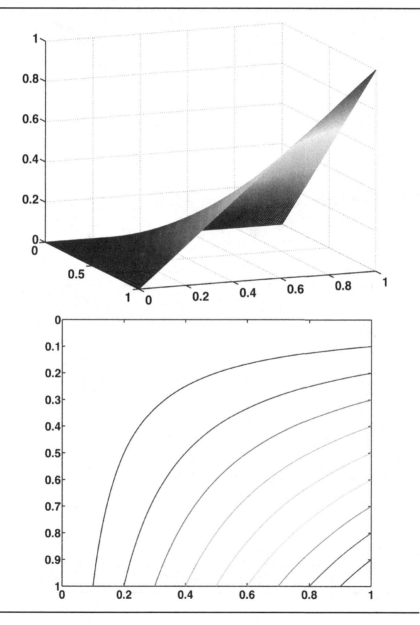

EXHIBIT 6.1 (Continued)
Panel b: Standard Normal Marginal Distributions.

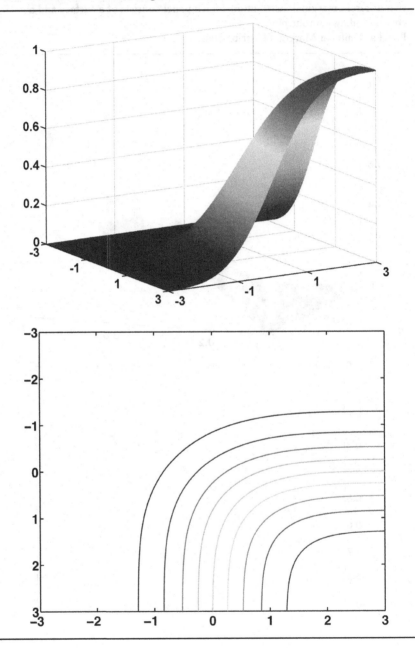

EXHIBIT 6.2 Visualization of the Bivariate Minimum Copula

The graphs show the joint distribution function of a bivariate random vector for two different marginal distributions. Each panel consists of a surface and a corresponding contour plot.

Panel a: Uniform Marginal Distributions.

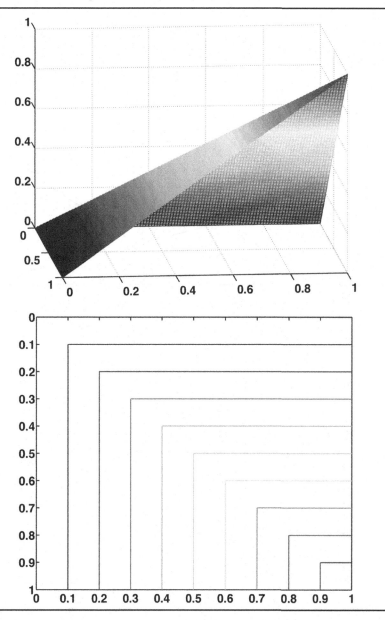

EXHIBIT 6.2 (Continued)
Panel b: Standard Normal Marginal Distributions.

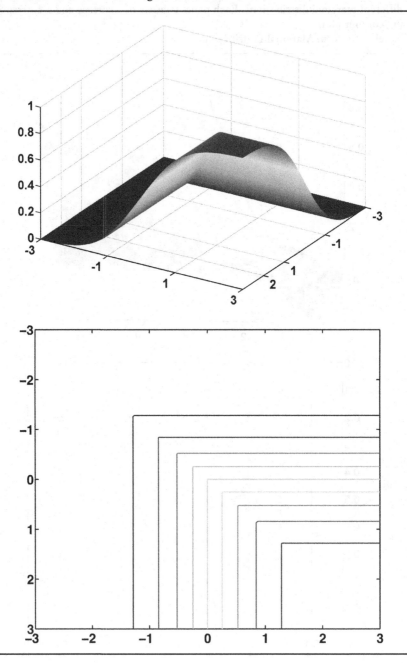

EXHIBIT 6.3   Visualization of the Gaussian Copula with Correlation $\rho = 0.8$
The graph shows the joint distribution function of a bivariate random vector for two
different marginal distributions. Each Panel consists of a surface and a correspnding
contour plot.
Panel a: Uniform Marginal Distributions.

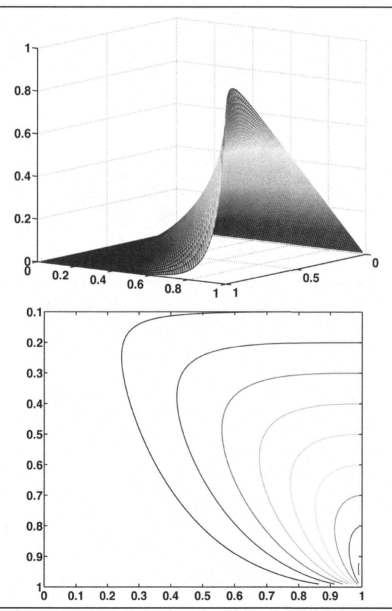

EXHIBIT 6.3 (Continued)
Panel b: Standard Normal Marginal Distributions.

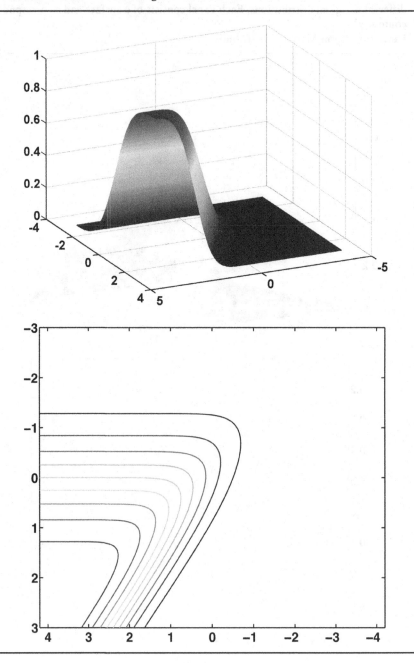

CHAPTER 7

Stable Distributions

Fat tails are observed in many asset price and return data, including well-known stock market indices and corporate bonds. Corporate bonds have nonnormal probability distributions that have negative skewness attributable to downgrading (i.e., a lowering of a bond's or issuer's credit rating) and default events. For assets whose returns or prices exhibit fat-tail attributes, nonnormal distribution models are required to accurately model the tail behavior and compute probabilities of extreme returns.

Various nonnormal distributions have been proposed for modeling extreme events, including:

- Mixtures of two or more normal distributions
- Student *t*-distributions, hyperbolic distributions, and other scale mixtures of normal distributions
- Gamma distributions
- Extreme value distributions
- Stable Paretian (also known as Lévy stable and alpha stable) non-Gaussian distributions.

The class of stable Paretian distributions will be simply referred to as *stable distributions*.

Among the above, only stable distributions have attractive enough mathematical properties to be a viable alternative to normal distributions in trading, optimization, and risk management systems. A major drawback of all alternative models is their lack of stability, where *stability* means that the distribution family of the returns does not depend on the time interval over which the returns are considered. More than four decades ago, Benoit Mandelbrot (1963) demonstrated that the stability

81

property is highly desirable for asset returns.[1] These advantages are particularly evident in the context of portfolio analysis and risk management. For this reason we will discuss stable distributions in this chapter. A more detailed treatment of the topic is provided in Rachev and Mittnik (2000).

PROPERTIES OF THE STABLE DISTRIBUTION

In only three cases discussed below does the density function of a stable distribution have a closed-form expression. In the general case, stable distributions are described by their *characteristic function* denoted by φ.[2] A characteristic function provides a third possibility (beside the cumulative distribution function and the probability density function) to uniquely define a probability distribution. The precise definition needs some more advanced mathematical concepts and is not of major interest for this book. At this point, we just state the fact, that knowing the characteristic function φ is mathematically equivalent to knowing the probability density function f or the cumulative distribution function F.

---

[1] The precise definition of stability is as follows: A probability distribution with distribution function F is stable if for any n there exists constants a_n and b_n such that the following equality holds in distribution:

$$a_n(X_1 + X_2 + \dots + X_n) + b_n = X$$

where $X, X_1, X_2, \dots, X_n$ are identically and independently distributed with distribution function F. In terms of financial returns, one could say that the sum of daily returns is up to scale and location equally distributed as the monthly return or yearly return.

[2] The characteristic function is a mapping from the set of real numbers $\mathbb{R}$ into the set of complex numbers $\mathbb{C}$ where $\varphi(t) = Ee^{itX}$ equals the so called "Fourier transform" of the distribution of the random variable X. The characteristic function of a stable distribution with distribution function F is given by the following expression:

$$\int e^{itx} dF(x) = \begin{cases} \exp\left\{-\sigma^\alpha |t|^\alpha \left[1 - i\beta \operatorname{sign}(t)\tan\dfrac{\pi\alpha}{2}\right] + i\mu t\right\}, & \text{if } \alpha \neq 1 \\[2ex] \exp\left\{-\sigma |t| \left[1 + i\beta\dfrac{2}{\pi}\operatorname{sign}(t)\ln|t|\right] + i\mu t\right\}, & \text{if } \alpha = 1 \end{cases}$$

where $\operatorname{sign}(t)$ is 1 if $t > 0$, 0 if $t = 0$, and -1 if $t < 0$. The characteristic exponent α is the *index of stability* and can also be interpreted as a *shape* parameter; β is the skewness parameter; μ is a location parameter; and σ is the scale parameter.

The connection among these three functions is given by two integral formulae, called the *Fourier inversion formulae*. What is important to understand is that the characteristic function (and thus the density function) of a stable distribution is described by four parameters. The parameters and their meaning are:[3]

- α, which determines the tail weight or the distribution's kurtosis with 0 < α ≤ 2
- β, which determines the distribution's skewness
- σ is a scale parameter
- μ is a location parameter

When the β of a stable distribution is zero, the distribution is symmetric around μ. Stable distributions allow for skewed distributions when β ≠ 0 and fat tails; this means a high probability for extreme events relative to the normal distribution when α < 2. The value of β can range from –1 to +1. When β is positive, a stable distribution is skewed to the right; when β is negative, a stable distribution is skewed to the left.

The value of α is greater than zero and does not exceed 2 (i.e., 0 < α ≤ 2). Exhibit 7.1 shows the effect of α on tail thickness of the density as well as peakedness at the origin relative to the normal distribution (collectively the "kurtosis" of the density), for the case of β = 0, μ = 0, and σ = 1. As the values of α decrease, the distribution exhibits fatter tails and more peakedness at the origin.

Exhibit 7.2 illustrates the influence of β on the skewness of the density function for α = 1.5, μ = 0, and σ = 1. Increasing (decreasing) values of β result in skewness to the right (left).

Three Special Cases of the Stable Distribution

As mentioned, only three stable distributions—that will now be discussed—possess a closed-form expression for their density function. The case where α = 2 (and β = 0, which plays no role in this case) and with the reparameterization in scale, $\tilde{\sigma} = \sqrt{2}\sigma$, yields the normal distribution, whose density function is given by equation (3.1) in Chapter 3. Thus, the normal distribution is one of the three special cases of the stable distribution, one which has a closed-form expression.

The case where α = 1 and β = 0 yields the *Cauchy distribution* with much fatter tails than the normal distribution. The Cauchy distribution

---

[3] There are many different possible parameterizations of stable distributions. For an overview the reader is referred to Zolotarev (1986). The parameterization used in this book is the one introduced by Samorodnitsky and Taqqu (1994).

EXHIBIT 7.1   Influence of α on the Resulting Stable Distribution

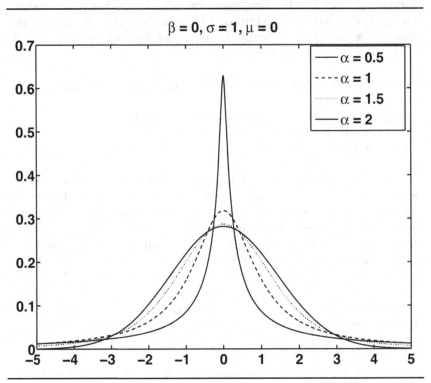

is the second case of the stable distribution where the density function has a closed-form expression given by:

$$f_{\mu,\sigma}(x) = \frac{1}{\pi \cdot \sigma}\left(1 + \left(\frac{x-\mu}{\sigma}\right)^2\right)^{-1}$$ (7.1)

From Exhibit 7.3, which compares the normal distribution and the Cauchy distribution, the fatter tails for the latter can be seen.

The third and last special case is obtained for α = 0.5 and β = 1. In this case, we have the *Lévy distribution* with density function:[4]

---

[4] Strictly speaking there is a fourth case with a closed-form density, namely the reflected Lévy distribution with parameters α = 0.5 and β = −1 which can be obtained from the Lévy distribution by reflecting the graph of the density at the vertical axis.

EXHIBIT 7.2 Influence of β on the Resulting Stable Distribution

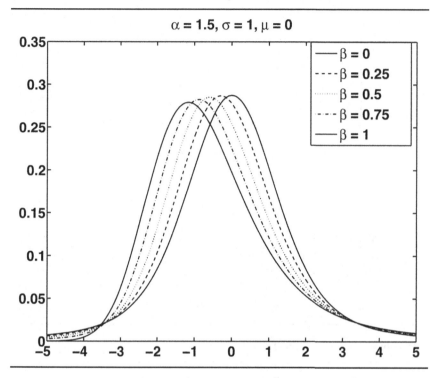

$$f_{\mu,\sigma}(x) = \left(\frac{\sigma}{2\pi}\right)^{\frac{1}{2}} \cdot \frac{1}{(x-\mu)^{3/2}} \cdot e^{-\frac{\sigma}{2(x-\mu)}}, \quad x > \mu \qquad (7.2)$$

The probability mass of the Lévy distribution is concentrated on the interval $(\mu, +\infty)$. The phenomenon that the domain of a stable distribution differs from the whole real line can only occur for values of α strictly less than one and in the case of maximal skewness, that is, for $\beta = +1$ or $\beta = -1$. In the former case, the support of the distribution equals the interval $(\mu, +\infty)$ whereas in the latter case it equals $(-\infty, \mu)$.

CONSIDERATIONS IN THE USE OF THE STABLE DISTRIBUTION

The question as to what theoretical distribution best describes the return on financial assets is an empirical question. There is a preponderance of

EXHIBIT 7.3   Comparison of Standard Cauchy and Standard Normal Distribution
Panel a: General Shape

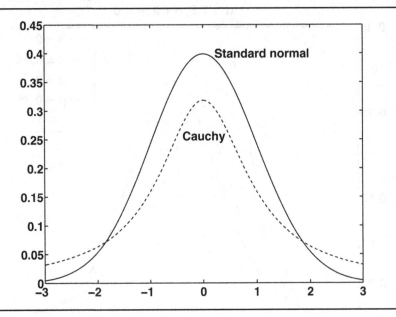

Panel b: Comparison of the Tails

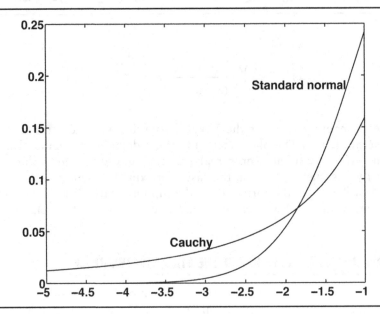

empirical evidence over the past four decades that supports the use of stable distributions in finance. In Chapter 11 we present evidence for U.S. stocks and fixed income securities in the largest sector of the U.S. bond market (mortgage passthrough securities). Despite this evidence, there have been several barriers to the application of stable distribution models, both conceptual and technical.

Computational Considerations

The major drawback that is put forth for rejecting the stable distribution is the problem that the variance of the stable nonnormal distributions equals infinity. This fact can be explained by the tail behavior of stable distributions. One can show that for large values of x the density function of a stable distribution with index of stability α "behaves like" $x^{-(\alpha+1)}$ and consequently all moments $E|X|^p$ with $p \geq \alpha$ do not exist. Particularly, the mean only exists for $\alpha > 1$.

A second issue of criticism concerns the fact that without a general expression for stable probability densities—except the three cases identified above—one cannot directly implement estimation methodologies for fitting these densities. Today, because of advances in computational finance, there are methodologies for fitting densities for stable distributions. We will briefly describe this methodology in the next chapter.

Desirable Properties of the Stable Distributions

The entire field of financial economic theory is based on the normal distribution and its statistical properties. However, an attractive feature of stable distributions, not shared by other probability distribution models, is that they allow generalization of financial theories based on normal distributions and, thus, allow construction of a coherent and general framework for financial modeling. These generalizations are possible only because of two specific probabilistic properties that are unique to stable distributions (both normal and nonnormal), namely:

■ Stability property
■ Central Limit Theorem

Let us discuss the significance of these properties.

The stability property was briefly mentioned before and denotes the fact that the sum of two independent α-stable random variables follows—up to some correction of scale and location—again the same stable distribution. For a special case, we already know this property from our description of the normal distribution. As mentioned earlier, this

characteristic becomes important in financial applications such as portfolio choice theory or when measuring returns on different time scales.

The second property is also well-known from the Gaussian framework and it generalizes to the stable case. Specifically, by the Central
Limit Theorem, appropriately normalized sums of independent and identically distributed (i.i.d) random variables with finite variance converge
weakly[5] to a normal random variable, and with infinite variance, the
sums converge weakly to a stable random variable. This gives a theoretical basis for the use of stable distributions when heavy tails are present
and stable distributions are the only distributional family that has its own
domain of attraction—that is a large sum of appropriately standardized
i.i.d random variables will have a distribution that converges to a stable
one. This is a unique feature and its fundamental implications for financial modeling are the following: If changes in a stock price, interest rate or
any other financial variable are driven by many independently occurring
small shocks, then the only appropriate distributional model for these
changes is a stable model, that is, normal or nonnormal stable.

Calculus for Stable Distributions

The previously discussed stability property, as well as the fact that the stable distributions form a location scale family, imply that a rescaled or
shifted stable random variable as well as the sum of two independent stable random variables is again stable. The question which we have not
addressed so far is how these manipulations change the values of the four
describing parameters. Let us therefore assume that X_1 and X_2 denote
two stable random variables with common index of stability α and
remaining parameters $(\beta_1, \sigma_1, \mu_1)$ and $(\beta_2, \sigma_2, \mu_2)$ respectively. Further, let
a and b denote two arbitrary real numbers with the additional assump-
tion that $a \neq 0$. Let us define three random variables Y_1, Y_2, and Y_3 by

$$Y_1 = a \cdot X_1, \; Y_2 = X_1 + b, \; Y_3 = X_1 + X_2$$

The first important statement is that Y_1, Y_2, and Y_3 follow again a
stable distribution with index of stability α. Second, the effect on the
remaining describing parameters $\tilde{\beta}_i, \tilde{\sigma}_i, \tilde{\mu}_i$, $i = 1, 2, 3$ is described by the
following expressions:[6]

---

[5] Weak converge of a sequence $X_1, X_2, \ldots$ of random variables to a distribution function F means that the distribution functions $F_1, F_2, \ldots$ of $X_1, X_2, \ldots$ converge point-
wise in every point of continuity of F to the distribution function F.
[6] A more detailed treatment and a proof for the correctness of these formulas can be
found in Samorodnitsky and Taqqu (1994).

$$\tilde{\beta}_1 = \text{sign}(a) \cdot \beta_1, \ \tilde{\beta}_2 = \beta_2, \ \tilde{\beta}_3 = \frac{\beta_1 \sigma_1^\alpha + \beta_2 \sigma_2^\alpha}{\sigma_1^\alpha + \sigma_2^\alpha}$$

$$\tilde{\sigma}_1 = |a| \cdot \sigma_1, \ \tilde{\sigma}_2 = \sigma_2, \ \tilde{\sigma}_3 = (\sigma_1^\alpha + \sigma_2^\alpha)^{1/\alpha}$$

$$\tilde{\mu}_1 = \begin{cases} (a \cdot \mu_1) & \text{if } \alpha \neq 1 \\ a \cdot \left(\mu - \dfrac{2}{\pi} \ln|a| \sigma_1 \beta_1 \right) & \text{if } \alpha = 1 \end{cases}, \tilde{\mu}_2 = \mu_2 + b, \ \tilde{\mu}_3 = \mu_1 + \mu_2$$

Implication of the Index of Stability for Financial Applications

When modeling asset returns with stable distributions, the index of stability (α) provides important financial insight. As we have already remarked, if it is below 2, then it follows that the data imply that extreme events happen more often than the Gaussian distribution would forecast. Even though the theoretical range of α is greater than zero but less than or equal to 2, not every value in the interval is meaningful from a financial viewpoint. On one hand, if α is less than or equal to 1, then the corresponding random variable does not have a finite mean. Any portfolio containing assets the returns of which follow a stable law with α less than or equal to 1 would have infinite expected return and it will not be a meaningful portfolio characteristic; decisions cannot be based on it. No risk diversification is possible for such a portfolio. In practice, when working with financial data, all estimated values of α are usually above 1, and if there is an exception, then the reason is most likely either a data problem or a numerical issue.[7]

SMOOTHLY TRUNCATED STABLE DISTRIBUTIONS

In some special cases of financial modeling it might occur that the infinite variance of stable distributions make their application impossible. We will see one example in Chapter 19, when we discuss the Black and Scholes type no-arbitrage models for the pricing of options. In many cases, the infinite variance of the return might lead to an infinite price for the derivative which clearly contradicts reality and intuition. The modeler is confronted with the following difficult situation: On the one hand, the skewed and heavy-tailed return distribution disqualify the

---

[7] For the details see, Rachev and Mittnik (2000).

normal distribution as an adequate candidate, on the other hand, theoretical restrictions in the option pricing problem do not allow us to use the stable distribution due to its infinite moments of order higher than α. For this reason, Rachev and Menn (2005) have suggested the use of appropriately truncated stable distributions.

The exact definition of truncated stable distributions is not that important at this point, that is why we restrict ourselves to a short outline of the idea. The density function of a *smoothly truncated stable distribution* (STS-distribution) is obtained by replacing the heavy tails of the density function g of some stable distribution with parameters (α, β, σ, μ) by the thin tails of two appropriately chosen normal distributions h_1 and h_2:

$$f(x) = \begin{cases} h_1(x), & x < a \\ g(x), & a \leq x \leq b \\ h_2(x), & x > b \end{cases} \qquad (7.3)$$

The parameters of the normal distributions are chosen such that the resulting function is the continuous density function of a probability measure on the real line. If it is possible to choose the cutting points a and b in a way that the resulting distribution possesses zero mean and unit variance, then we have found an easy way to characterize standardized STS-distributions. In Exhibit 7.4 the influence of the stable parameters on the appropriate cutting points is examined. As α approaches 2 (i.e., when the stable distribution approaches the normal distribution), we observe that the cutting points move to infinity. For small values of α, in contrast, the interval $[a,b]$ shrinks, reflecting the increasing heaviness of the tails of the stable distribution in the center.

Due to the thin tails of the normal density functions, the STS-distributions admit finite moments of arbitrary order but nevertheless are able to explain extreme observations. Exhibit 7.5 provides a comparison of tail probabilities for an arbitrarily chosen STS-distribution with zero mean and unit variance and the standard normal distribution. As one can see, the probability for extreme events is much higher under the assumption of an STS-distribution.

Consequently, one can see the class of STS-distribution as an appropriate class for modeling the return distribution of various financial assets. STS-distributions allow for skewness in the returns and the tails behave like fat tails but are light tails in the mathematical sense. That is, all moments of arbitrary order exist and are finite.

EXHIBIT 7.4   Influence of the Stable Parameters on the Cutting Points a and b

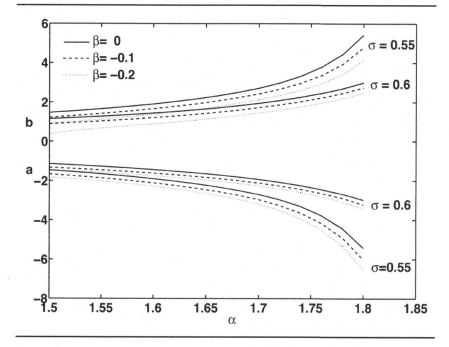

EXHIBIT 7.5   Comparison of Tail Probabilities between a Standard Normal and a Standardized STS-Distribution

x	$P(X \leq x)$ with $X \sim N(0,1)$	$P(X \leq x)$ with $X \sim STS$
−10	7.6198530242 E-24	0.00009861132775
−9	1.1285884060 E-19	0.00019210547239
−8	6.2209605743 E-16	0.00036395064728
−7	0.00000000000128	0.00067063777602
−6	0.00000000098659	0.00120208371192
−5	0.00000028665157	0.00209626995052
−4	0.00003167124183	0.00355718712680
−3	0.00134989803163	0.00669781592407
−2	0.02275013194818	0.02013650454786
−1	0.15865525393146	0.11793584416637

REFERENCES

Mandelbrot, B. B. 1963. "The Variation of Certain Speculative Prices." *Journal of Business* 36: 394–419.

Menn, C., and S. T. Rachev. 2005. "Smoothly Truncated Stable Distributions, GARCH-Models and Option Pricing" Technical report, University of California at Santa Barbara.

Rachev, S. T., and S. Mittnik. 2000. *Stable Paretian Models in Finance*. Chichester: John Wiley & Sons.

Samorodnitsky, G., and M. S. Taqqu. 1994. *Stable Non-Gaussian Random Processes*. New York: Chapman & Hall.

Zolotarev, V. M. 1986. *One-Dimensional Stable Distributions. Translation of Mathematical Monographs*, Vol. 65. Providence, RI: American Mathematical Society.

CHAPTER 8

Estimation Methodologies

In previous chapters, we described probability distributions in general and treated in detail some specific distributions of interest in finance. Our primary focus in the previous chapter was on the stable Paretian distribution and how it compared to the normal distribution. But how do you (1) determine whether the probability distribution for a time series of returns or prices for a particular asset is normally distributed or follows some other distribution and (2) estimate a probability distribution from an empirical distribution? Our purpose in this chapter is to explain how this is done. Specifically, we give a brief introduction to the different approaches to the testing and estimation of probability distributions.[1]

FITTING PROBABILITY DISTRIBUTIONS BY MAXIMUM LIKELIHOOD ESTIMATION

This section introduces the reader to one of the most popular concepts of determining an adequate probability distribution for a given set of observations. A set of observations is called a *sample*. Usually it is assumed that the observations are realizations that are independently drawn from the same probability distribution. In this book, we always assume that a given sample fulfills these properties. One method that can be applied in most of the practical applications and that possesses several appealing theoretical properties is called *maximum likelihood estimation*. The theory of maximum likelihood estimation can probably be understood best by looking at the following two examples:

---

[1] The reader may want to supplement the coverage in this chapter with a popular textbook in statistics such as Larsen and Marx (1986).

Example 1: Imagine that you have a coin for which you do not know the probability that it will show "tails" or "heads" when it is tossed. Let us denote the unknown probability for "tails" with the parameter p and, consequently, the unknown probability for "heads" is $1 - p$. After a small experiment of throwing the coin 10 times we observe "tails" three times and "heads" seven times. What will be the best guess for p on the basis of this observation? If we asked different people, the most frequent guess for p would be $\hat{p} = 0.3$. What is the theoretical foundation for this answer?

Example 2: Consider a Budweiser filling machine that is supposed to fill every can with 8 ounces of beer. The engineer responsible for the filling machine tells us that there are small random fluctuations in the volume that is filled in every can and that it is common to assume that the volume, V, that we will observe in a randomly chosen beer can varies according to a normal distribution, $V \sim N(\mu, \sigma^2)$, with unknown parameters μ and σ^2. As in Example 1, we consider a sample of 10 randomly chosen beer cans and examine their content. The result is the following list of measured volumes (in ounces):

Observation	Measured volume (ounces)
1	7.80
2	8.13
3	7.94
4	7.95
5	8.02
6	7.87
7	8.09
8	8.18
9	8.21
10	7.91

What would be your guess, on the basis of these observations, for the two unknown parameters? This question is more complicated than in the previous example, but we will try to explain one possible idea: From Chapter 4 we know that μ represents the mean of the distribution and σ^2 the variance. As the sample mean is the empirical counterpart for the mean and, as the variance is the mean of the random variable $(V - EV)^2$, we can calculate the sample counterparts as given in Chapter 4:

$$\hat{\mu} = \frac{1}{10} \sum_{i=1}^{10} v_i = 8.01$$

$$\hat{\sigma}^2 = \frac{1}{10} \sum_{i=1}^{10} (v_i - \hat{\mu}^2) = 0.0172$$

where v_i denotes the i-th observation. These values seem to be reasonable estimates for the two unknown parameters as common sense implies that for large samples, the difference between the estimates and the true values will vanish. But what is the theoretical foundation for these estimates?

The common principle in these two examples becomes obvious if we look at the probability for observing the specific sample. In the first example, the probability of observing three tails and seven heads is given by the expression (this follows from the general formula for the binomial distribution as described in Chapter 2):

$$P(3 \text{ tails, } 7 \text{ heads}) = 120 \cdot p^3 \cdot (1-p)^7$$

Obviously this probability (which is often called *likelihood*) depends upon the unknown parameter p. Now we could choose the estimate p such that the probability for the concrete observation is maximized. In other words, just roll out a usual maximization of a function with respect to its argument by setting the first derivative equal to zero and solving for the argument. In our case this maximization yields the above mentioned solution $\hat{p} = 0.3$ or in general form $\hat{p}$ = number of tails observed/number of observations.[2]

In the second example, the described procedure cannot be applied as we are dealing with a continuous distribution, the normal distribution. The probability for a specific observation is always zero. Nevertheless, the value $f(x)$ of the density function contains information about "how likely an observation will fall in the neighborhood of x." Consequently, we do not consider the probability to observe the sample but we consider the joint probability density function at the sample observations as a function of the unknown parameters μ and σ^2:

---

[2] The first derivative of the likelihood is

$$120 \cdot (3p^2(1-p)^7 - 7\,p^3(1-p)^6) = 0$$

Setting the above equal to zero and solving for p we find $p = 0.3$.

$$f(v_1, ..., v_n) = \left(\frac{1}{\sqrt{2\pi\sigma^2}}\right)^{10} \cdot e^{-\frac{\sum_{i=1}^{10}(v_i-\mu)^2}{2\sigma^2}} \tag{8.1}$$

As above, we call this expression the "likelihood of the sample observation."

Now we can proceed in the same way as above: We try to maximize the likelihood with respect to the two unknown parameters. Usually it is convenient to consider the logarithm of the likelihood and to maximize the logarithm:

$$\log(f(v_1, ..., v_n)) = -\frac{\sum_{i=1}^{10}(v_i-\mu)^2}{2\sigma^2} - 5\log(2\pi\sigma^2) \to \max \tag{8.2}$$

In this case we will obtain after some standard maximization calculus the result given earlier for μ and σ.

The idea of maximizing the likelihood of a given sample can be generalized to the following "maximum likelihood estimation" (denoted ML-estimation) approach: Choose the estimates for the unknown parameter(s) such that the likelihood given by the probability of observing the specific sample or by the joint density function evaluated at the observed sample points is maximal. The only ingredients to realize this approach is the distribution function (for discrete probability distributions) or the joint density function (for continuous probability distributions) and some sample values. Exhibit 8.1 lists some ML-estimates for popular distributions.

CONFIDENCE BOUNDS

Let us consider again the estimates for the statistical moments reported in Exhibit 4.4 of Chapter 4. Imagine that we have generated by computer 10 random draws from a normal distribution with zero mean and standard deviation σ equal to 3. Thus, we know that the true mean μ equals zero. Now we calculate the sample mean $\bar{x}$ and consider the result as an estimator for the true population mean μ. Is it very likely that our sample mean $\bar{x}$ coincides with the true mean μ? Actually not. As $\bar{x}$ is the realization of a continuous distribution, the probability of getting the true value equals zero, i.e., $P(\bar{x} = \mu) = 0$. But certainly we can expect that the sample mean will be in most cases somewhere in the neighborhood of μ.

EXHIBIT 8.1 Maximum Likelihood Estimates for the Parameters of Popular Probability Distributions

The estimators are expressed in terms of a sample $(x_1, \ldots, x_n)$ of independent observations of the respective distribution.

Probability Distribution	Probability Density/Probability Function	ML Estimate
Bernoulli	$P(X = x) = p^x \cdot (1-p)^{1-x}$	$\hat{p} = \dfrac{1}{n} \displaystyle\sum_{i=1}^{n} x_i$
Binomial	$P(X = k) = \dbinom{m}{k} p^k (1-p)^{m-k}$	$\hat{p} = \dfrac{1}{n} \displaystyle\sum_{i=1}^{n} x_i$
Poisson	$P(X = k) = \dfrac{\lambda^k}{k!} \cdot e^{-\lambda}$, $k = 0, 1, 2, \ldots$	$\hat{\lambda} = \dfrac{1}{n} \displaystyle\sum_{i=1}^{n} x_i$
Normal	$f(x) = \dfrac{1}{\sqrt{2\pi}\sigma} \cdot e^{-\frac{(x-\mu)^2}{2\sigma^2}}$	$\hat{\mu} = \dfrac{1}{n} \displaystyle\sum_{i=1}^{n} x_i,\ \hat{\sigma} = \sqrt{\dfrac{1}{n} \displaystyle\sum_{i=1}^{n} (x_i - \hat{\mu})^2}$
Exponential	$f(x) = \dfrac{1}{\beta} \cdot e^{-\frac{x}{\beta}}$, $x > 0$	$\hat{\beta} = \dfrac{1}{n} \displaystyle\sum_{i=1}^{n} x_i,\ \hat{\lambda} = \dfrac{n}{\displaystyle\sum_{i=1}^{n} x_i}$

97

EXHIBIT 8.1 (Continued)

Probability Distribution	Probability Density Function	ML Estimate
Weibull[a]	$f(x) = \dfrac{\alpha x^{\alpha-1}}{\beta^\alpha} \cdot e^{-\left(\frac{x}{\beta}\right)^\alpha}$, $x > 0$	$\hat{\alpha} = \left(\dfrac{\displaystyle\sum_{i=1}^{n} x_i^{\hat{\alpha}} \log x_i}{\displaystyle\sum_{i=1}^{n} x_i^{\hat{\alpha}}} - \dfrac{1}{n}\displaystyle\sum_{i=1}^{n} \log x_i \right)^{-1}$ $\hat{\beta} = \left(\dfrac{1}{n}\displaystyle\sum_{i=1}^{n} x_i^{\hat{\alpha}} \right)^{1/\hat{\alpha}}$
Gamma[a,b]	$f(x) = \dfrac{1}{\beta \cdot \Gamma(\alpha)} \cdot e^{-x/\beta} \cdot \left(\dfrac{x}{\beta}\right)^{\alpha-1}$, $x > 0$	$\dfrac{1}{n}\displaystyle\sum_{i=1}^{n} \log x_i - \log\left(\dfrac{1}{n}\displaystyle\sum_{i=1}^{n} x_i\right) = \psi(\hat{\alpha}) - \log(\hat{\alpha})$ $\hat{\beta} = \dfrac{\dfrac{1}{n}\displaystyle\sum_{i=1}^{n} x_i}{\hat{\alpha}}$
Beta[b,c]	$f(x) = \dfrac{\Gamma(\alpha_1 + \alpha_2)}{\Gamma(\alpha_1) \cdot \Gamma(\alpha_2)} \cdot x^{\alpha_1-1} \cdot (1-x)^{\alpha_2-1}$, $0 < x < 1$	$\psi(\alpha_1) - \psi(\alpha_1 + \alpha_2) = \dfrac{1}{n}\displaystyle\sum_{i=1}^{n} \log x_i$ $\psi(\alpha_2) - \psi(\alpha_1 + \alpha_2) = \dfrac{1}{n}\displaystyle\sum_{i=1}^{n} \log(1 - x_i)$

EXHIBIT 8.1 (Continued)

Probability Distribution	Probability Density Function	ML Estimate
Lognormal	$f(x) = \dfrac{1}{x\sigma\sqrt{2\pi}} \cdot e^{-\frac{(\ln x - \mu)^2}{2\sigma^2}}$, $x > 0$	$\hat{\mu} = \dfrac{1}{n}\sum_{i=1}^{n}\log x_i$, $\hat{\sigma} = \sqrt{\dfrac{1}{n}\sum_{i=1}^{n}(\log x_i - \hat{\mu})^2}$
Logistic[c]	$f(x) = \dfrac{e^{-(x-\alpha)/\beta}}{\beta\left(1 + e^{-(x-\alpha)/\beta}\right)^2}$	$\dfrac{2}{n}\sum_{i=1}^{n}\left(1 + e^{\frac{x_i-\alpha}{\beta}}\right)^{-1} = 1$ $\dfrac{1}{n}\sum_{i=1}^{n}\dfrac{x_i-\alpha}{\beta}\cdot\dfrac{1 - e^{\frac{x_i-\alpha}{\beta}}}{1 + e^{\frac{x_i-\alpha}{\beta}}} = 1$
Extreme Value[c]	$f(x) = \dfrac{1}{b}\cdot e^{-\frac{x-a}{b} - e^{-\frac{x-a}{b}}}$	$\dfrac{1}{n}\sum_{i=1}^{n} e^{-\frac{x_i-a}{b}} = 1$, $\dfrac{1}{n}\sum_{i=1}^{n}\dfrac{x_i-a}{b}\left(1 - e^{-\frac{x_i-a}{b}}\right) = 1$

[a] No explicit solution available, the first equation must be solved numerically.

[b] ψ denotes the derivative of the log-gamma function, that is,

$$\psi(x) = \frac{\partial}{\partial x}\log\Gamma(x) = \frac{\Gamma'(x)}{\Gamma(x)}$$

[c] The system of equations must be solved numerically. Analytical solutions are not available.

Formalizing the use of "most cases" and "neighborhood" leads to the concept of confidence bounds for estimators. Suppose we want to estimate a distributional parameter γ with an estimator $\hat{\gamma}$. Due to profound statistical results, we are able to determine in most of the cases an interval $[\hat{\gamma} - c_1, \hat{\gamma} + c_2]$, called a *confidence interval*, which covers the true parameter with a prespecified probability, the so-called *confidence level*. The width of the interval depends on the number of sample observations used to estimate the parameter and on the variance of the specific distribution. In our example, the confidence interval possesses the following form:

$$\left[\bar{x} - \frac{\sigma}{\sqrt{n}} q_{1-\frac{\alpha}{2}} \; , \; \bar{x} + \frac{\sigma}{\sqrt{n}} q_{1-\frac{\alpha}{2}} \right]$$

where

n = number of observations

$q_{1-\frac{\alpha}{2}}$ = quantile of the standard normal distribution

σ = standard deviation of the distribution generating the sample

How can this result be obtained? We will explain the crucial steps here. The first important fact is that the expression

$$\bar{x} = \frac{1}{n} \sum_{i=1}^{n} x_i$$

is normally distributed with mean $\tilde{\mu} = \mu$ and variance

$$\tilde{\sigma}^2 = \frac{1}{n}\sigma^2$$

Therefore, we know that the following relation holds true:

$$P(q_{\alpha/2} \leq \bar{x} \leq q_{1-\alpha/2}) = \alpha$$

where α denotes the desired level of significance and q_β denotes the β-quantile of a normal distribution with mean $\tilde{\mu}$ and variance $\tilde{\sigma}^2$. Now let u_β denote the β-quantile of a standard normal distribution. Then the following relation holds true:

$$q_\beta = \tilde{\mu} + \tilde{\sigma} \cdot u_\beta$$

Using this equation we can manipulate our initial equation as follows:

$$P(q_{\alpha/2} \leq \bar{x} \leq q_{1-\alpha/2}) = \alpha$$
$$\Leftrightarrow P(\tilde{\mu} + \tilde{\sigma} \cdot u_{\alpha/2} \leq \bar{x} \leq \tilde{\mu} + \tilde{\sigma} \cdot u_{1-\alpha/2}) = \alpha$$
$$\Leftrightarrow P(\bar{x} + \tilde{\sigma} \cdot u_{\alpha/2} \leq \tilde{\mu} \leq \bar{x} + \tilde{\sigma} \cdot u_{1-\alpha/2}) = \alpha$$

Given the fact that $\tilde{\mu}$ equals μ and u_β equals $-u_{1-\beta}$, we obtain exactly the claimed result.

A naturally arising question is whether the same methodology can be applied to any distribution? The answer is "yes almost." Assume that we are given a sample $(x_1, ..., x_n)$ of size n, where the observations are independent realizations of the same fixed but unknown probability distribution P. Let us additionally assume that m denotes the mean and v the variance of this unknown distribution P. The already mentioned Central Limit Theorem states that under these assumptions the sum

$$\sum x_i$$

of our sample observations behaves—at least for large n—like a normally distributed random variable with mean $\mu = n \cdot m$ and variance $\sigma^2 = n \cdot v$. Therefore, the same approach as described above can be used to obtain the following approximate confidence interval with a level of significance α for the mean m:

$$\left[\bar{x} - \sqrt{\frac{v}{n}} u_{1-\alpha/2}, \bar{x} + \sqrt{\frac{v}{n}} u_{1-\alpha/2} \right]$$

In the case where the variance v of the data generating distribution is unknown—which will be the case in most practical applications—we will be forced to estimate the variance with the sample variance σ^2. For large samples and "well-behaved" distributions, the approximation error of the approximate confidence interval tends to be acceptably small.

HYPOTHESIS TESTS AND P-VALUE

Sometimes statisticians are not only interested in giving confidence bounds for an unknown parameter. They also want to affirm the validity of assumptions about a specific unknown parameter. This discipline is referred to as *hypothesis testing*. As an example, we will test hypotheses about the parameters of probability distributions.

To illustrate the concepts and the basic elements of hypothesis testing, suppose that we are considering a shipment of 10,000 bulbs. The vendor guarantees that at least 99% of the bulbs are faultless. Usually we denote the claimed hypothesis as H_0 (referred to as the *null hypothesis*) and the logical opposite hypothesis as H_1 (referred to as the *alternative hypothesis*). So in our case we have

$$H_0: q = 1\%$$

$$H_1: q \neq 1\%$$

where q denotes the true but unknown percentage of bad bulbs.

To check the assertion, we take a random sample of 10 bulbs. We find that 2 of the 10 bulbs do not work. Our empirically observed estimate will be denoted by $\hat{q}$ and is 20% in our case. Should we believe the vendor's statement that 99% of the bulbs will be faultless (i.e., accept the null hypothesis H_0) and, if not, how could we theoretically underpin our doubts? What we can do is compare the empirically observed percentage of "bad bulbs" of $\hat{q} = 20\%$ in our sample of 10 bulbs with the theoretically predicted percentage of bad bulbs of $q = 1\%$.

It is intuitively clear that large deviations militate against the null hypothesis, H_0. In the parlance of statisticians, a function that decides on the basis of a sample whether we should reject H_0 and believe in H_1—or whether we cannot reject H_0—is called a *decision function*. The decision function takes only two possible values, usually encoded as d_0 and d_1. d_0 means "don't reject H_0" and d_1 means "reject H_0". It is clear that, unless our sample contains the whole shipment, the output of our decision function might be wrong. The following table visualizes the two errors which can occur:

	True State	
Decision	H_0 (null hypothesis)	H_1 (alternative hypothesis)
d_0	Correct decision	Incorrect decision: Type II error
d_1	Incorrect decision: Type I error	Correct decision

Making a possibly wrong decision with a decision function based upon a sample is called a *statistical test*. Most of us know applications of statistical tests from our daily life: A pregnancy test, an AIDS test, or the result of a lie detector is simply the application of a statistical test and we know that errors can occur. But a natural question is whether it is possible to construct for every specific problem "a best test," that is, a test which minimizes the probability that our decision is wrong.

Notice in the previous table there are two incorrect decisions, labeled "Type I error" and "Type II error." The former error is the rejection of the null hypothesis when it is the true state.[3] The latter error is the acceptance of the null hypothesis when it is not the true state.[4]

After thinking about this task, it becomes immediately obvious that we cannot minimize both error probabilities simultaneously: A test which regardless of the outcome of the sample rejects H_0 has a probability of zero for the second type error, whereas a test which never rejects H_0 has a probability of zero for the first type error. The way out of this tricky situation is that we define a *level of significance*, usually denoted as α, which represents the maximally tolerated probability for the occurrence of the first type error. Under all tests which have a probability for observing the first type error of less than α, we seek the one with the smallest probability for the occurrence of the second type error. Coming back to our example, we are defining the following decision function:

$$\delta(x) = \begin{cases} d_1 \text{ if } \hat{q} < c_1 \text{ or } \hat{q} > c_2 \\ d_0 \text{ if } c_1 \leq \hat{q} \leq c_2 \end{cases}$$

where c_1 and c_2 denote two appropriately chosen constants.

As already mentioned, this decision function is based on the fact that large deviations of the empirically observed percentage $\hat{q}$ of bad bulbs, from the theoretically predicted one, will militate against H_0 (i.e., against $q = 1\%$). To determine the barriers c_1 and c_2, we must choose first a level of significance α (i.e., an upper bound for the tolerated probability for the Type I error). The Type I error in our example means that we decide on the basis of our sample that the shipment has a percentage of bad bulbs different from 1% (H_1), whereas in reality this percentage equals 1% (H_0). Typically, in hypothesis testing, the value for α used is 1%, 5%, or 10%.

The probability of observing less than c_1 bad bulbs or more than c_2 in a sample of 10 if the true percentage of bad bulbs is 1% can now be calculated with the help of the binomial distribution. As the probability for the occurrence of a Type I error should be smaller than the level of significance α, we end up with the following inequality:

---

[3] Type I error is also called the "α error."
[4] Type II error is also called the "β error."

$$P(N < c_1 \text{ or } N > c_2) = P(N < c_1) + P(N > c_2) < \alpha$$

where N denotes the number of bad bulbs in our sample. For $\alpha = 5\%$ we obtain the following decision function:

$$\delta(x) = \begin{cases} d_1 \text{ if } \hat{q} > 0 \\ d_0 \text{ if } \hat{q} = 0 \end{cases}$$

This means that if we observe only one defective bulb in our sample of size 10, this will already militate against the null hypothesis H_0. Our sample contained two bad bulbs and, consequently, we reject the null hypothesis.

As we have shown, the probability of wrongly rejecting the null hypothesis, that is, the probability for the Type I error, is less than or equal to 5%. This means that our decision is statistically assured. In the case that the null hypothesis cannot be rejected, we can make no statement about the validity of H_0. The reason for that is the fact that in most applications, the maximal probability for the occurrence of the Type I error and Type II error add up to at least one. As the probability for the Type I error is usually bounded by a small number (like 1% or 5%), we can conclude that the probability of wrongly accepting H_0 might be very high, even close to one.

Alternative Formulation: *p*-Value

Another way of formulating the testing problem and obtaining the same result is provided by a concept called the *p-value*. For a specific sample, the *p*-value is the maximal level of significance for which a rejection of the null hypothesis is not possible. In our case, we have to determine the probability of obtaining 2 or more bad bulbs in a sample of 10 under the assumption that the percentage of bad bulbs in the shipment equals 1%. We obtain—again with the help of the binomial distribution:

$$\begin{aligned} p &= P(N \geq 2) = 1 - P(N < 2) = 1 - P(N = 0) - P(N = 1) \\ &= 1 - \binom{10}{0} \cdot 0.01^0 \cdot 0.99^{10} - \binom{10}{1} \cdot 0.01^1 \cdot 0.99^9 \\ &= 0.004266 \end{aligned}$$

A rule for rejecting the null hypothesis which is equivalent to the previously described decision function is given by the following decision function:

$$\delta(x) = \begin{cases} d_1 \text{ if } p < \alpha \\ d_0 \text{ if } p \geq \alpha \end{cases}$$

Again, the $\alpha\%$ is referred to as the level of significance.

RELATIONSHIP BETWEEN HYPOTHESIS TESTS AND CONFIDENCE BOUNDS

The following example tries to clarify the relationship between the concepts that we have introduced so far in this chapter. We consider a data set of 1,000 daily returns from the S&P 500. We assume that these daily returns can be regarded as independent and identically distributed. For the ease of computation, we simply assume that these returns follow a normal distribution with zero mean and unknown variance σ^2. The task is to determine the 95% quantile of the return distribution. (In Chapter 14, we see that the task of determining the $1 - \alpha$-quantile of a return distribution corresponds to calculating the so-called Value-at-Risk at level α, an important controlling tool in risk management applications.)

We divide our data sample in two equally large subsamples where the first will serve as our estimation sample whereas the second will be used as our verification sample. Exhibit 8.2 visualizes the return series and indicates its division into two subsamples, with the estimation sample and verification sample labeled "estimation window" and "verification window," respectively.

Approaches to Quantile Estimates

One possible way of estimating the 95% quantile is to estimate in a first step the data generating distribution. As we know per assumption that the distribution belongs to the class of normal distributions with zero mean, we just need to calculate the ML-estimate $\hat{\sigma}^2$ for the unknown variance σ^2:

$$\hat{\sigma}^2 = \frac{1}{n}\sum_{i=1}^{n}(r_i - \mu)^2$$

and since by assumption $\mu = 0$,

$$= \frac{1}{500}\sum_{i=1}^{500}r_i^2 = 10.4$$

The connection between the α-quantile q_α of a normal distribution with mean μ and variance σ^2 and the α-quantile u_α of a standard normal distribution is given by the following formula:

EXHIBIT 8.2   Sample of 1,000 Daily Returns for S&P 500: Estimation Window and Verification Window

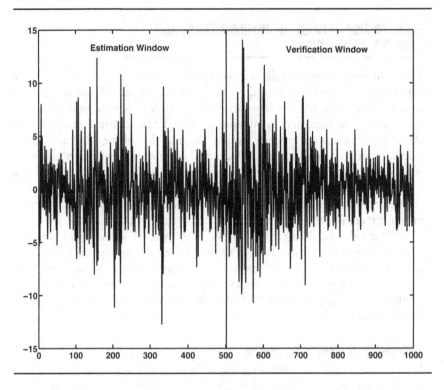

$$q_\alpha = \mu + \sigma \cdot u_\alpha$$

In our illustration, σ^2 is 10.4 and μ is 0. For a normal distribution, $u_{0.95}$ is equal to 1.64.[5] Substituting these values into the above equation, we obtain the following estimate for the 95% quantile $q_{0.95}$:

$$
\begin{aligned}
\hat{q}_\alpha^{ML} &= \mu + \hat{\sigma} \cdot u_\alpha \\
&= 0 + \sqrt{10.4} \cdot 1.64 = 5.30
\end{aligned}
$$

We have equipped the estimate with the superscript "ML" to emphasize the fact that the estimate is based on a ML-estimate for the unknown variance σ^2.

---

[5] This value can be looked up in any statistics textbook.

Another possibility of estimating the 95% quantile $q_{0.95}$ is to consider the empirical 95% quantile in the estimation sample. We know that the probability of observing a realization greater than or equal to the 95% quantile equals 5% and the probability for a realization smaller than or equal to the 95% quantile equals 95%. A natural estimate for the value of the quantile may be obtained by dividing the sorted sample in the proportion 95:5 and then taking the average of the greatest value in the first part and the smallest value in the second part. This leads to the following estimate, which will be denoted as empirical quantile (emp):

$$\hat{q}_{0.95}^{\mathrm{emp}} = 4.97$$

Obviously the two estimates differ substantially.

Now we could be interested in testing whether these estimates provide reliable proxies for the true but unknown 95% quantile.

Testing for the Reliability of Quantile Estimates

One possibility to obtain information about the reliability of our quantile estimates is the determination of confidence bounds. Confidence bounds can easily be obtained for the ML-method. It is possible to show that the following expression is Chi-square distributed with n degrees of freedom:

$$\frac{n \cdot \hat{\sigma}^2}{\sigma^2} \sim \chi^2(n)$$

Therefore, the following relation holds true:

$$P\left(\chi_{\alpha/2}^2(n) \leq \frac{n \cdot \hat{\sigma}^2}{\sigma^2} \leq \chi_{1-\alpha/2}^2(n)\right) = 1 - \alpha$$

where $\chi_\beta^2(n)$ denotes the β-quantile of the Chi-square distribution with n degrees of freedom.

After a few manipulations we obtain the following equation:

$$P\left(\frac{n \cdot \hat{\sigma}^2}{\chi_{1-\alpha/2}^2(n)} \leq \sigma^2 \leq \frac{n \cdot \hat{\sigma}^2}{\chi_{\alpha/2}^2(n)}\right) = 1 - \alpha$$

From the last equation we can deduce that

$$\left[\frac{n \cdot \hat{\sigma}^2}{\chi^2_{1-\alpha/2}(n)}, \frac{n \cdot \hat{\sigma}^2}{\chi^2_{\alpha/2}(n)} \right]$$

forms a confidence interval for the unknown variance σ^2 with confidence level $1 - \alpha$.

In our example we obtain with $\alpha = 5\%$ the confidence interval [9.229, 11.832]. From the confidence interval for σ^2 we deduce the following 95%-confidence interval for the unknown 95% quantile:

$$[\mu + \sqrt{9.229} \cdot u_{0.95}, \mu + \sqrt{11.832} \cdot u_{0.95}] = [5.00, 5.66]$$

The interpretation of this interval is the following: Under the assumption that the data consist of independent observations of a normal distribution with zero mean, the random interval constructed according to the above description will contain the true but unknown 95% quantile with a probability of 95%.

An alternative use of this confidence interval could arise when we want to test whether the true but unknown quantile equals 5.30 as computed above from the ML-estimate. If we choose a significance level of $\alpha = 5\%$, then we obtain the following decision function:

$$\delta(r_1, ..., r_n) = \begin{cases} d_1 \text{ reject } H_0 \text{ if } \hat{q}^{ML}_{0.95} \notin [5.00, 5.66] \\ d_0 \text{ do not reject } H_0 \text{ if } \hat{q}^{ML}_{0.95} \notin [5.00, 5.66] \end{cases}$$

where $\notin$ means "does not belong to".

For our second quantile estimate, the situation is more difficult: The empirical quantile is not based on any assumption on the underlying distribution; it is a *nonparametric estimate*. On the one hand, this fact is a great advantage as the method can be applied to any data sample; on the other hand, it makes it nearly impossible to determine a confidence interval for our estimate.[6] But nevertheless we can test the reliability of our estimate. This is where the verification sample enters the game.

---

[6] For the calculation of a confidence interval, the distribution of the estimator and therefore the distribution of the data is needed.

Imagine that we knew the true 95% quantile $q_{0.95}$. Then we know that the probability of realizing a return greater than $q_{0.95}$ equals 5%. Realizing a return and seeing whether it is greater than $q_{0.95}$ can be interpreted as realizing a Bernoulli distributed random variable with parameter $p = 5\%$. Let us repeat this experiment 500 times and let N denote the number of *exceedances*; that is, the number of realizations greater than $q_{0.95}$. We know from Chapter 2 that the random variable N will follow a binomial distribution with parameters $n = 500$ and $p = 5\%$. Knowing the distribution of N, we are able to calculate a confidence interval for N. We have

$$P(b_{\alpha/2}(n, p) < N \le b_{1-\alpha/2}(n, p)) \ge 1 - \alpha$$

where $b_\beta(n,p)$ denotes the β-quantile of a binomial distribution with parameters n and p. For $\alpha = 5\%$, $n = 500$, and $p = 5\%$ we obtain the following 95%-confidence interval for the number of exceedances: [15.5, 34.5].

Knowing this, we can count the number of exceedances we observe in the verification sample for our two estimates for the unknown 95% quantile. With $\hat{q}_{0.95}^{emp} = 4.97$ we obtain 29 exceedances and for $\hat{q}_\alpha^{ML} = 5.30$ we have 28 exceedances. Both values are covered by the confidence interval. If we observed a number of exceedances outside of our confidence interval, then we could reject the null hypothesis of $q_{0.95} = \hat{q}_{0.95}$ at the 5% level of significance.

FITTING STABLE DISTRIBUTIONS

In this section, we introduce two popular methodologies for the parameter estimation of stable Paretian distributions.[7] The problem with stable distributions is the fact that with a few exceptions there are no closed-form expressions for the density function of a general stable distribution. As already mentioned in Chapter 7, stable distributions are uniquely characterized through their characteristic function. Concretely, the characteristic function of a general stable distribution possesses the following form:

$$\varphi(t) = Ee^{itX} = \begin{cases} \exp\left(-\sigma|t|^\alpha\left[1 - i\beta \operatorname{sign}(t)\tan\left(\frac{\alpha\pi}{2}\right)\right] + i\mu t\right), \alpha \ne 1 \\ \exp\left(-\sigma|t|\left[1 + i\beta\frac{2}{\pi}\operatorname{sign}(t)\ln(t)\right] + i\mu t\right), \alpha = 1 \end{cases} \quad (8.3)$$

---

[7] For an overview, see Stoyanov and Racheva-Iotova (2004b).

Now, the question is how can we use the characteristic function to estimate the four different describing parameters (α, β, σ, μ) on the basis of a given sample of observations $x = (x_1, \ldots, x_n)$. Principally there are two approaches:

■ Try to calculate a proxy for the characteristic function denoted as sample characteristic function out of the observations given by $x = (x_1, \ldots, x_n)$ and to estimate the unknown parameters (α, β, σ, μ) such that the sample characteristic function is as close as possible to the theoretical characteristic function.[8]

■ Try to derive a numerical approximation of the density function of the stable distribution and estimate the unknown parameters (α, β, σ, μ) by maximizing the numerical density.[9]

Fitting the Characteristic Function

To implement the first approach, we use the fact that the characteristic function is in fact nothing other than an expectation. It is the expected value of the random variable e^{itX}, where X follows a stable distribution with parameter vector (α, β, σ, μ). Consequently we can calculate a proxy for φ by computing the following arithmetic mean for different values of t:

$$\hat{\varphi}(t) = \frac{1}{n} \sum_{i=1}^{n} e^{itx_i} \tag{8.4}$$

By using mathematical optimization software, it is easy to determine estimates ($\hat{\alpha}$, $\hat{\beta}$, $\hat{\sigma}$, $\hat{\mu}$) such that the theoretical function φ is as close as possible to its sample counterpart $\hat{\varphi}$. This approach is referred to as "fitting the characteristic function." For a detailed description of this approach, see Kogon and Williams (1998).

MLE with Numerical Approximation of the Density Function

The second approach requires a way to determine a numerical approximation of the density function of a stable probability law. There are two main different methodologies as to how to proceed. The first approach is based on the following so-called Fourier-inversion formulae: Let P be a continuous probability distribution on the real line with characteristic function φ and density function f. The following equation describes the relation between these two functions:

---

[8] This approach goes back to Press (1972).
[9] This approach was first proposed and examined by DuMouchel (1971,1973).

$$f(x) = \frac{1}{2\pi} \cdot \int_{-\infty}^{\infty} e^{-itx} \varphi(t) dt \qquad (8.5)$$

Given this relation and the characteristic function of a stable distribution as described in equation (8.3), we are able (at least theoretically) to calculate the value $f(x)$ of the stable density function at every given point x. This task can be performed in a very efficient way by using the so-called Fast Fourier Transform (FFT)—an algorithm that can be used for a simultaneous evaluation of the integral in equation (8.5) for many different x-values. This approach is, for example, used by the methodology presented in Rachev and Menn (2005) and provides a fast calculation of the desired approximative density while guaranteeing an acceptable level of accuracy.

When the main focus is on calculating, a highly accurate value for $f(x)$, the second approach is more favorable. The idea is to express the value $f(x)$ of the stable density at point x in terms of a so-called Zolotarev integral which can then be evaluated numerically. This approach is pursued in Nolan (1997) and implemented in a freely distributed software package called STABLE.[10]

Consequently, we can calculate with one of the two described methods the likelihood corresponding to our sample $x = (x_1, ..., x_n)$ in dependence of the unknown parameter vector $(\alpha, \beta, \sigma, \mu)$. The estimate $(\hat{\alpha}, \hat{\beta}, \hat{\sigma}, \hat{\mu})$ is now obtained by maximizing the likelihood with respect to the unknown parameters with the help of a numerical optimization software.

COMPARING PROBABILITY DISTRIBUTIONS: TESTING FOR THE GOODNESS OF FIT

When examining the empirical distribution of observations, it is not only interesting to fit a representative of a given class of probability distributions to the observations, but it is also quite important to determine how well the fit between the empirical and the theoretical distribution is. The reason why this question is so important is that when estimating the parameters of a given distribution family one determines the best candidate in exactly this distribution class to explain the observations. But it very might be that the real distribution generating the data does not belong to the pre-specified distribution family and consequently the esti-

---

[10] http://academic2.american.edu/~jpnolan/stable/stable.html.

mated distribution will not be able to explain the observed realizations, neither in the past nor in the future. This question leads us to the concept of probability metrics.

Generally speaking a *probability metric*[11] is a function that assigns distances to two given probability distributions. This concept helps in addressing the above mentioned problems because we can proceed in the following way: Given a sample of observations, we can compare the empirical distribution with the presumed distribution in order to determine whether it is plausible that the data were generated by the estimated distribution or not. Another application could be to determine whether the data generating distribution belongs to a certain class of probability distributions such as the class of normal distributions.

Kolmogorov-Smirnov Distance and Quantile-Quantile Plots

One of the most famous (simple) probability distances is the *Kolmogorov-Smirnov distance* (KS-distance). Given two probability distributions P and Q on the real line with cumulative distribution functions F and G, we can assess a distance between these two distributions by calculating the highest distance between the values $F(x)$ and $G(x)$ for varying x. Mathematically, this means calculating the supremum distance between F and G:

$$d(P, Q) = \|F - G\|_\infty = \sup_x |F(x) - G(x)| \qquad (8.6)$$

The *supremum* is the least upper bound of a set and is denoted by "sup."

It was understood by statisticians that the distribution of this distance calculated between an empirical distribution function and the theoretical one on the basis of a sample, does not depend on the concrete type of distribution as long as it is a continuous distribution. This fact can be used to perform the famous Kolmogorov-Smirnov test of goodness of fit, which is outlined below.

Given a sample of observations $x = (x_1, ..., x_n)$, the empirical distribution function F_n is given by the following expression

$$F_n(t) = \frac{1}{n} \#\{x_i | x_i \leq t\} \qquad (8.7)$$

---

[11] Strictly speaking, one has to distinguish between two types of probability metrics. The so-called "simple probability" metrics (or "simple distances") measure the distance between two probability distributions; whereas the "compound probability" metrics (distances) measure the distance between two (possibly dependent) random variables. For a rigorous description of probability metrics, see Rachev (1991).

where #{...} denotes the number of elements contained in the set {...} and F_n defines a discrete probability distribution on the real line and for large values of n the empirical distribution converges to the theoretical one. Under the hypothesis that the sample was generated by a probability distribution with distribution function F, the distribution of the KS-distance between F and F_n is tabulated. That means that depending on the concrete value of n and the observed distance (denoted by d), it is possible to calculate the p-value and to decide whether we should believe in the hypotheses or not.

Sometimes it is helpful to plot the distance between the empirical and theoretical distribution function to illustrate the deviation graphically. In order to generate a maximum of comparability, it is common to standardize the two distributions in the following way: Instead of plotting the x-values versus the difference of distribution function values, we plot the quantiles of the first distribution versus the quantiles of the second. The result is called the *quantile-quantile plot* or simply the *QQ-plot*.

Let us illustrate the concepts presented with an example. Suppose that we are given the following sample of 20 observations (e.g., daily stock return data in percent over one trading month):

i	Observation	i	Observation
1	–2.1	11	0.4
2	0.1	12	0.1
3	0.3	13	–1.1
4	–0.8	14	–0.3
5	1.7	15	0.9
6	1.3	16	0.1
7	0.2	17	–3.1
8	–0.4	18	–0.7
9	0.0	19	–0.2
10	–0.1	20	1.5

We want to determine whether it is reasonable to assume that the underlying distribution is standard normal. We can use the QQ-plot in Exhibit 8.3, which shows the differences between the empirical distribution and the standard normal distribution.

The line in the exhibit embodies the perfect coincidence, whereas the dots represent the actual observations. We can see that there are notable differences between the corresponding quantiles. In order to interpret these deviations, we calculate additionally the KS-distance. The calculations are shown in Exhibit 8.4. The KS-distance is given by

EXHIBIT 8.3   Q-Q Plot Illustration

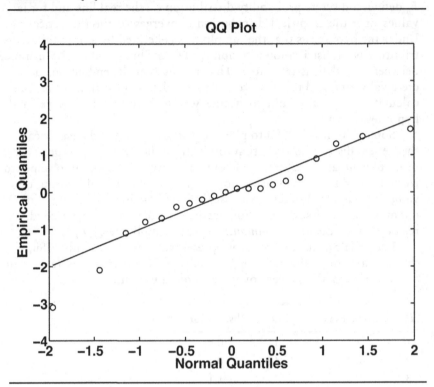

$$d = \max_{1 \le i \le 20} \left| F_n(x_i) - \Phi(x_i) \right| = 0.1446$$

and the critical value[12] for a confidence level of 95% is $d_n = 0.2647$. The latter value can be interpreted as follows: If we draw randomly 20 values from a standard normal distribution and calculate the KS distance (which will also be denoted as "KS statistic" if we plan to use it to test a distributional assumption, i.e., if we plan to perform a KS test), then we will obtain in 95% of the cases a value which is below 0.2467 and only in 5% of the cases a value above. Consequently, a value higher than 0.2467 will speak against the hypothesis that the data are generated by a standard normal distribution. In our case, the value is below and we cannot reject the standard normal hypothesis.

---

[12] These values can be found in any statistics textbook.

EXHIBIT 8.4 Calculation of the KS-Distance

i	x_i	$\Phi(x_i)$	$F_{20}(x_i) = i/n$	$|F_{20}(x_i) - \Phi(x_i)|$
1	−3.1	0.00096767	0.05	0.04903233
2	−2.1	0.01786436	0.1	0.08213564
3	−1.1	0.1356661	0.15	0.0143339
4	−0.8	0.21185533	0.2	0.01185533
5	−0.7	0.24196358	0.25	0.00803642
6	−0.4	0.3445783	0.3	0.0445783
7	−0.3	0.38208864	0.35	0.03208864
8	−0.2	0.42074031	0.4	0.02074031
9	−0.1	0.4601721	0.45	0.0101721
10	0	0.5	0.5	0
11	0.1	0.5398279	0.55	0.0101721
12	0.1	0.5398279	0.6	0.0601721
13	0.1	0.5398279	0.65	0.1101721
14	0.2	0.57925969	0.7	0.12074031
15	0.3	0.61791136	0.75	0.13208864
16	0.4	0.6554217	0.8	0.1445783
17	0.9	0.81593991	0.85	0.03406009
18	1.3	0.90319945	0.9	0.00319945
19	1.5	0.93319277	0.95	0.01680723
20	1.7	0.95543457	1	0.04456543

Anderson-Darling Distance

Sometimes it is important to assign different weights to the same deviations between two probability distribution functions. In financial applications, for example, one might be interested in estimating the tails of a return distribution very accurately. The reason for that is that the tails are responsible for the unexpected events and if such an unexpected event takes place, we want to know how much money we lose (or win) and, therefore, we need information about the tail of the return distribution. If we assume a certain probability distribution with distribution function F and measure the distance between F and the empirical distribution function F_n by the KS-distance, then the same importance is assigned to the tails as to the center. The reason is that the KS-distance measures the uniform distance between the two functions (i.e., the maximum deviation regardless where it occurs).

An alternative way is provided by the following empirical variant of
the *Anderson Darling statistic* (AD-statistic):

$$AD = \sup_x \frac{|F_n(x) - F(x)|}{\sqrt{F(x)(1 - F(x))}} \tag{8.8}$$

As with the KS-statistic, the AD-statistic measures the distance between
the empirical and theoretical distribution function but is rescaled by
dividing the distance through the "standard deviation" of this distance,
given by the denominator in equation (8.8). As can be seen, the denominator becomes small for very large and very small x-values. Thus, the
same absolute deviation between F and F_n in the tails gets a higher
weight as if it occurs in the center of the distribution. The drawback of
this approach is the fact that the distribution of the statistic depends on
the concrete choice of F and consequently tests about the validity of the
assumption cannot be performed as easy as with the KS-distance.

Tests for Normality

The class of normal or Gaussian distributions is certainly the most popular distribution family in applied statistics and many procedures, tests,
and estimators are based on normal or asymptotical normal distributions. The reason for that is the previously mentioned Central Limit Theorem which roughly states that a sum of many independent observations
behaves like a normal random variable. This result is often applied to
stock market returns: A return or change in the stock price is the result
of many small influences and shocks and thus the return can be treated
as a normal random variable.

There is only one condition which must be fulfilled for the theorem to
apply: The individual random variables must possess finite variances.
Because statisticians want to treat a sample as if it is generated by a normal distribution, many tests have been developed to check whether it is
reasonable to assume that a sample is generated by a normal distribution
or not. We have already seen one example using the KS-test. The test can
always be applied if we want to test whether the data are generated by a
specific continuous distribution as, for example, the standard normal distribution. But the test cannot be applied to answer questions such as: Are
the data generated by *any* normal distribution?

Consequently, other concepts have been developed to address this
question and we will briefly describe the most popular one: The *Jarque-
Bera test* (JB-test) of normality. The test statistic is given by the following
expression:

$$JB = \frac{n}{6}\hat{\gamma}^2 + \frac{n}{24}(\hat{\kappa}-3)^2 \qquad (8.9)$$

Here we denote by

$$\hat{\gamma} = \frac{1}{n}\sum_{i=1}^{n}\left(\frac{x_i - \bar{x}}{\hat{\sigma}}\right)^3 \text{ the sample skewness}$$

$$\hat{\kappa} = \frac{1}{n}\sum_{i=1}^{n}\left(\frac{x_i - \bar{x}}{\hat{\sigma}}\right)^4 \text{ the sample kurtosis}$$

$$\hat{\sigma}^2 = \frac{1}{n-1}\sum_{i=1}^{n}(x_i - \bar{x})^2 \text{ the sample variance}$$

It has been proven that under the hypothesis that the x_i are independent observations from a normal distribution, for large n the distribution of the JB-test statistic is asymptotically Chi-square distributed, $\chi^2(2)$.[13] This enables us to roll out a test on normality. For a given large sample $x = (x_1, ..., x_n)$ we calculate the JB-test statistic and compare it with the 95%-quantile of the $\chi^2(2)$ distribution which equals 5.99. Under the null-hypothesis that the data were generated by a normal distribution, we know that in 95% of the cases the value of the JB-test statistic will be smaller than 5.99. Consequently, we reject the hypothesis of normality if the value of JB-test statistic exceeds 5.99 and accept it otherwise.

REFERENCES

DuMouchel, W. 1971. *Stable Distributions in Statistical Inference*. Doctoral Dissertation, Yale University.

DuMouchel, W. 1973. "Stable Distributions in Statistical Inference: 1. Symmetric Stable Distribution Compared to Other Symmetric Long-Tailed Distributions." *Journal of the American Statistical Association* 68: 469–477.

Kogon, S. M., and B. W. William. 1998. "Characteristic Function Based Estimation of Stable Distribution Parameters." In *A Practical Guide to Heavy Tails*, ed. R. J. Adler, R. E. Feldman, and M. S. Taqqu, 311–336. Boston: Birkhäuser.

Larsen, R. J., and M. L. Marx. 1986. *An Introduction to Mathematical Statistics and its Applications*. Englewood Cliffs, NJ: Prentice Hall.

---

[13] In Chapter 3 we explained the Chi-square distribution.

Menn, C., and S. T. Rachev. 2005. "Calibrated FFT-Based Density Approximations For Alpha-Stable Distributions." Forthcoming in *Computational Statistics and Data Analysis*.

Nolan, J. P. 1997. "Numerical Calculation of Stable Densities and Distribution Functions." *Communications in Statistics—Stochastic Models* 13: 759–774.

Press, S. J. 1972. "Estimation of Univariate and Multivariate Stable Distributions." *Journal of the American Statistical Association* 67: 842–846.

Rachev, S. T. 1991. *Probability Metrics and the Stability of Stochastic Models*. Chichester: John Wiley & Sons.

Stoyanov, S., and B. Racheva-Iotova. 2004a. "Univariate Stable Laws in the Field of Finance—Approximations of Density and Distribution Functions." *Journal of Concrete and Applicable Mathematics* 2 (1): 38–57.

Stoyanov, S., and B. Racheva-Iotova. 2004b. "Univariate Stable Laws in the Field of Finance—Parameter Estimation." *Journal of Concrete and Applicable Mathematics* 2 (4): 24–49.

Stochastic Processes

CHAPTER 9

Stochastic Processes in Discrete Time and Time Series Analysis

In this chapter we provide an introduction to the theory of stochastic processes. In our exposition, we seek to motivate the reader as to why an understanding of this theory is important, rather than set forth a rigorous analytical presentation. While we provide an explanation for the most important issues, the technical details are not presented. Instead, we provide references where technical issues are discussed further.

STOCHASTIC PROCESSES IN DISCRETE TIME

The theory of stochastic processes in discrete time is an important tool when examining the characteristics of financial data. In this section, we think of the sample $x = (x_1, ..., x_n)$ as being a sample of return data. From our discussion in Chapter 8, we know how to fit a probability distribution to these observations and we are able to examine the goodness of fit. This approach is denoted as "fitting the unconditional distribution." Unfortunately, almost every classical estimation technique for distribution parameters assumes that the return observations are independent. This itself is an assumption that can be tested (or at least the weaker formulation of uncorrelated observations) and which is violated by most real return samples. That is the point where stochastic process comes into the game: Stochastic processes describe the evolution of a random variable (here the return) through time. That is, it describes the relationship between the probability distribution of yesterday's return, today's return. and tomorrow's return, and the like.

Autoregressive Moving Average Models

One of the simplest time series models is formed by the linear models of the *autoregressive moving average* (ARMA) class, described in the following subsections.[1]

White Noise

The building block of all time series models is the so-called *white noise process* given by a sequence of independently and identically distributed (iid) random variables which are usually assumed to have zero mean and unit variance:[2]

$$\varepsilon_t \overset{iid}{\sim} P, \text{ with } E\varepsilon_t = 0 \text{ and } V\varepsilon_t = 1 \qquad (9.1)$$

One popular candidate for the white noise distribution is the standard normal distribution. Exhibit 9.1 presents a plot with the evolution of a normal white noise process. As we can see from the exhibit, there are no trends or clusters in the realizations which can be explained by the fact that the observations are independent from each other. This is not always what is needed for practical applications, so we continue to introduce more complex and flexible time series models.

Autoregressive Processes

Consider the following model, which is called an *autoregressive process of order 1*:

$$x_t = c + ax_{t-1} + \sigma\varepsilon_t \qquad (9.2)$$

Here c denotes a real constant. Usually it is assumed that:

1. The parameter σ, which scales the influence of the white noise process, is positive.
2. The value of the parameter a, which measures the impact of the previous observation, lies between -1 and 1.

---

[1] A detailed description of all classical time series concepts can be found in Hamilton (1994).
[2] There are different types of white noise: Sometimes it is only imposed that the process possesses uncorrelated elements.

EXHIBIT 9.1   Realizations of Standard Normal White Noise Process

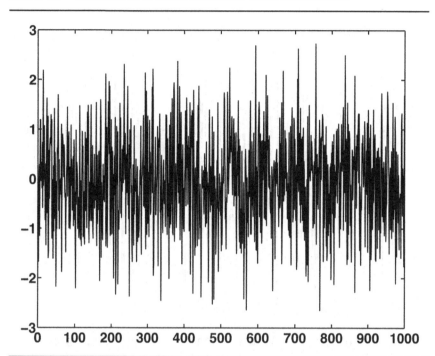

The name "autoregressive" can be explained by looking at the defining equation (9.2): The value of x_t is obtained as an affine function (i.e., a linear function with an intercept) of x_{t-1} plus an error term. Due to the similarity with univariate regression models (i.e., regression models with a single explanatory variable) and the fact the regressor equals the time lagged regressand, the models are called "autoregressive."

Exhibit 9.2 illustrates one possible path of an AR(1) process with $c = 0$, $a = 0.8$, and $\sigma = 1$. As we can immediately see, the path differs substantially from the previous white noise process. Highly positive returns are followed by positive returns and vice versa. We can recognize patterns; these are called "trends." The reason for that is clearly the fact, that the realization of the current return depends strongly on the previous one. We can calculate the mean and the variance of the return given the AR(1) model as follows:

$$Ex_t = E(c + ax_{t-1} + \sigma\varepsilon_t) = c + aEx_{t-1} + \sigma E\varepsilon_t \Rightarrow Ex_t = \frac{c}{1-a} \qquad (9.3)$$

EXHIBIT 9.2   Realizations of an AR(1) Process

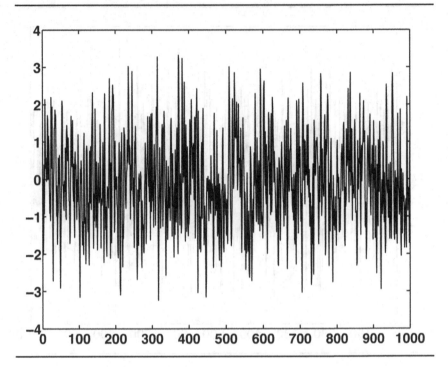

$$Vx_t = V(c + ax_{t-1} + \sigma\varepsilon_t) = a^2 V(x_{t-1}) + \sigma^2 \Rightarrow Vx_t = \frac{\sigma^2}{1 - a^2} \qquad (9.4)$$

In the derivation of the mean and variance expression, we have implicitly used the fact that the x_t form a stationary sequence of second order (i.e., the mean and variance do not depend on the time index t). Mean and variance given in the above equations are called "unconditional mean and variance" because we make no assumptions about possible additional knowledge about the process.

Sometimes it is more important to consider the so-called "conditional mean" or "conditional variance." Imagine that we have observed a return series $x_0, \ldots, x_t$ and we want to get information about the return of tomorrow x_{t+1}. Then an appropriate method would be to consider the mean of x_{t+1} given the information until today. The information available at time t is usually denoted by $\mathfrak{I}_t$ and we write:

$$E(x_{t+1}|\mathfrak{I}_t) = E(c + ax_t + \sigma\varepsilon_{t+1}|\mathfrak{I}_t) = c + ax_t \qquad (9.5)$$

$$V(x_{t+1}|\mathfrak{I}_t) = V(c + ax_t + \sigma\varepsilon_{t+1}|\mathfrak{I}_t) = \sigma^2 \qquad (9.6)$$

What is important about equations (9.5) and (9.6) is the fact that the conditional mean of an AR(1) time series model changes through time (it depends on the current state x_t), whereas the conditional variance remains constant.

After having discussed the autoregressive process of order 1, it is not too difficult to guess what an autoregressive process of higher order will look like. The dynamic of an AR(n) process is given by the following equation:[3]

$$x_t = c + \sum_{i=1}^{n} a_i x_{t-i} + \sigma\varepsilon_t \qquad (9.7)$$

The AR(n) process is useful to incorporate possible dependencies of the current return from several previous returns. One possibility to measure the dependence between past and current returns is provided by the *autocorrelation function* (ACF). The autocorrelation function, denoted by ρ, is defined by the following equation:

$$\rho(h) = \frac{\text{Cov}(x_t, x_{t+h})}{\sqrt{V(x_t)}\sqrt{V(x_{t+h})}} \qquad (9.8)$$

For the special case of an AR(1) process given by equation (9.2), we obtain the following simple expression:

$$\rho(h) = \frac{\sigma^2}{1-a} \cdot a^h \qquad (9.9)$$

We can see that the correlation between two elements of the time series with a lag of h time steps is nonzero. In terms of our example, this means that a return which has occurred one year ago still influences the return of today, but the influence decreases geometrically with the time lag. This

---

[3] For the AR(n) process to form a stationary sequence, the coefficient must fulfill some technical condition. For details, see Hamilton (1994).

means that the influence becomes quickly negligible when the time lag increases.

There is another possibility to measure the influence of past observations on the current value of the time series, the so-called *partial autocorrelation function* (PACF), denoted by ζ. The partial autocorrelation coefficient of order h is simply defined as the slope coefficient of x_{t-h} if we perform a regression of x_t on $x_{t-1}, ..., x_{t-h}$. In the AR(1) case we can easily see that we obtain the following partial autocorrelation function ζ:

$$\zeta(h) = \begin{cases} a, & h = 1 \\ 1, & h = 0 \\ 0, & \text{otherwise} \end{cases} \tag{9.10}$$

whereas, in the general case of an AR(n)-process, we obtain nonzero partial autocorrelation for the first n lags and zero partial autocorrelation otherwise. In contrast to the ACF, the PACF jumps immediately to zero when the lag exceeds the order of the autoregressive process.

In some applications, we might want to model another situation where the ACF behaves in this way; that is, for the first 1, 2, or m lags we observe autocorrelation and then the autocorrelation jumps immediately to zero. One possibility to realize this concept is provided by the so-called *moving average* (MA) processes described below.

Moving Average Processes

The dynamic of a moving average process of order m (MA(m) process) is given by:[4]

$$x_t = c + \sum_{i=1}^{m} b_i \sigma \varepsilon_{t-i} + \sigma \varepsilon_t \tag{9.11}$$

As above we denote by c a real constant, $\sigma > 0$ is a scaling factor for the innovation process, and the b_i, $i = 1, ..., m$ are the moving average coefficients. The name "moving average" comes from the fact that the next return is given by a weighted average of today's and the m previous observations of the white noise process. The set of observations taken into account moves through time and explains the name.

---

[4] For the MA(m) process to form a stationary sequence, the coefficient must fulfill some technical condition. For Hamilton (1994) for details.

The mean and variance of the moving average process are calculated as follows:

$$Ex_t = E\left(c + \sum_{i=1}^{m} b_i \sigma \varepsilon_{t-i} + \sigma \varepsilon_t\right)$$

$$= c + \sum_{i=1}^{m} b_i \sigma E\varepsilon_{t-i} + \sigma E\varepsilon_t = c \tag{9.12}$$

$$Vx_t = V\left(c + \sum_{i=1}^{m} b_i \sigma \varepsilon_{t-i} + \sigma \varepsilon_t\right)$$

$$= \sum_{i=1}^{m} b_i^2 \sigma^2 V\varepsilon_{t-i} + \sigma^2 V\varepsilon_t \tag{9.13}$$

$$= \sigma^2 \left(1 + \sum_{i=1}^{m} b_i^2\right)$$

As in the autoregressive case, we recognize that the unconditional mean and the variance do not depend upon the specific date of time we consider.

Additionally, we consider again the conditional mean and variance:

$$E(x_{t+1}|\Im_t) = E\left(c + \sum_{i=1}^{m} b_i \sigma \varepsilon_{t-i} + \sigma \varepsilon_t \middle| \Im_t\right) = c + \sum_{i=1}^{m} b_i \sigma \varepsilon_{t-i} \tag{9.14}$$

$$V(x_{t+1}|\Im_t) = V\left(c + \sum_{i=1}^{m} b_i \sigma \varepsilon_{t-i} + \sigma \varepsilon_t \middle| \Im_t\right) = \sigma^2 \tag{9.15}$$

Again, the conditional mean changes through time, whereas the conditional variance remains constant. This is a property which is connected to the stationarity of these time series models.

Now we will consider the *autocorrelation function* (ACF) for the special case $m = 1$ and $c = 0$ and check whether the claimed property holds true:

$$\rho(h) = \frac{\text{Cov}(x_t, x_{t+h})}{\sqrt{V(x_t)}\sqrt{V(x_{t+h})}} = \frac{\text{Cov}(\sigma b \varepsilon_{t-1} + \sigma \varepsilon_t, \sigma b \varepsilon_{t+h-1} + \sigma \varepsilon_{t+h})}{\sigma^2(1+b^2)}$$

$$= \frac{\sigma^2[b^2\text{Cov}(\varepsilon_{t-1}, \varepsilon_{t+h-1}) + b\text{Cov}(\varepsilon_{t-1}, \varepsilon_{t+h})}{\sigma^2(1+b^2)}$$

$$\frac{+ b\text{Cov}(\varepsilon_t, \varepsilon_{t+h-1}) + \text{Cov}(\varepsilon_t, \varepsilon_{t+h})]}{\sigma^2(1+b^2)} \qquad (9.16)$$

$$= \begin{cases} 1, & h = 0 \\ \dfrac{b}{1+b^2}, & h = \pm 1 \\ 0, & |h| > 1 \end{cases}$$

As we can see, we obtain exactly the structure we have asked for:

1. A perfect correlation of the current return with itself
2. A correlation between the current return and its direct predecessor and successor
3. Zero correlation otherwise

A graphical illustration of a moving average process of order 1 is presented in Exhibit 9.3. Obviously the fluctuations in the path of the MA(1) process are not as randomly as in the white noise case. This can be explained by the correlation between subsequent observations, but the process is less "regular" than the AR(1) path shown in Exhibit 9.2.

Autoregressive Moving Average Processes with Exogenous Variables

The two concepts of autoregressive and moving average process can be fitted together to obtain the *general linear time series model*, the ARMA(n,m)-process. Its dynamic is given by the following equation:

$$x_t = c + \sum_{i=1}^{n} a_i x_{t-i} + \sum_{i=1}^{m} b_i \sigma \varepsilon_{t-i} + \sigma \varepsilon_t \qquad (9.17)$$

Processes of this type are called "linear" because the describing equation is a linear equation in the past observations and the white noise process.

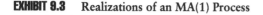

EXHIBIT 9.3   Realizations of an MA(1) Process

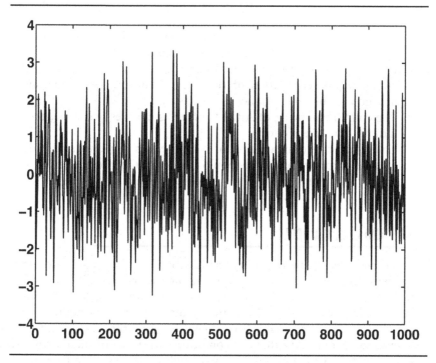

The models can be extended to an even more general framework, which is called ARMAX processes. These processes allow for the incorporation of known exogenous effects which are described by a set of exogenous variables $(e^{(1)}, ..., e^{(d)})$. In the context of asset returns, these exogenous variables could play the role of macroeconomic factors or business data. We obtain the following general ARMAX(n,m,d) process:

$$x_t = c_0 + \sum_{i=1}^{d} c_i e_t^{(i)} + \sum_{i=1}^{n} a_i x_{t-i} + \sum_{i=1}^{m} b_i \sigma \varepsilon_{t-i} + \sigma \varepsilon_t \qquad (9.18)$$

Summary of Properties of Linear Time Series Models

The key properties regarding stochastic processes presented in this section are:

■ The stochastic structure in ARMAX processes is generated by a white noise process ε_t, $t = 1, 2, ...$ of independent and identically distributed random variables with zero mean and (if defined) unit variance.

- ARMAX processes are linear in the exogenous variables, the lagged observations of the dependent variable, and the lagged white noise observations.
- ARMA processes are covariance stationary (under suitable conditions on the coefficients and white noise distribution); that is, the mean and the variance do not depend on the specific date of time under consideration and the correlation of two components x_t, x_{t+h} is a function uniquely of the time distance h.
- The conditional mean of ARMA processes changes over time; the conditional variance is constant.
- The autocorrelation function of AR processes is geometrically decaying; the autocorrelation function of the MA(m) process is zero for lags greater than the order m of the process.

ARCH AND GARCH MODELS

Sometimes it might be necessary, especially when the focus is on modeling financial return data, to incorporate time-varying conditional volatility. In calm market periods, you expect that the stock market variation of the next days will not be dramatically high, whereas in highly volatile periods (e.g., after a crash), you expect large market movements. This observation simply says that the conditional variance of the return series is not constant through time. This issue will be addressed in this section.

Time series models with time varying conditional variance (so-called *conditional heteroskedasticity*) were first presented by Engle (1982) and later refined by Bollerslev (1986). The idea is to use the property of ARMA models which possess unconditionally constant and time varying conditional mean for the variance process. This leads to the following innovation process with time-varying variance, called *generalized autoregressive conditional heteroskedasticity* (GARCH) process and denoted by GARCH(p,q) process:

$$u_t = \sigma_t \varepsilon_t, \text{ with } \sigma_t^2 = \alpha_0 + \sum_{i=1}^{p} \alpha_i u_{t-i}^2 + \sum_{i=1}^{q} \beta_i \sigma_{t-i}^2 \qquad (9.19)$$

where $(\varepsilon_t)_{t=1, 2, \ldots}$ denotes a standard white noise process.

In the special case where $q = 0$, the process is called an *autoregressive conditional heteroskedasticity* (ARCH) process, denoted by ARCH(p), and coincides with the original process suggested by Engle. If the coefficients fulfill some suitable conditions, the GARCH(p,q) process has the following properties:

$$E(u_t) = 0 \text{ and } E(u_t|\Im_t) = 0 \tag{9.20}$$

$$Vu_t = E\sigma_t^2 = \frac{\alpha_0}{1 - \sum_{i=1}^{p} \alpha_i - \sum_{i=1}^{q} \beta_i}$$

$$\text{and} \tag{9.21}$$

$$V(u_t|\Im_{t-1}) = \sigma_t^2 = \alpha_0 + \sum_{i=1}^{p} \alpha_i u_{t-i}^2 + \sum_{i=1}^{q} \beta_i \sigma_{t-i}^2$$

Thus, the GARCH(p,q) innovation process possesses exactly the above mentioned and desired properties:

■ constant unconditional mean and variance
■ constant conditional mean but time varying conditional variance.

Exhibit 9.4 shows the path of a GARCH(1,1)-innovation process. In comparison to Exhibit 9.1, where a path of a standard homoskedastic white noise process is plotted, we observe the effect of "volatility clustering." That is, periods of high volatility are followed by calm periods.

Having now defined a conditional heteroskedastic innovation process $(u_t)_{t=1,2,\ldots}$ we combine our results with those of the previous section and obtain the most general linear discrete time stochastic process with conditional heteroskedastic innovations, called ARMAX-GARCH process, expressed is:

$$x_t = c_0 + \sum_{i=1}^{d} c_i e_t^{(i)} + \sum_{i=1}^{n} a_i x_{t-i} + \sum_{i=1}^{m} b_i \sigma \varepsilon_{t-i} + \sigma_t \varepsilon_t$$

$$\sigma_t^2 = \alpha_0 + \sum_{i=1}^{p} \alpha_i \sigma_{t-i}^2 \varepsilon_{t-i}^2 + \sum_{i=1}^{q} \beta_i \sigma_{t-i}^2 \tag{9.22}$$

It should be mentioned at this point that the presented specification of an innovation process providing conditional heteroskedasticity is by far not unique. After the publication of the pathbreaking article by Engle

EXHIBIT 9.4   Realizations of an GARCH(1,1) Innovation Process and the Conditional Volatility ($\alpha_0 = 0.1$, $\alpha_1 = 0.4$, $\beta_1 = 0.5$)

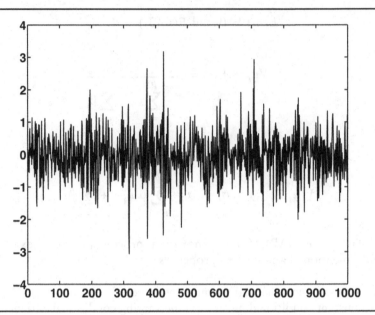

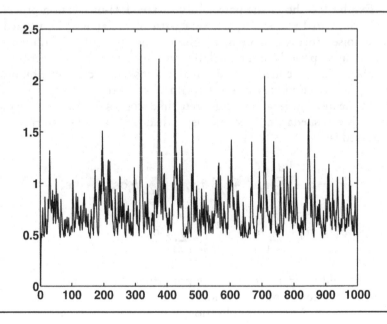

(1982) on the subject, various generalizations and adaptions have been suggested in the literature.[5]

Before concluding our introduction to the classical time series models with a walk-through example, we provide a short discussion of the limitations and possible extensions of the above presented ARMA-GARCH framework. One phenomenon which is often observed in real life data is called *long-range dependence* or *long-memory effect*. This effect was first observed and described by Hurst (1951) when examining the annual minima of the water level in the Nile river. Trying to explain long-range dependence verbally one could state that a time series exhibits a long memory or long-range dependence when past observations have a persistent impact on future realizations in a way that cannot be explained by an exponentially decaying autocorrelation function. A possibility to introduce this long memory effect into an ARMA time series model is provided by the so-called *fractional Gaussian noise* and GARCH models can be extended to so-called FIGARCH models (fractional integrated GARCH).[6] A formal treatment of long-memory processes is beyond the scope of this book. An understandable introduction to the theory of long-range dependence also covering the presence of heavy tails is provided by Samorodnitsky and Racheva-Iotova (2003).

ARMA-GARCH ILLUSTRATION

In order to recapitulate all the concepts described in the last two sections of the chapter and to show the potential power of the time series models introduced, we illustrate how one might fit ARCH and GARCH models to a dataset.[7] Our dataset consists of 1,000 daily returns of a hypothetical risky financial asset. The return data are visualized in Exhibit 9.5.

As we can see from the return plot, the data exhibit volatility clustering which could indicate a GARCH-innovation process and the data exhibit trends which indicate the presence of autocorrelation.

---

[5] These include EGARCH, IGARCH, TS-GARCH, A-GARCH2, NA-GARCH, V-GARCH, Thr.-GARCH, GJR-GARCH, log-ARCH, NGARCH, APARCH, GQ-ARCH, H-GARCH, and Aug-GARCH. Duan (1997) provides a description of the most prominent representatives.

[6] FIGARCH models have been introduced by Baillie, Bollerslev, and Mikkelsen (1996). Fractional Gaussian noise and its extensions are covered in Samorodnitsky and Taqqu (1994).

[7] The methodology described here is inspired by the Box-Jenkins-philosophy, which was presented in Box and Jenkins (1976).

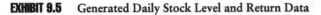

EXHIBIT 9.5 Generated Daily Stock Level and Return Data

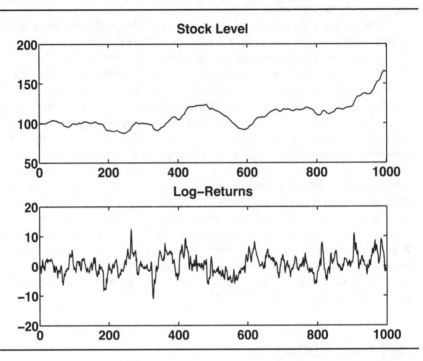

Autocorrelation and Partial Autocorrelation

Let us start with examining the autocorrelation and partial autocorrelation function of the return series. As the autocorrelation consists of covariance and variance expressions, we can estimate the autocorrelation function by the following expression:

$$\rho(h) = -\frac{\text{Cov}(x_t, x_{t-h})}{V(x_t)} \approx \frac{\frac{1}{T}\sum\limits_{i=h+1}^{T}(x_i - \bar{x})(x_{i-h} - \bar{x})}{\frac{1}{T}\sum\limits_{i=h+1}^{T}(x_i - \bar{x})^2} = \hat{\rho}(h) \qquad (9.23)$$

where T denotes the length of the sample and $\bar{x}$ the sample mean.

It can be shown that if the data were generated by a white noise process, then the estimate $\hat{\rho}(h)$, $h = 1, 2, \ldots$ lies between $\pm 2/\sqrt{T}$ in 95% of the cases. Consequently, we can estimate the moving average order of the data generating process by looking at the estimates $\hat{\rho}(h)$, $h = 1, 2, \ldots$, which lay outside the confidence interval. In Exhibit 9.6 we have plotted the first 20 autocorrelations.

The shape of the estimated ACF indicates a monotonically decaying ACF and from this we conclude the data generating process contains an autoregressive component. In order to determine the length of the autoregressive component, we additionally estimate the PACF which should be zero for lags greater than the order of the autoregressive term. Exhibit 9.7 shows the PACF estimate together with the 95%-confidence bound.

The plot suggests an AR(2) or AR(3) process. In order to capture eventual moving average components in the data generating process, we will estimate an ARMA(2,1)-process. The estimation results for the coefficients are summarized below:

$\hat{c}$	$\hat{a}_1$	$\hat{a}_2$	$\hat{b}_1$	$\hat{\sigma}$
0.0506	0.8788	0.0199	0.4402	0.9852

And we obtain the following estimated process dynamic:

$$x_t = 0.05 + 0.88x_{t-1} + 0.02x_{t-2} + 0.43\varepsilon_{t-1} + 0.99\varepsilon_t$$

EXHIBIT 9.6   First 20 Autocorrelations

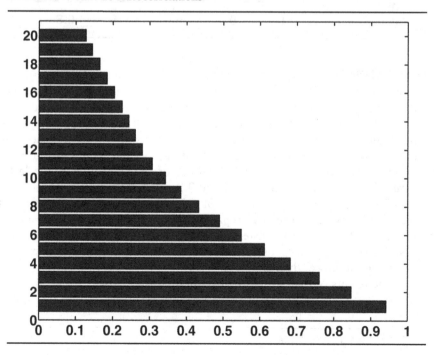

EXHIBIT 9.7   PACF Estimate

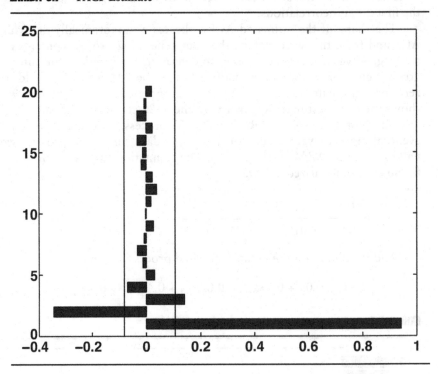

GARCH Estimate

Now the question arises whether the empirical residuals $\hat{\varepsilon}_t$, $t = 1, 2, \ldots$ satisfy the assumptions of a white noise process. Therefore, we consider the ACF of the empirical residuals and the ACF of the squared empirical residuals. For a true white noise process, both would be zero; if there are moving average components left in the data, the first would significantly differ from zero whereas in the presence of GARCH effects, the latter would be significant. Exhibits 9.8 and 9.9 show the results.

The graphs show the presence of GARCH effects. This conjecture is manifested by the graphical representation of the empirical residuals which exhibit volatility clustering which is the standard choice in such cases (Exhibit 9.10). Consequently we estimate a GARCH(1,1) process on the empirical residuals.

The results of the estimation are summarized below:

$\hat{\alpha}_0$	$\hat{\alpha}_1$	$\hat{\beta}_0$
0.2959	0.5309	0.2366

EXHIBIT 9.8   ACF of the Empirical Residuals

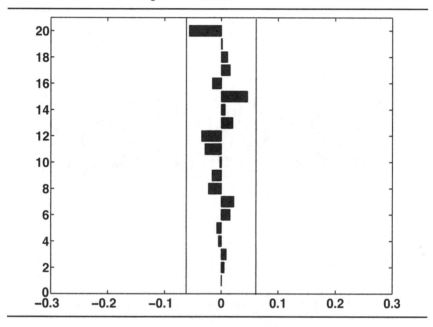

EXHIBIT 9.9   ACF of the Squared Empirical Residuals

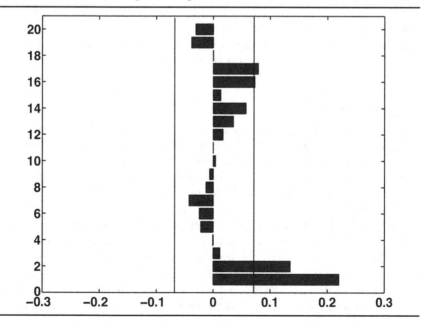

EXHIBIT 9.10   Empirical Residuals after ARMA Estimation

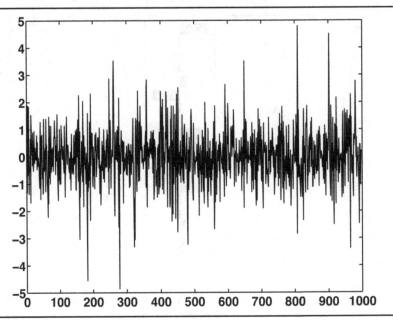

From these GARCH-process estimates, we can now calculate the empirical residuals, which, hopefully, will behave like standard normal white noise. At least the graphical illustration in Exhibit 9.11 looks quite similar to our white noise example in Exhibit 9.1. Additionally, the ACF-estimate in Exhibit 9.12 shows no significant remaining autocorrelation in the residuals.

Testing the Residuals

Now we have shown that our estimated model fits the data quite well. The only remaining hypothesis we must investigate is the distribution of the residuals. By assumption, the residuals are standard normally distribution and this can be graphically verified by a QQ-plot and statistically verified by a Kolmogorov-Smirnov (KS) test. The QQ-plot is shown in Exhibit 9.13. The KS statistic has a value of $d = 0.0198$ with a p-value of nearly 90%. So the graphical as well as statistical examination lead to the conclusion that the empirical distribution of the residuals does not significantly differ from the standard normal distribution. This completes our case study.

Unfortunately, things do not go as easily when we confront a real data set. First, we cannot expect to always capture the whole structure of

EXHIBIT 9.11   Empirical Residuals after ARMA-GARCH Estimation

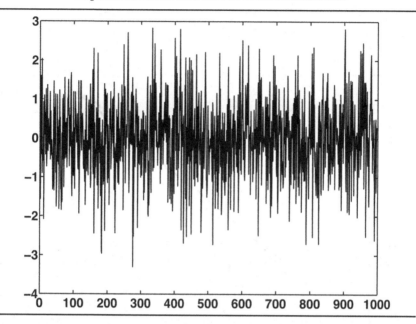

EXHIBIT 9.12   ACF for Empirical Residuals after ARMA-GARCH Estimation

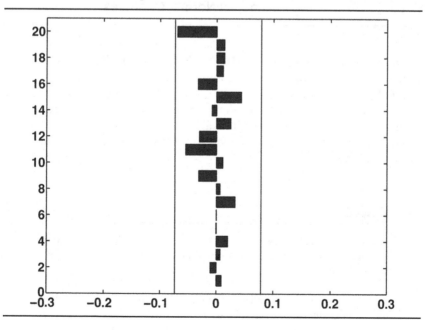

EXHIBIT 9.13   QQ-Plot

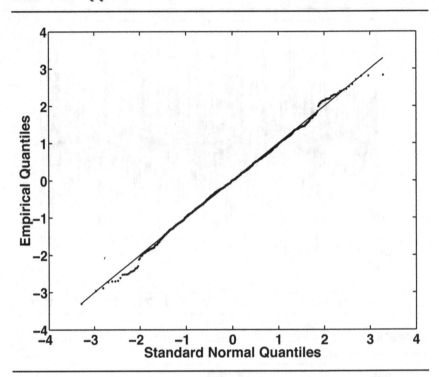

the time series inherent to the data with the prespecified model. Compromises are needed and the aim should be to find the most parsimonious model under all models that yield a satisfiable fit. In Chapter 11, where we provide some empirical evidence from the U.S. financial markets, we will see that the KS test leads in nearly all cases to a rejection of the normal distribution assumption, which was not the case in our walk through example here.

REFERENCES

Baillie, Richard T., T. Bollerslev, and H. O. Mikkelsen. 1996. "Fractionally Integrated Generalized Autoregressive Conditional Heteroskedasticity." *Journal of Econometrics* 74: 3–30.

Bollerslev, T. 1986. "Generalized Conditional Autoregressive Heteroscedasticity." *Journal of Econometrics* 52: 115–127.

Box, G. E. P., and G. M. Jenkins. 1976. *Time Series Analysis: Forecasting and Control.* San Francisco: Holden-Day.

Duan, J-C. 1997. "Augmented GARCH(p,q) Process and its Diffusion Limit." *Journal of Econometrics* 79: 97–127.

Engle R.F., 1982. "Autoregressive Conditional Heteroscedasticity and Variance Estimates of UK Inflation." *Econometrica* 50: 987–1007.

Hamilton, J. D. 1994. *Time Series Analysis.* Princeton, NJ: Princeton University Press.

Hurst, H. 1951. "Long-Term Storage Capacity of Reservoirs." *Transactions of the American Society of Civil Engineers* 116: 770–808.

Racheva-Iotova, B. and G. Samorodnitsky. 2001. "Long Range Dependence in Heavy Tailed Stochastic Processes." OR&IE Technical Reports, Cornell University.

Samorodnitsky, G., and M. S. Taqqu. 1994. *Stable Non-Gaussian Random Processes: Stochastic Models with Infinite Variance.* New York: Chapman and Hall.

CHAPTER 10

Stochastic Processes in Continuous Time

In the previous chapter, we discussed the case where the time scale of a stochastic process consists of discrete points. In some applications and for various reasons, it might be more useful to model stochastic phenomena on a continuous-time scale. One purely pragmatic reason for the popularity of continuous-time models in financial applications is their analytical tractability. Another appealing issue, albeit difficult to realize, is that if trading time is modeled as a continuum, much more powerful hedging strategies are possible than in the discrete time setup. In this chapter, we introduce the most important notions on a purely heuristic level.[1]

Probably, the two most prominent representatives of the class of continuous-time stochastic processes are Brownian motion and the Poisson process. The name of the former is due to the botanist Robert Brown who in 1827 described the movement of pollen suspended in water. Brownian motion has later been examined and applied by Bachelier (1900) for modeling stock price dynamics. The theory of Brownian motion was founded by the work of Norbert Wiener who was the first to prove its existence and, as a result, Brownian motion is sometimes also referred to as a *Wiener process*. The Poisson process owes its name to the Poisson distribution, which governs the realizations of the process in a way that will be explained in the next section. Both processes belong to the larger class of Lévy processes; on the other hand, they are fundamentally different concerning their path properties.

---

[1] The interested reader is referred to the textbooks of Oksendal (2000) or Karatzas and Shreve (1991) for a complete treatment of continuous-time stochastic processes. Shiryaev (1999) contains a complete treatment of the topic with a special focus on financial applications.

Before we continue with the discussion and the construction of the two processes, we will briefly introduce some notions. We assume in the following that for every point in time $t \geq 0$, we are given a random variable X_t over the same probability space. The family of random variables $(X_t)_{t \geq 0}$ is called a *stochastic process in continuous time*. The function that describes the evolution of one specific realization of X through time is called a path of the process.

THE POISSON PROCESS

In basic insurance theory, it is commonly assumed that the time T between the occurrence of two loss events—denoted as *interarrival time*—is exponentially distributed with intensity parameter λ. Additionally, we can assume that no inference between the different loss events is present, i.e., the interarrival times are stochastically independent.

Let us denote the current date as $t = 0$. For every $t \geq 0$, we define a random variable N_t that will tell us how many loss events have occurred up to time t. It is possible to show that we have the following result:

$$P(N_t = k) = \frac{(\lambda t)^k}{k!} e^{-\lambda t}, \, k = 0, 1, 2, \dots \qquad (10.1)$$

The process $(N_t)_{t \geq 0}$ is called a Poisson process with intensity λ. Equation (10.1) says that the number of losses which have occurred until time t is Poisson distributed with parameter λt. Possible paths of this process are illustrated in Exhibit 10.1.

From the definition of the process we can immediately derive the following properties:

- The paths of the process are piecewise constant and exhibit jumps of size one.
- The paths are monotonically increasing.
- The paths are discontinuous.
- The process is integer valued and nonnegative with $N_0 = 0$.
- The expected value of N_t (the expected number of losses that have occurred until time t) is given by $EN_t = \lambda t$.

Transforms of the Poisson Process

For practical applications, not only the basic Poisson process but generalizations of it are needed. It is beyond the scope of this book to present in-depth coverage of the topic, which leads to the field of point pro-

EXHIBIT 10.1   Possible Paths of a Poisson Process where the Interarrival Times are Exponentially Distributed with Parameter $\lambda = 0.5$

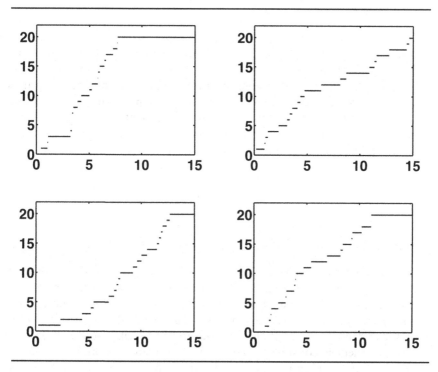

cesses. We restrict ourself to the introduction of the *inhomogeneous Poisson process*, the Cox process—or doubly stochastic Poisson process—and a concept called *compound Poisson process*.

Inhomogeneous Poisson Processes

The underlying idea of the inhomogeneous Poisson process is closely related to the notion of intensity of a Poisson process. In Chapter 3, we discussed how the parameter λ of the exponential distribution can be interpreted as an intensity parameter. As the Poisson process is generated by exponentially distributed interarrival times, the concept can be carried over.

The easiest and most intuitive way is to define the *jump intensity* at time t as the expected number of jumps in the interval $[t, t + \Delta t]$ divided by Δt, where Δt denotes a small time interval. In our case, we obtain:

$$\text{Jump intensity} = \frac{E(N_{t+\Delta t} - N_t)}{\Delta t} = \frac{\lambda \Delta t}{\Delta t} = \lambda$$

We see that the jump intensity of the Poisson process is constant, as we could already expect from the fact that the intensity of the exponential distribution is constant.

Now we can define a generalization of the Poisson process by introducing a time dependence of the intensity. Given a nonnegative function $\lambda(t)$, a stochastic process $(N_t)_{t \geq 0}$ with independent increments and starting at zero is said to be an inhomogeneous Poisson process if the following equation holds true for every real $t \geq s \geq 0$:

$$P(N_t - N_s = k) = \frac{\left(\int_s^t \lambda(u)\,du \right)^k}{k!} \cdot e^{-\int_s^t \lambda(u)\,du} \tag{10.2}$$

For the inhomogeneous Poisson process many properties of the basic Poisson process remain valid. The paths are still piecewise constant and exhibit jumps of size one. The increments $N_t - N_s$ are Poisson distributed, but as can be seen from equation (10.2), the distribution depends not only on the distance $h = t - s$. It also depends on the specific point in time where this increment is considered. This time dependence of the jump intensity may be very useful in practical applications. As previously stated, the first jump of a Poisson process is used in some credit risk models to determine the time of default. Now it is well known that in recession periods the probability of default for most companies increases, whereas in boom periods it decreases. This effect can be accomplished by a time-varying jump intensity $\lambda(t)$, that is, an inhomogeneous Poisson process.

Cox Processes

A *Cox process* is a natural generalization of the inhomogeneous Poisson process. In most practical applications, we will perhaps know that the jump intensity is varying through time—but not how. Therefore, the jump intensity can be modeled itself as a stochastic process. Let therefore a non-negative stochastic process $(\lambda_t)_{t \geq 0}$ be given. Then, we call a stochastic process $(N_t)_{t \geq 0}$ Cox process if the following relation holds true:[2]

---

[2] For a proper definition of a Cox process, more technical details are needed. The interested reader is referred to more advanced probability textbooks such as Kallenberg (1977).

$$P(N_t - N_s = k | (\lambda_u)_{s \le u \le t}) = \frac{\left(\int_s^t \lambda(u)du\right)^k}{k!} \cdot e^{-\int_s^t \lambda(u)du} \tag{10.3}$$

Equation (10.3) says nothing more than that for every given specific path of the intensity process, the Cox process behaves like an inhomogeneous Poisson process. For the Cox process, we have again that the paths are piecewise constant and exhibit jumps of size one.

Compound Poisson Processes

Compound processes have been used for a long time as a basic model to describe the claim process in insurance theory. The idea is the following. Every time when a damage event occurs, that is, when the Poisson process admits a jump, then we model the claim amount by drawing from a probability distribution Q. The claims are drawn independently from each other and independently from the Poisson process, being denoted as $Y_1, Y_2, \ldots$. The total claim amount C_t faced by the insurance company at time t can now be formally expressed as

$$C_t = \sum_{k=1}^{N_t} Y_k \tag{10.4}$$

Exhibit 10.2 provides a graphical illustration of the construction of the claim process. A process $(C_t)_{t \ge 0}$, with the representation given by equation (10.4), is generally called a *compound Poisson process*. The main difference to the previous generalizations of the Poisson process is that although being a piecewise constant pure jump process, the jump sizes may vary according to the values supported by the probability distribution Q. For insurance applications, one usually assumes continuous positive probability distributions such as the Lognormal or Weibull distribution. In financial applications when modeling stock price movements, one possibility to account for extreme up and downward movements is to add a jump component into the stock price dynamic. The distribution of the jumps could then, for example, be chosen to be a normal distribution.

BROWNIAN MOTION

We will introduce Brownian motion with an example. We begin with a short summary of the most important and defining properties of a standard Brownian motion $(W_t)_{t \ge 0}$:

EXHIBIT 10.2   Four Different Paths of a Compound Poisson Process with Jump Intensity $\lambda = 2$ and Lognormal Jump Size Distribution with $\mu = 1$, $\sigma = 1$

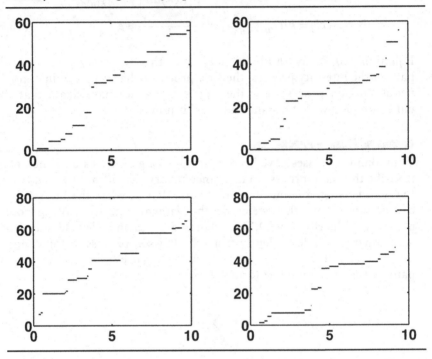

1. $W_0 = 0$, that is, Brownian motion starts at zero.
2. $(W_t)_{t \geq 0}$ is a process with homogeneous and independent increments.[3]
3. Any increment $W_{t+h} - W_t$ is normally distributed with mean zero and variance h.
4. The paths of $(W_t)_{t \geq 0}$ are continuous.

Every process fulfilling the above four properties is denoted as a *standard Brownian motion*. From the second and third conditions it can be deduced that Brownian motion W_t at time t (which equals the increment from time 0 to time t) is normally distributed with mean zero and variance t. Actually the second condition is much stronger than that. Loosely speaking, one could say that the distribution of the future changes does not depend on past realizations. Generally we call pro-

---

[3] A process possesses homogeneous increments if the distribution of any increment $W_{t+h} - W_t$ depends solely on h and not on t. The process has independent increments if the random variables $W_{t_2} - W_{t_1}$, $W_{t_3} - W_{t_2}$, ..., $W_{t_n} - W_{t_{n-1}}$ are independent for every n and every choice of $t_1, t_2, \ldots t_n$.

cesses that fulfill the first two conditions together with a technical requirement referred to as "stochastic continuity" Lévy processes. The Lévy processes form a rich class of stochastic processes, which include, for example, the previously discussed Poisson process. Other Lévy processes are mentioned in a later section of this chapter.

Exhibit 10.3 tries to visualize possible paths of Brownian motion. Due to its characteristic path properties, it is impossible to draw a real path of Brownian motion. As it will become clear from the constructive methodology described below, the paths of Brownian motion are highly irregular and nowhere differentiable. In order to draw a true path, one would have to calculate the value of the process for every real number, which is clearly not feasible.

From the above definition of the process, it does not become clear how one can imagine a Brownian motion or how one could construct it. Therefore, we will present a constructive method demonstrating how

EXHIBIT 10.3   Possible Paths of a Standard Brownian Motion (Every path consists of 10.000 equally spaced observations)

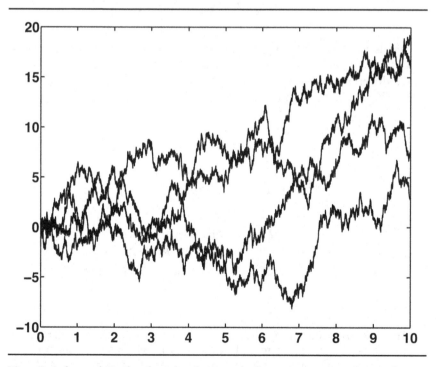

Note: Strictly speaking the plotted paths are only discrete approximations to the true paths. The process can only be evaluated for a discrete set of points.

one can generate a Brownian motion as a limit of very simple processes.[4] We restrict the presentation to the unit interval, that is, we assume $0 \leq t \leq 1$ but the generalization to the abstract case is obvious. The procedure is iterative, which means that on the k-th step of the iteration we define a process $(X_t^{(k)})_{0 \leq t \leq 1}$, which will serve as an approximation for standard Brownian motion.

Let us start with $k = 0$ and define

$$X_0^{(1)} = 0, \; X_1^{(1)} = \begin{cases} 1 \text{ with probability } p = 0.5 \\ -1 \text{ with probability } p = 0.5 \end{cases}$$

For values of t between 0 and 1, we simply perform a linear interpolation. By doing so, we get a stochastic process with continuous paths. At any time t the random variable $X_1^{(1)}$ can take only two possible values namely $-t$ and t. At any time, the process has zero mean and the variance at time $t = 1$ equals

$$VX_1^{(1)} = 1^2 \cdot 0.5 + (-1)^2 \cdot 0.5 = 1$$

That is not so bad for the beginning. But obviously the distribution of $X_1^{(1)}$ is far from being normal. What we do in the next step is allow for two different values until time $t = \frac{1}{2}$ and three different values for $\frac{1}{2} \leq t \leq 1$. We do so by defining

$$X_0^{(2)} = 0$$

$$X_{0.5}^{(2)} = \begin{cases} 1/\sqrt{2} \text{ with probability } p = 0.5 \\ -1/\sqrt{2} \text{ with probability } 1 - p = 0.5 \end{cases}$$

$$X_{0.5}^{(2)} = \begin{cases} \sqrt{2} \text{ with probability } p^2 = 0.25 \\ 0 \text{ with probability } 2p(1-p) = 0.5 \\ -\sqrt{2} \text{ with probability } (1-p)^2 = 0.25 \end{cases}$$

---

[4] The reader is encouraged to compare the presented methodology with the convergence of the binomial model to the Black-Scholes model outlined in Chapter 17. The original construction of Brownian motion differs from the one presented and is based on the so-called Donsker invariance principle. The interested reader is referred to Billingsley (1968).

As before, we define the missing values by linear interpolation.

In total, the process $X_t^{(2)}$ now has four possible paths. The mean of $X_t^{(2)}$ is zero and the variance of $X_1^{(2)}$ equals

$$VX_1^{(2)} = \sqrt{2}^2 \cdot 0.25 + (-\sqrt{2})^2 \cdot 0.25 = 1$$

but still the distribution of $X_t^{(2)}$ is far from being normal. However, by iterating the stated procedure, we get on the k-th step a stochastic process which has 2^k continuous paths, zero mean, and perhaps the distribution $X_t^{(2)}$ will approach the normal distribution due to the Central Limit Theorem. Indeed, this is the case and we provide a visualization of the convergence in Exhibits 10.4 and 10.5 where possible paths of $(X_t^{(k)})_{0 \le t \le 1}$ are plotted for $k = 1, 2, 5$ and the distribution of is shown for $k = 1, 2, 5, 25, 100,$ and 400.

EXHIBIT 10.4   Possible Paths and the Probability Distribution of $X_1^{(k)}$ for $k = 1, 2, 5$

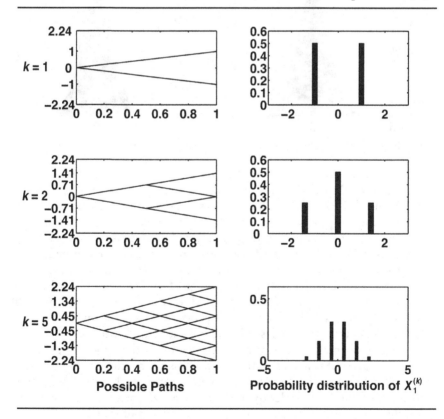

Possible Paths   Probability distribution of $X_1^{(k)}$

EXHIBIT 10.5 Histogram for the Distribution of $X_1^{(k)}$ for $k = 25, 100, 400$ and for the Density Function of a Standard Normal Distribution

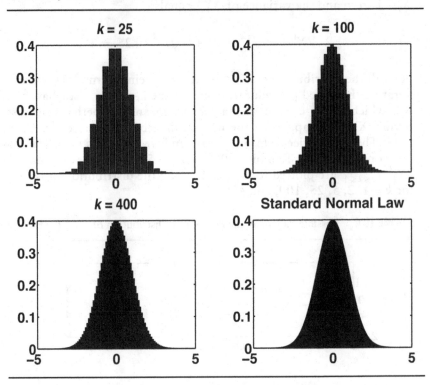

The exhibits provide insight into the convergence of the distribution of $X_1^{(k)}$ toward the standard normal distribution. Because we are not providing the needed concepts for fully understanding the underlying theory, it is not possible to provide a reason why even a much stronger result holds: The process $(X_t^{(k)})_{0 \le t \le 1}$ converges in distribution to the standard Brownian motion $(W_t)_{0 \le t \le 1}$. But if we believe in the result we can deduce and understand some of the above mentioned properties of Brownian motion.

First, we recognize that at every stage of the iteration all paths of the process $(X_t^{(k)})_{0 \le t \le 1}$ are continuous and it is, therefore, quite reasonable that this property holds for the limit process as well. Second, we see that the increments of the process always have an expectation of zero. As an increment we mean the possible realizations of the process in the next time step given its current state. The process does either take the upward moving branch or the downward moving branch each with a probability of one half and independently of the past realizations or its current state. On the k-th stage of iteration, the process consists of $(k/2)(k + 1)$ rescaled versions of the initial process ($k = 1$). The time scale is rescaled by a factor of $1/k$ and the state space by a factor of $1/\sqrt{k}$. This explains why not only the process itself, but also the increments of every size, are normally distributed and independent of the past. Thus we have found all the defining properties of a Brownian motion in this simple approximating process.

Transforms of Brownian Motion

In the context of financial applications, there are two main variants of the standard Brownian motion that have to be mentioned: the arithmetic and the geometric Brownian motion. Both are obtained as a function of the standard Brownian motion.

Arithmetic Brownian Motion

Given a Brownian motion $(W_t)_{t \geq 0}$ and two real constants μ and σ, the arithmetic Brownian motion $(X_t)_{t \geq 0}$ is obtained as

$$X_t = \mu \cdot t + \sigma \cdot W_t$$

The process (X_t) consists of a sum of a purely deterministic linear trend function $\mu \cdot t$ and a rescaled Brownian motion $\sigma \cdot W_t$. The latter has the property that at time t, $\sigma \cdot W_t$ is normally distributed with mean 0 and variance $\sigma^2 t$. The paths will, therefore, randomly jitter around the deterministic trend with a variance proportional to the point in time t under consideration. The arithmetic Brownian motion is a simple but popular model for financial returns.

Geometric Brownian Motion

Given a Brownian motion $(W_t)_{t \geq 0}$, two real constants μ and σ, and a starting value $S_0 > 0$, the geometric Brownian motion $(S_t)_{t \geq 0}$ is obtained as

$$S_t = S_0 \cdot e^{\mu \cdot t + \sigma \cdot W_t}$$

The process (S_t) is just the exponential of an arithmetic Brownian motion multiplied by a factor. S_t / S_0 is, therefore, lognormally distributed and its mean equals

$$e^{\mu + 0.5\sigma^2}$$

The geometric Brownian motion forms the basis of the seminal Black and Scholes theory and many of its extensions described in Part Four of this book.

Fractional Brownian Motion

A stochastic process that possesses normally distributed marginals, and which is related to the Brownian motion, is the so-called *fractional Brownian motion*. It is defined as a stochastic process that possesses the following properties:

1. $W_0^H = 0$, that is, fractional Brownian motion starts in zero.
2. (W_t^H, W_s^H) are bivariate normally distributed with mean vector $(0,0)$ and variance-covariance matrix:

$$\Sigma = \begin{pmatrix} s^{2H} & \tfrac{1}{2}(s^{2H} + t^{2H} - |t-s|^{2H}) \\ \tfrac{1}{2}(s^{2H} + t^{2H} - |t-s|^{2H}) & t^{2H} \end{pmatrix}$$

3. W^H has continuous paths.

The fractional Brownian motion depends on a real parameter $0 < H < 1$ which is also called the *Hurst parameter*. For $H = 0.5$, the fractional Brownian motion reduces to the ordinary Brownian motion. Due to the dependence structure imposed by the second defining property, the increments of the fractional Brownian motion are not independent if $H \neq 0.5$. More specifically, we obtain for $t > s \geq 0$:

$$\begin{aligned} \mathrm{Cov}(W_t^H - W_s^H, W_s^H) &= \mathrm{Cov}(W_t^H, W_s^H) - \mathrm{Cov}(W_s^H, W_s^H) \\ &= \tfrac{1}{2}(s^{2H} + t^{2H} - (t-s)^{2H}) - s^{2H} \\ &= \tfrac{1}{2}(t^{2H} - s^{2H} - (t-s)^{2H}) = \begin{cases} < 0, \; 0 < H < 0.5 \\ = 0, \; H = 0.5 \\ > 0, \; 0.5 < H < 1 \end{cases} \end{aligned}$$

For $H > 0.5$, the increments of the fractional Brownian motion are positively correlated which means that if a path is moving upwards than it tends to continue moving upwards and vice versa. When $H < 0.5$, the opposite effect occur: The paths are likely to exhibit reversals which means that an up movement is followed by a down movement.

An important concept deduced from fractional Brownian motion is the fractional Gaussian noise which can be used as an innovation process in time series models. Fractional Gaussian noise is defined as the increments of a fractional Brownian motion over time intervals of length one:

$$\varepsilon_t^H = W_t^H - W_{t-1}^H, \quad t = 1, 2, 3 \ldots$$

Fractional Brownian motion and fractional Gaussian noise have become attractive for financial modeling as they offer the possibility to incorporate the long memory effect. For $0.5 < H < 1$, the fractional Brownian motion and also the fractional Gaussian noise exhibit long-range dependence.[5]

STOCHASTIC DIFFERENTIAL EQUATIONS

Modeling the future evolution of a financial asset, a financial return or an economic risk factor as a stochastic process can be realized by using a powerful mathematical discipline, namely the *theory of stochastic differential equations*. In this section, we provide an intuitive idea of what a stochastic differential equation is and how it can be used.

When searching for an appropriate stochastic model in continuous time based on the processes described so far for the return series generated by the S&P 500, we could start with the following ingredients. We assume a deterministic dividend yield of d%, we know that in the long run we expect an annualized total return of say μ%, and we know that the usual yearly return volatility equals σ%. Additionally, we know that there might be some extreme movements in the market, which occur on average λ times per year and which cause an additional volatility of τ%. For the ease of exposition, we assume so far that the mean jump size equals zero, that is, on average the downward jumps and the upward jumps are offsetting each other.

Putting this together, we can say that the return over a very small time interval Δt can be described as

$$\frac{S_{t+\Delta t} - S_t}{S_t} = (\mu - \delta) \cdot \Delta t + \sigma \cdot (W_{t+\Delta t} - W_t) + Y \cdot (N_{t+\Delta t} - N_t) \qquad (10.5)$$

where we have chosen the increments of a Brownian motion $(W_t)_{t \geq 0}$ as a model for the "usual" random fluctuation and the increments of a compound Poisson process as model for the extreme market movements.

The expression $N_{t+\Delta t} - N_t$ will vanish with probability $1 - \lambda \cdot \Delta t$ (no jump of the Poisson process occurs) and will equal one with probability $\lambda \cdot \Delta t$ (jump has occurred).[6] In this case we draw a realization of Y from a distribution with mean zero and variance τ^2. Calculating the expected return

---

[5] For further insights into this topic, and the possible extensions to fractional Lévy motion, see Samorodnitsky and Taqqu (1994).

[6] The case that more than one jump occurs can be neglected when the length of the considered time interval tends to zero.

for the time interval of length Δt, the second and the third addend in equation (10.5) will vanish. The second one will vanish because the increments of the Brownian motion have zero mean and the third due to the zero mean jump size $EY = 0$. So we have the desired result that the expected return equals the expected growth rate minus the dividend rate. Additionally, the return will randomly vary around its expected value and these variations can be split into two components: a *regular component* (also called *diffusion term*) which creates continuous paths and an *extreme component* caused by jumps of compound Poisson process (*jump term*).

In the limit, we obtain the following stochastic differential equation, also called a *jump diffusion*:

$$\frac{dS_t}{S_t} = (\mu - \delta)\,dt + \sigma\,dW_t + Y\,dN_t \qquad (10.6)$$

A process of this type was first used in the jump diffusion framework to option pricing by Merton (1976) and in many subsequent publications.[7]

The stochastic differential equation (10.6) can now be generalized in various ways. First, we can introduce time-dependent parameters, that is, the parameters μ, σ, and δ are no longer constant but functions of the time t. Another possibility would be that these constants depend on the current index level S_t and clearly a combination of these two is possible as well. All these generalizations lead to the family of *Markov processes*.[8] We will finish our exposition with a different view on the processes discussed so far which will show a natural connection between the Poisson process and Brownian motion and lead to a large class of processes which have become increasingly popular in financial applications.

LÉVY PROCESSES

We have already mentioned that the Poisson process as well as the Brownian motion belong to one and the same class of stochastic processes called Lévy processes. Now, the question arises what is the joint property which relates the two. Obviously, their path properties are fundamentally different. The Poisson process has very regular paths which are constant up to some rare jumps which have a prespecified size of one.

---

[7] For an overview of the application of jump processes in finance, see Cont and Tankov (2004).

[8] To gain further insights in the corresponding mathematical theory, see Oksendal (2000) or Karatzas and Shreve (1991).

Brownian motion has paths which are fluctuating around and, which apart from the fact that they are continuous, behave very irregularly and jitter around. And, indeed, it can be proven that the paths of a Brownian motion are nowhere differentiable. The answer to that question is that both processes possess independent and stationary increments.

What does this mean? The first property was already treated in the context of a Brownian motion and it simply means that you cannot gain any information from the historic realizations in order to predict the future. One classical example occurs when we are playing roulette. What would your choice be if you enter a table and you see that the past 10 realizations have been red numbers? Are you betting on red or on black? Usually people tend to bet on black and their reasoning is as follows. Because the probability for black and red is equally high, we must observe—at least in the long run—the same number of red and black realizations. Therefore, after having observed red 10 times, black has to catch up and consequently people would bet on black. Clearly this is foolish! The next realization is independent of the past and, therefore, the probability for observing red or black in the next throw is $p = 18/37$. And with the Brownian motion and the Poisson process it is the same: The fact that we have not observed a jump for a long time does not increase the jump intensity nor the fact that Brownian motion has moved up for a long time increases or decreases the probability for up or down movements for the future.

The second property is the stationarity of the increments. This simply means that the distribution of the increment $X_{t+h} - X_t$ does not depend on the single point in time t, where we define the increment, but simply on the length h of the time interval over which the increment is defined.

The class of Lévy processes contains many other important stochastic processes.[9] Generally, a Lévy process consists of three components. The first and easiest one is a deterministic and linear drift term. The second one is a multiple of a Brownian motion and the third is a pure jump process.

In general, the jump process can differ substantially from the described Poisson process. When describing a pure jump process we must distinguish between two ingredients: (1) the distribution that governs when the next jump will happen (an exponential distribution in the Poisson process case) and (2) the distribution that describes the jump size (deterministic and equal to one in the Poisson case). But even without further explanations, one can imagine that there exist many possibilities for choosing these two ingredients and therefore the resulting class of Lévy processes is very large.

---

[9] For a more detailed treatment of Lévy processes with a special focus on its applications in finance, see Schoutens (2003) and Samorodnitsky and Taqqu (1994).

α-Stable Lévy Motion

At this point we note one special representative, the so-called α-*stable Lévy motion* $(L_t)_{t \geq 0}$, which is the stable analogue to the Brownian motion. It is defined as a stochastic process with the following properties:

1. $L_0 = 0$, that is, Lévy motion starts in zero.
2. $(L_t)_{t \geq 0}$ is a process with homogeneous and independent increments.
3. Any increment $L_{t+h} - L_t$ is α-stable distributed, with

$$L_{t+h} - L_t \sim S_\alpha(h^{1/\alpha}, \beta, 0)$$

4. The paths of $(L_t)_{t \geq 0}$ are right continuous and possess left-side limits.

Comparing the definition to the definition of the Brownian motion, we recognize that they are virtually identical. Only the property of continuity is missing which can be explained by the fact that the Lévy motion actually exhibits jumps and can, therefore, not be continuous.

REFERENCES

Bachelier, L. 1900. "Théorie de la Spéculation." *Annales d'Ecole Normale Superieurea* 3: 21–86.

Billingsley, P. 1968. *Convergence of Probability Measures.* New York: John Wiley & Sons.

Cont, R., and P. Tankov. 2004. *Financial Modelling with Jump Processes.* New York: CRC Press.

Kallenberg, O. 1997. *Foundations of Modern Probability: Second Edition.* New York: Springer.

Karatzas, I., and S. E. Shreve. 1991. *Brownian Motion and Stochastic Calculus: Second Edition.* New York: Springer.

Merton, R. C. 1976. "Option Pricing When the Underlying Stock Returns are Discontinuous." *Journal of Financial Economics* 3: 125–144.

Oksendal, B. 2000. *Stochastic Differential Equations: An Introduction with Applications: Fifth Edition.* New York: Springer.

Samorodnitsky, G., and M. S. Taqqu. 1994. *Stable Non-Gaussian Random Processes: Stochastic Models with Infinite Variance.* New York: Chapman and Hall.

Schoutens, W. 2003. *Lévy Processes in Finance: Pricing Financial Derivatives.* Chichester: John Wiley & Sons.

Shiryaev, A. N. 1999. *Essentials of Stochastic Finance.* Singapore: World Scientific.

PART Three

Portfolio Selection

CHAPTER 11

Equity and Bond Return
Distributions

In this chapter and those that follow, we apply the probability and statistical concepts in Parts One and Two to three areas of finance: portfolio selection, risk management, and option pricing. This chapter is the first of three chapters in Part Three that covers portfolio selection. Here we provide a description of recent empirical evidence on the return distribution for the two major asset classes, common stock and bonds, that supports the stable Paretian hypothesis and clearly refutes the normal (Gaussian) hypothesis. In the next chapter, we look at the desirable features of investment risk measures and present several portfolio risk measures. In Chapter 13, we explain how to determine the optimal portfolio choice for an investor under very weak distributional assumptions and describe various performance measures for portfolio selection.

EVIDENCE FROM THE U.S. STOCK MARKET

Since the 1960s, there have been a good number of studies that have investigated whether the stable Paretian distribution fairly represents the return distribution for stocks. Typically, these studies have been limited to stock indexes. In studies where individual stock returns have been analyzed, the samples have been small, typically limited to the constituent components of the Dow Jones Industrial Average or a non-U.S. stock index with no more than 40 stocks. The most likely explanation as to why researchers have not investigated a large sample of companies is the computational time involved to calculate the maximum likelihood estimate of the parameters of the stable distribution.

Recently, Stoyanov et al. (2005) compared the normal and stable
Paretian cases for a large sample of U.S. stocks. The sample included all
the companies that were included in the S&P 500 index over the 12-year
time period from January 1, 1992 to December 12, 2003 that had a complete return history (3,026 observations). Daily continuous returns (the
adjusted for dividends) were calculated.

Stoyanov et al. estimate and test two models. The first model assumes
that daily return observations are *independent and identically distributed*
(iid) and, therefore, is an unconditional, homoskedastic distribution
model. In the second test, it is assumed that the daily returns follow an
ARMA(1,1)–GARCH(1,1) process and, for that reason, belong to the
class of conditional heteroskedastic models. For both models, Stoyanov
et al. test whether the Gaussian hypothesis holds. The normality tests
employed are based on the *Kolmogorov distance (KD)*. For both the iid
and the ARMA–GARCH models, they compare the goodness-of-fit, in
the case of the Gaussian hypothesis, and the stable Paretian hypothesis
using the *KD*-statistic and the *Anderson-Darling (AD)* statistic.

In the unconditional model, Stoyanov et al. estimated the values for
the four parameters of the stable Paretian distribution using the method
of maximum likelihood. Exhibit 11.1 shows the distribution of the estimated index of stability and Exhibit 11.2 shows the distribution of the
estimated asymmetry value. Stoyanov et al. find that for the return distribution of *every* stock in their sample (1) the estimated values of the
index of stability are below 2 and (2) there is asymmetry ($\beta \neq 0$). These
two facts alone would strongly suggest that the Gaussian assumption is
not a proper theoretical distribution model for describing the return distribution of stocks. Note, however, for the firms in the sample, β is
found to be positive for most of the firms.

Additional support for the stable Paretian hypothesis is contained in
Exhibit 11.3. The exhibit shows that the normality hypothesis can be
rejected using the standard Kolmogorov-Smirnov test for (1) more than
95% of the stocks at the extremely high confidence level of 99.9% and
(2) 100% of the stocks at the traditional levels of 95% and 99%. In
contrast, the stable Paretian hypothesis is rejected in much fewer cases.

The superiority of the stable Paretian hypothesis over the normal
hypothesis is clearly supported from the computed *KD* and *AD* statistics
for all stocks under the two distributional assumptions. For *every* stock
in the Stoyanov et al. sample, the *KD* statistic in the stable Paretian case
is below the *KD* statistic in the Gaussian case. The same is true for the
AD statistic. The *KD* statistic implies that for their sample firms there
was a better fit of the stable Paretian model around the center of the distribution while the *AD* statistic implies that there was a better fit in the tails.
The huge difference between the *AD* statistic computed for the stable

EXHIBIT 11.1   Distribution of the Estimated Values of Stable Parameter α for Daily Returns of 382 Stocks

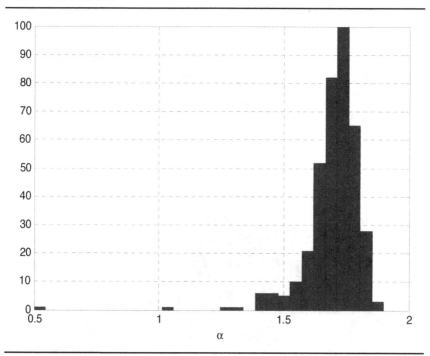

Source: Stoyanov, Biglova, Rachev, and Fabozzi (2005)

Paretian model relative to the Gaussian model strongly suggests a much better ability for the stable Paretian model to explain extreme events and confirms an already noticed phenomenon—the Gaussian distribution fails to describe observed large downward or upward asset price shifts, that is, in reality, extreme events have a larger probability than predicted by the Gaussian distribution.

Because the simple iid model does not account for the clustering of the volatility phenomenon, the second model considers the more advanced ARMA–GARCH model. For the general form of the ARMA(p,q)–GARCH(r,s) model, Stoyanov et al. found that $p = q = r = s = 1$ proved appropriate for the stock returns time series in their sample because the serial correlation in the residuals disappeared. The model parameters were estimated using the method of maximum likelihood assuming the normal distribution for the innovations. After estimating the ARMA(1,1)–GARCH(1,1) parameters, they computed the model residuals and verified which distributional assumption is more appropriate. For every return distribution in their sample, the estimated index of

EXHIBIT 11.2 Distribution of the Estimated Values of Stable Parameter β for Daily Returns of 382 Stocks

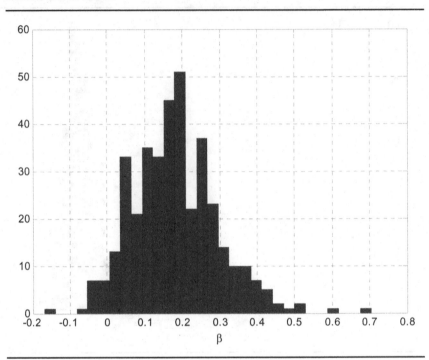

Source: Stoyanov, Biglova, Rachev, and Fabozzi (2005)

EXHIBIT 11.3 Percentage of Stocks Rejected at Different Confidence Levels using Kolmogorov Distance Statistic for the Independent and Identically Distributed Model

Confidence Level	95%	99%	99.50%	99.90%
Normal Distribution Hypothesis	100.00%	100.00%	99.74%	99.21%
Stable Paretian Distribution Hypothesis	28.54%	15.71%	11.78%	7.07%

Source: Adapted from Stoyanov, Biglova, Rachev, and Fabozzi (2005)

stability was greater than 1. Even though the estimated values of α are closer to 2 than in the iid model, they were found to be significantly different from 2. This is suggested by Exhibits 11.4 and 11.5.

Comparing the results reported Exhibit 11.6 to those reported in Exhibit 11.3, one can observe that the Gaussian model is rejected in fewer cases in the ARMA–GARCH model than in the simple iid model;

EXHIBIT 11.4   Distribution of the Estimated Values of Stable Parameter α of the
Residuals in the ARMA–GARCH Model for All 382 Stocks

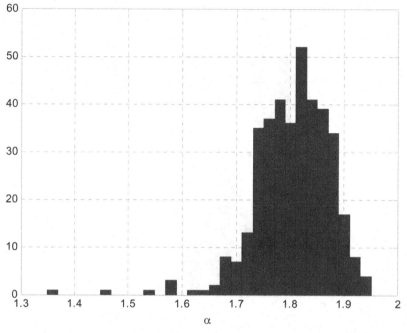

Source: Stoyanov, Biglova, Rachev, and Fabozzi (2005)

nevertheless, the Gaussian assumption is rejected for more than 82% of
the stocks at the 99% confidence level. The stable Paretian assumption
is rejected in only about 6% of the stocks at the same confidence level.

EVIDENCE FROM THE U.S. BOND MARKET

Now we turn to evidence in the U.S. bond market. The three largest sectors of the U.S. bond market are the Treasury sector, corporate sector,
and mortgage sector. Several studies in the 1990s show that distribution
of value changes of debt obligations are skewed and heavy tailed.[1]
Below we describe two studies that provide emirical evidence that the
daily return distribution of these three sectors is better characterized as
a stable Paretian distribution.

---

[1] Gupton, Finger, and Bhatia (1997), Federal Reserve System Task Force on Internal
Credit Risk Models (1998), and Basel Committee on Banking Supervision (1999).

EXHIBIT 11.5   Distribution of the Estimated Values of Stable Parameter of the Residuals in the ARMA–GARCH Model for All 382 Stocks

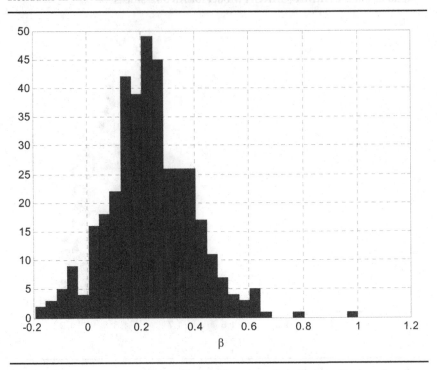

Source: Stoyanov, Biglova, Rachev, and Fabozzi (2005)

EXHIBIT 11.6   Percentage of Stocks for Rejected at Different Confidence Levels using Kolmogorov Distance in the ARMA–GARCH Model

Confidence Level	95%	99%	99.50%	99.90%
Normal Distribution Hypothesis	97.38%	92.94%	89.79%	79.58%
Stable Paretian Distribution Hypothesis	12.05%	5.76%	4.98%	2.62%

Source: Adapted from Stoyanov, Biglova, Rachev, and Fabozzi (2005)

Treasury and Corporate Bonds

The most extensive study of the distribution of Treasury and corporate bond returns for individual bond series and portfolios is the Rachev, Schwartz, and Khindanova (2003) study. They estimated the daily return distribution of bond returns for the Merrill Lynch indices for U.S. government and corporate bonds with maturities from one to 10 years and credit ratings from AAA to BB.[2] With one exception, each index set includes 2,418 daily observations from 3/13/90 to 7/29/99. The stable and normal parameter estimates for the bond indices are presented in Exhibit 11.7. For all 17 considered indices, the tail index α is less than 2, which reveals heavy tailedness, and the skewness parameter β is below zero, which implies skewness to the left.

In order to assess riskiness of the individual credit series and properties of stable modeling in risk evaluation, the 99% and 95% Value-at-Risk (VaR) measurements were computed. (This risk measure is described in more detail in Chapter 14.) The stable and normal VaR estimates are reported in Exhibit 11.8. The differences between empirical and modeled VaR are given in Exhibit 11.9. The VaR evaluation for the 5–7 year Treasury series (G302) is illustrated in Exhibit 11.10, for the 5–7 year A rated corporate bond series (C3A3) in Exhibit 11.11, and for the BB rated corporate bond (H0A1 series) in Exhibit 11.12.

Results of VaR estimations lead Rachev, Schwartz, and Khindanova (2003) to conclude:[3]

■ Returns on the credit series investigated have skewed and heavy-tailed distributions and, as a result, VaR mesurements provide a more adequate indication of risk than symmetric measurements (standard deviation or, in case of stable distributions, scale parameter).
■ Stable modeling produces conservative and accurate 99% VaR estimates "Conservative" VaR estimates exceed empirical VaR, implying that forecasts of losses were greater than observed losses.
■ Stable modeling underestimates the 95% VaR.
■ Overly optimistic forecasts of losses in the 99% VaR estimation are found when normal modeling is used.
■ Normal modeling is acceptable for the 95% VaR estimation.

They then go on to examine properties of stable modeling in evaluation of portfolio risk under the assumptions of independent and symmetric dependent instruments and the most general case—skewed dependent instruments. They evaluate portfolio risk for equally

---

[2] For the corporate series, a digit after the letter "C" denotes the maturity band: 1, from one to three years; 2, from three to five years; 3, from five to seven years; and 4, from seven to 10 years. A digit after letter "A" denotes credit rating: 1, AAA rated; 2, AA rated; 3, A rated; and 4, BBB rated.
[3] While the Rachev, Schwartz, Khindanova (2003) computes "in-sample" VaR and for that reason, the conclusions consider only in-sample VaR properties, Khindanova, Rachev, and Schwartz (2001) have examined forecasting VaR properties and reported excellent performance of stable modeling in forecast evaluation of VaR and measurements of potential losses.

weighted returns on indices of the investment-grade corporate bonds in
Exhibit 11.7. Their conclusion is the same regarding the superiority of
the stable Paretian distribution.

EXHIBIT 11.7 Normal and Stable Parameter Estimates of Bond Indices

			Normal		Stable			
Index[a]	Rating or Issuer	Maturity (years)	Mean	Standard deviation	Tail Index α	Skewness β	Location μ	Scale σ
G102	US gov-t	1–3	0.026	0.096	1.696	−0.160	0.029	0.055
G202	US gov-t	3–5	0.030	0.204	1.739	−0.134	0.036	0.122
G302	US gov-t	5–7	0.032	0.275	1.781	−0.134	0.032	0.169
G402	US gov-t	7–10	0.033	0.352	1.808	−0.172	0.033	0.218
C1A1	AAA	1–3	0.027	0.096	1.654	−0.080	0.053	0.027
C2A1	AAA	3–5	0.029	0.175	1.695	−0.112	0.029	0.099
C3A1	AAA	5–7	0.032	0.249	1.710	−0.116	0.031	0.145
C4A1	AAA	7–10	0.032	0.319	1.739	−0.155	0.031	0.190
C1A2	AA	1–3	0.028	0.099	1.686	−0.105	0.027	0.056
C2A2	AA	3–5	0.029	0.177	1.722	−0.111	0.029	0.104
C3A2	AA	5–7	0.032	0.250	1.757	−0.121	0.032	0.150
C4A2	AA	7–10	0.033	0.325	1.778	−0.148	0.033	0.198
C1A3	A	1–3	0.028	0.098	1.688	−0.135	0.027	0.056
C2A3	A	3–5	0.030	0.180	1.702	−0.122	0.029	0.104
C3A3	A	5–7	0.032	0.255	1.743	−0.133	0.033	0.151
C4A3	A	7–10	0.033	0.333	1.753	−0.167	0.033	0.199
C1A4	BBB	1–3	0.029	0.112	1.653	−0.113	0.029	0.054
C2A4	BBB	3–5	0.032	0.183	1.662	−0.042	0.033	0.096
C3A4	BBB	5–7	0.034	0.249	1.690	−0.125	0.035	0.140
C4A4	BBB	7–10	0.035	0.316	1.694	−0.136	0.035	0.180
H0A1	BB	1–3	0.027	0.185	1.686	−0.252	0.042	0.104

[a] Each index set, except H0A1, includes 2,418 daily observations from 3.13.90 to
7.29.99. Source of index series: Merrill Lynch, used with permission.
Source: Rachev, Schwartz, and Khindanova (2003).

EXHIBIT 11.8   Empirical, Normal, and Stable VaR Estimates for Bond Indices

Index	99% VaR estimates			95% VaR estimates		
	Empirical	Normal	Stable	Empirical	Normal	Stable
G102	0.242	0.198	0.275	0.127	0.132	0.119
G202	0.518	0.446	0.576	0.303	0.306	0.283
G302	0.739	0.609	0.747	0.412	0.421	0.399
G402	0.928	0.785	0.932	0.545	0.545	0.518
C1A1	0.238	0.196	0.284	0.129	0.130	0.119
C2A1	0.437	0.377	0.509	0.244	0.258	0.236
C3A1	0.687	0.548	0.734	0.369	0.378	0.353
C4A1	0.883	0.712	0.931	0.480	0.494	0.467
C1A2	0.237	0.201	0.285	0.132	0.134	0.125
C2A2	0.443	0.382	0.505	0.254	0.261	0.244
C3A2	0.663	0.550	0.689	0.373	0.380	0.355
C4A2	0.870	0.722	0.890	0.482	0.501	0.474
C1A3	0.237	0.207	0.286	0.135	0.134	0.125
C2A3	0.469	0.390	0.530	0.260	0.267	0.248
C3A3	0.705	0.560	0.719	0.376	0.386	0.361
C4A3	0.893	0.741	0.949	0.487	0.514	0.485
C1A4	0.262	0.231	0.290	0.124	0.155	0.119
C2A4	0.478	0.392	0.511	0.243	0.268	0.228
C3A4	0.711	0.545	0.741	0.361	0.375	0.343
C4A4	0.862	0.702	0.960	0.467	0.486	0.451
H0A1	0.557	0.403	0.570	0.258	0.277	0.245

The U.S. Agency Mortgage Passthrough Securities

A mortgage passthrough security is created when one or more holders of mortgage loans form a collection (pool) of mortgage loans and sell shares or participation certificates in the pool. U.S. agency mortgage passthrough securities are issued by the Government National Mortgage Association (Ginnie Mae, a U.S. government agency), the Federal Home Loan Mortgage Association (Freddie Mac, a U.S. government-sponsored enterprise), and the Federal National Mortgage Association (Fannie Mae, a U.S. government-sponsored enterprise).

EXHIBIT 11.9 Deviations of VaR Estimates for Bond Indices

Index	99% VaR_{model} – 99% $VaR_{empirical}$		95% VaR_{model} – 95% $VaR_{empirical}$	
	Normal	Stable	Normal	Stable
G102	–0.044	0.033	0.005	–0.008
G202	–0.072	0.058	0.003	–0.020
G302	–0.130	0.008	0.009	–0.013
G402	–0.143	0.004	0.000	–0.027
C1A1	–0.042	0.046	0.001	–0.010
C2A1	–0.060	0.072	0.014	–0.008
C3A1	–0.139	0.047	0.009	–0.016
C4A1	–0.171	0.048	0.014	–0.013
C1A2	–0.036	0.048	0.002	–0.007
C2A2	–0.061	0.062	0.007	–0.010
C3A2	–0.113	0.026	0.007	–0.018
C4A2	–0.148	0.020	0.019	–0.008
C1A3	–0.030	0.049	–0.001	–0.010
C2A3	–0.079	0.061	0.007	–0.012
C3A3	–0.145	0.014	0.010	–0.015
C4A3	–0.152	0.056	0.027	–0.002
C1A4	–0.031	0.028	0.031	–0.005
C2A4	–0.086	0.033	0.025	–0.015
C3A4	–0.166	0.030	0.014	–0.018
C4A4	–0.160	0.098	0.019	–0.016
H0A1	–0.154	0.013	0.019	–0.013

Source: Rachev, Schwartz, and Khindanova (2003).

The agency mortgage passthrough securities sector is included in the broad-based bond market indexes created by Lehman Brothers, Salomon Smith Barney, and Merrill Lynch. Lehman Brothers labels this sector of its bond market index the "mortgage passthrough sector." This sector is the largest one in the U.S. investment-grade fixed income market. It is approximately 40% of the Lehman Brothers U.S. Aggregate Bond Index. Dealer positions in mortgage-backed securities products is large and must be hedged. For example, a report by Lehman Brothers in October 2004 was that the aggregate net long position in mortgage-backed securities for 22 dealers had reached $40 billion (see Goodwin, 2004). With-

EXHIBIT 11.10   VAR Estimation for the G302 Index

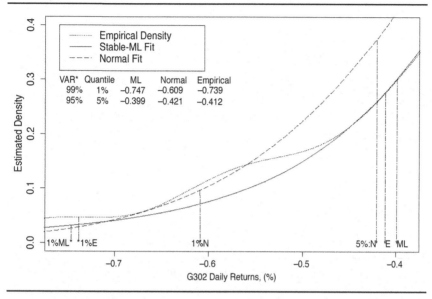

Source: Rachev, Schwartz, and Khindanova (2003).

EXHIBIT 11.11   VAR Estimation for the C3A3 Index

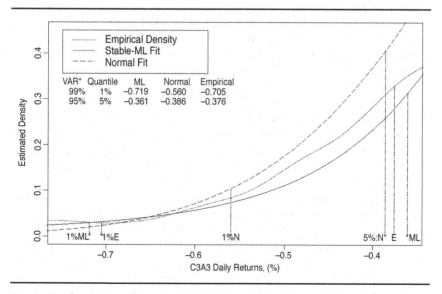

Source: Rachev, Schwartz, and Khindanova (2003).

EXHIBIT 11.12 VAR Estimation for the H0A1 Index

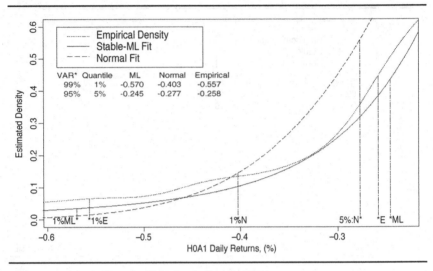

Source: Rachev, Schwartz, and Khindanova (2003).

out a firm understanding of the return distribution properties of these securities, dealers cannot adequately hedge positions.

Lehman Brothers employs a rule-based methodology to produce the index to represent each major sector of the bond market. The securities to be included in the index for a given sector are identified by a set of rules that involve the characteristics of a security that is a potential candidate for inclusion in the index. The methodology is straightforward for all sectors except the agency mortgage passthrough sector where there are challenge because in the aggregate there are more than a half a million pools (i.e., mortgage passthrough securities) created by Ginnie Mae, Fannie Mae, and Freddie Mac. The other sectors of the fixed income market have only a small fraction of the number of issues that are included in the index. The creators of bond indexes do not include all of these pools in the index. Instead, they create composites of these securities, what Lehman Brothers refers to as "index generics."

A recent study by Fabozzi, Racheva-Iotova, and Stoyanov (2005) examined six index generics that would be representative of the market. The six index generics were FGB06001, FNA07001, FNC05401, GNA06001, GNA07001, and FNA06001. For each of the six index generics, daily return data were provided for the period March 1, 2001 through May 5, 2004.

They compared the stable and normal distributional assumptions in the independent and identically distributed (iid) returns model and the

ARMA(1,1)–GARCH(1,1) model. These models are the same as used in Stoyanov et al. (2005) and discussed above for equity returns. The risk statistics computed and reported for all cases are VaR at 99% and 95% confidence levels and *expected tail loss* (ETL) at 99% VaR and 95% VaR. (We will discuss ETL in Chapter 14.)

The back-testing period that Stoyanov et al. used for the iid model is 556 days—a moving window of 250 observations was used for parameter estimation. Exhibit 11.13 summarizes the results of the iid model. Based on these results Fabozzi, Racheva-Iotova, and Stoyanov conclude that:

- In the 99% VaR case, both the stable Paretian and the normal show equal performance. The number of exceedances is within the 95% confidence bounds for a back-testing period of 556 days, which is [0, 10].
- In the 95% VaR case, the normal model has less exceedances and therefore is more conservative than the stable Paretian model. Actually the number of exceedances in the stable Paretian model are within the 95% confidence bound for a back-testing period of 556 days—[17, 37]—while the normal model is almost always below the lower bound making it unrealistically conservative.

Even though the stable distribution were found to have a heavier tail, the normal distribution appears to provide a more conservative

EXHIBIT 11.13 Results of the Independent, Identically Distributed Returns Model for Index Generic Passthrough Securities

| Index Generic Passthrough | Number of Exceedances | | | |
| | Normal | | Stable Paretian | |
	99% VaR[a]	95% VaR[b]	99% VaR[a]	95% VaR[b]
FGB06001	5	15	5	27
FNA07001	6	9	8	27
FNC05401	6	15	5	26
GNA06001	6	17	5	26
GNA07001	6	15	6	26
FNA06001	4	14	4	27

[a] The 95% confidence bounds for the exceedances of the 99% VaR for a back-testing period of 556 days equals [0,10].
[b] The 95% confidence bounds for the exceedances of the 95% VaR for a back-testing period of 556 days equals [17,37].
Source: Fabozzi, Racheva-Iotova, and Stoyanov (2005)

VaR estimate leading to less exceedances and in the 95% VaR case their number is almost always below the corresponding lower confidence bound. The reason is that because of the observed extreme passthrough returns, the estimated variance is unusually higher, leading to fitted normal density which is inadequate to describe the real data.

In addition, Fabozzi, Racheva-Iotova, and Stoyanov computed the *KD* and statistics. Exhibit 11.14 reports the average *KD* for the entire back-testing period for all mortgage passthrough securities in their study. The results suggest that the stable hypothesis better explains not only the left tail but the entire distribution of all six mortgage passthrough securities daily returns within the iid model. The average values of the *AD* statistics reported in Exhibit 11.14 confirm the conclusion from the VaR analysis that the stable Paretian assumption better models the tails of the empirical data.

For the ARMA(1,1)–GARCH(1,1) model, Fabozzi, Racheva-Iotova, and Stoyanov used a back-testing period of 349 days; for parameter estimation, they used a moving window of 457 observations. A longer time window was necessary because the parameters are more and the estimation procedure is more involved. Their results are summarized in Exhibit 11.15 and suggested that:

- In all but one case, the number of exceedances for the stable Paretian model is within the 99% confidence bound of [0, 7] for a back-testing period of 349 days. This suggests a realistic estimation of real loss. In the normal case, there are only two examples with the number of exceedances being on the upper confidence bound. Therefore, in the 99% VaR case, the stable model has superior performance.
- In contrast to the iid model and the EWMA model, the ARMA–GARCH model for both 95% stable Paretian and normal VaR shows equal performance with respect to the number of exceedances—it is within the 95% confidence interval of [9, 25] for a back-testing period of 349 days. Nevertheless the estimate of the expected tail loss of the stable Paretian model is more conservative than that of the Gaussian model.

Apart from the analysis concerning the modeling of the left tail, Fabozzi, Racheva-Iotova, and Stoyanov consider the *KD* between the residuals of the ARMA(1,1)–GARCH(1,1) model with stable or normal innovation process and the corresponding fitted error distribution—stable Paretian or normal respectively. The results are shown in Exhibit 11.16 and from them they concluded that the stable Paretian assumption better explains the corresponding model residuals for all mortgage passthrough securities they examined. Again, as in the iid model, the average *AD* statistics reported in Exhibit 11.16 reinforces the conclusion that stable Paretian model better explains the tails.

EXHIBIT 11.14 Average Kolmogorov Distance and Anderson-Darling Statistics for the Back-Testing Period for the Independent, Identical Distributed Model

	FGB06001	FNA07001	FNC05401	GNA06001	GNA07001	FNA06001
Stable Paretian, KD	0.042481	0.067248	0.041636	0.047098	0.058849	0.050903
Normal, KD	0.088459	0.116047	0.087744	0.101551	0.111152	0.095703
Stable Paretian, AD	0.110631	0.162174	0.108324	0.121099	0.167603	0.123031
Normal, AD	0.236203	0.310677	0.233643	0.265416	0.293394	0.248093

Source: Fabozzi, Racheva-Iotova, and Stoyanov (2005)

EXHIBIT 11.15 Results of the ARMA(1,1)–GARCH(1,1) Model

Index Generic Passthrough	Number of Exceedances			
	Normal		Stable Paretian	
	99% VaR[a]	99% VaR[b]	99% VaR[a]	95% VaR[b]
FGB06001	9	18	5	21
FNA07001	8	10	5	10
FNC05401	7	19	5	20
GNA06001	9	19	4	19
GNA07001	10	16	8	15
FNA06001	7	14	4	16

[a] The 95% confidence bounds for the exceedances of the 99% VaR for a back-testing period of 556 days equals [0,10].
[b] The 95% confidence bounds for the exceedances of the 95% VaR for a back-testing period of 556 days equals [17,37].
Source: Fabozzi, Racheva-Iotova, and Stoyanov (2005)

REFERENCES

Basel Committee on Banking Supervision. 1999. "Credit Risk Modelling: Current Practices and Applications."

Fabozzi, F. J., B. Racheva-Iotova, and S. Stoyanov. 2005. "An Empirical Examination of the Return Distribution Characteristics of Agency Mortgage Pass-Through Securities." Technical report, Chair of Econometrics, Statistics and Mathematical Finance, School of Economics, University of Karlsruhe, Postfach 6980, D-76128, Karlsruhe, Germany and Technical Report, Department of Statistics and Applied Probability, UCSB, CA 93106, USA.

Federal Reserve System Task Force on Internal Credit Risk Models. 1998. "Credit Risk Models at Major U.S. Banking Institutions: Current State of the Art and Implications for Assessment of Capital Adequacy."

Goodwin, S. 2004. "Lehman Warns of Risks in Dealers' Mortgage Exposure." *BondWeek* (18 October), 1, 11.

Gupton, G. M., C. C. Finger, and M. Bhatia. 1997. "CreditMetrics™—Technical Document." New York: J. P. Morgan.

Khindanova, I., S.T. Rachev, and E. Schwartz. 2001. "Stable Modeling of Value at Risk." *Mathematical and Computer Modelling* 34: 1223–1259.

EXHIBIT 11.16 Average Kolmogorov Distance and Anderson-Darling Statistics between the ARMA(1,1)–GARCH(1,1) Residuals and the Fitted distribution for the Back-Testing Period

	FGB06001	FNA07001	FNC05401	GNA06001	GNA07001	FNA06001
Stable Paretian, KD	0.028443	0.041978	0.029432	0.02997	0.04114	0.030697
Normal, KD	0.055325	0.066767	0.060623	0.06853	0.074795	0.060423
Stable Paretian, AD	0.090792	0.117915	0.089638	0.097586	0.125346	0.142087
Normal, AD	0.160486	0.166855	0.162895	0.176109	0.181541	0.150505

Source: Fabozzi, Racheva-Iotova, and Stoyanov (2005)

Rachev, S. T., E. Schwartz, and I. Khindanova. 2003. "Stable Modeling of Credit Risk." In *Handbook of Heavy Tailed Distributions in Finance*, ed. S. T. Rachev, 249–328. Amsterdam: North Holland Handbooks of Finance.

Rachev, S. T., S. Stoyanov, A. Biglova, and F. J. Fabozzi, 2005. "An Empirical Examination of Daily Stock Return Distributions for U.S. Stocks." Forthcoming in *Data Analysis and Decision Support*, Springer Series in *Studies in Classification, Data Analysis, and Knowledge Organization*. eds. R. Decker, L. Schmidt-Thieme, and D. Baier.

CHAPTER 12

Risk Measures and Portfolio Selection

In the previous chapter, we discussed the evidence against the normal distribution assumption for describing asset returns. In this chapter, we look at alternative risk measures that can be employed in portfolio selection, which can accommodate nonnormal return distributions. We begin with a discussion of the desirable features of investment risk measures.

DESIRABLE FEATURES OF INVESTMENT RISK MEASURES

In portfolio theory, the variance of a portfolio's return has been historically the most commonly used measure of investment risk. However, different investors adopt different investment strategies in seeking to realize their investment objectives. Consequently, intuitively, it is difficult to believe that investors have come to accept only one definition of risk. Regulators of financial institutions and commentators to risk measures proposed by regulators have proffered alternative definitions of risk. As noted by Dowd (2002, 1):

> The theory and practice of risk management—and, included with that, risk measurement—have developed enormously since the pioneering work of Harry Markowitz in the 1950s. The theory has developed to the point where risk management/measurement is now regarded as a distinct sub-field of the theory of finance . . .

Swegö (2004, 1) categorizes risk measures as one of the three major revolutions in finance and places the start of that revolution in 1997. The other two major revolutions are mean-variance analysis (1952–1956) and continuous-time models (1969–1973). He notes that alternative risk measures have been accepted by practitioners but "rejected by the academic establishment and, so far discarded by regulators!" (Swegö 2004, 4).

In the next chapter, we will describe many of the alternative risk measures proposed in the literature. We look at some of these risk measures more closely when we cover risk management in Part Three.

Basic Features of Investment Risk Measures

Balzer (2001) argues that a risk measure is investor specific and, therefore, there is "no single universally acceptable risk measure." He suggests the following three features that an investment risk measure should capture:[1]

- Relativity of risk
- Multidimensionalility of risk
- Asymmetry of risk

The relativity of risk means that risk should be related to performing worse than some alternative investment or benchmark. Balzer (1994, 2001) and Sortino and Satchell (2001), among others, have proposed that investment risk might be measured by the probability of the investment return falling below a specified risk benchmark. The risk benchmark might itself be a random variable, such as a liability benchmark (e.g., an insurance product), the inflation rate or possibly inflation plus some safety margin, the risk-free rate of return, the bottom percentile of return, a sector index return, a budgeted return, or other alternative investments. Each benchmark can be justified in relation to the goal of the portfolio manager. Should performance fall below the benchmark, the consequences could have major adverse consequences for the portfolio manager.

In addition, the same investor could have multiple objectives and, hence, multiple risk benchmarks. Thus, risk is also a *multidimensional* phenomenon. However, an appropriate choice of the benchmarks is necessary in order to avoid an incorrect evaluation of opportunities available to investors. For example, too often little recognition is given to liability targets. This is the major factor contributing to the underfunding of U.S. corporate pension sponsors of defined benefit plans.[2]

Intuition suggests that risk is an asymmetric concept related to the downside outcomes, and any realistic risk measure has to value and

---

[1] There are other features he suggests but they are not discussed here.
[2] See Ryan and Fabozzi (2002).

consider upside and downside differently. The standard deviation considers the positive and the negative deviations from the mean as a potential risk. In this case overperformance relative to the mean is penalized just as much as underperformance.

Intertemporal Dependence and Correlation with Other Sources of Risk

The standard deviation is a measure of dispersion and it cannot always be used as a measure of risk. The preferred investment does not always present better returns than the other. It could happen that the worst investment presents the greatest return in some periods. Hence, time could influence the investor's choices. We illustrate this feature of investment risk in this section with a realistic example.

Exhibit 12.1 shows the S&P 500 daily return series from January 4, 1995 to January 30, 1998. The dispersion around the mean changes sensibly in particular during the last period of our observations, when the Asian market crisis began (i.e., the spike in the series). Therefore, in some periods, big oscillations are around zero and in other periods the oscillations are reduced.

Clearly, if the degree of uncertainty changes over time, the risk has to change during the time as well. In this case, the investment return process is not stationary; that is, we cannot assume that returns maintain their distribution unvaried in the course of time. In much of the research published, stationary and independent realizations are assumed. The lat-

EXHIBIT 12.1 S&P 500 Return Time Series from 1/4/1995 to 1/30/1998

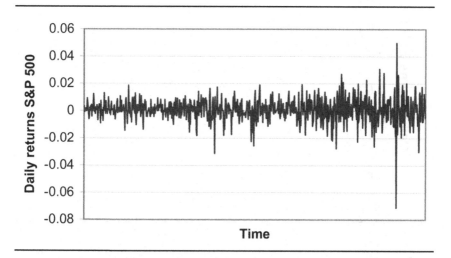

ter assumption implies that history has no impact on the future. More concrete, the distribution of tomorrow's return is the same independent of whether the biggest stock market crash ever recorded took place yesterday or yesterday's return equaled 10%.[3]

As a result, the oldest observations have the same weight in our decisions as the most recent ones. Is this assumption realistic? Recent studies on investment return processes have shown that historical realizations are not independent and present a clustering of the volatility effect (time-varying volatility). That phenomena lead to the fundamental time-series model Autoregressive Conditional Hetroscedascity (ARCH) formulated by Engle (1981) and described in Chapter 9. In particular, the last observations have a greater impact in investment decisions than the oldest ones. Thus, any realistic measure of risk changes and evolves over time taking into consideration the heteroscedastic (time-varying volatility) behavior of historical series.

Exhibit 12.2 shows the S&P 500 daily return series from September 8, 1997 to January 30, 1998. The wavy behavior of returns also has a *propagation effect* on the other markets. This can be seen in Exhibit 12.3, which describes the DAX 30 daily return series valued in U.S. dollars during the same period as the S&P 500 series. When we observe the highest peaks in the S&P 500 returns, there is an analogous peak in the DAX 30 series.

EXHIBIT 12.2   S&P 500 Return Time Series from 9/8/1997 to 1/30/1998

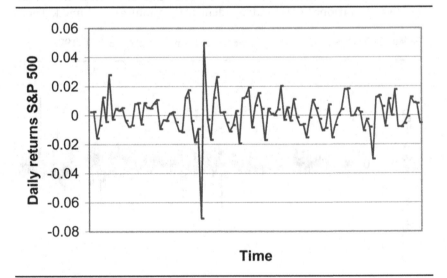

---

[3] See also the discussion of the properties of ARMAX processes in Chapter 9.

EXHIBIT 12.3 DAX 30 Return Time Series from 9/8/1997 to 1/30/1998

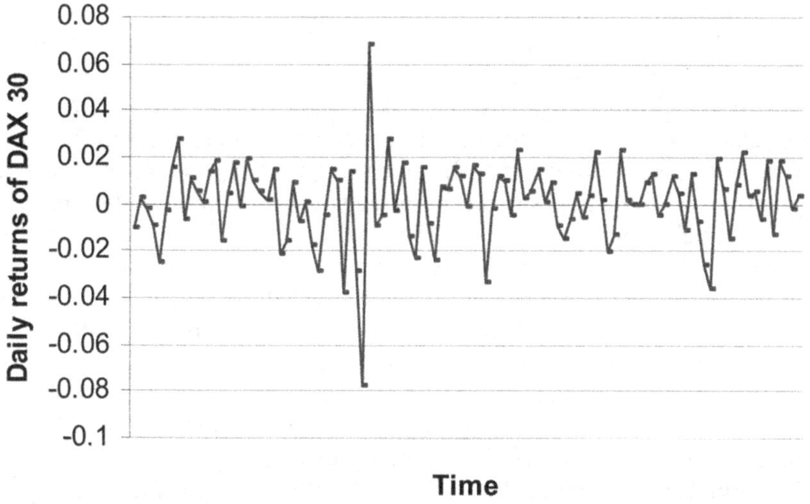

This propagation effect is known as cointegration of the return series, introduced by the fundamental work of Granger (1981) and elaborated upon further by Engle and Granger (1987). The propagation effect in this case is a consequence of the globalization of financial markets—the risk of a country/sector is linked to the risk of the other countries/sectors. Therefore, it could be important to limit the propagation effect by *diversifying the risk*. As a matter of fact, it is largely proven that the diversification, opportunely modeled, diminishes the probability of big losses. Hence, an adequate risk measure values and models correctly the *correlation* among different investments, sectors, and markets.

ALTERNATIVE RISK MEASURES FOR PORTFOLIO SELECTION

The goal of portfolio selection is the construction of portfolios that maximize expected returns consistent with individually acceptable levels of risk. Using both historical data and investor expectations of future returns, portfolio selection uses modeling techniques to quantify "expected portfolio returns" and "acceptable levels of portfolio risk," and provides methods to select an optimal portfolio.

It would not be an overstatement to say that modern portfolio theory as developed by Harry Markowitz (1952, 1959) has revolutionized the world of investment management. Allowing managers to appreciate that the investment risk and expected return of a portfolio can be quantified has provided the scientific and objective complement to the subjective art of investment management. More importantly, whereas previously the focus of portfolio management used to be the risk of individual assets, the theory of portfolio selection has shifted the focus to the risk of the entire portfolio. This theory shows that it is possible to combine risky assets and produce a portfolio whose expected return reflects its components, but with considerably lower risk. In other words, it is possible to construct a portfolio whose risk is smaller than the sum of all its individual parts.

Though practitioners realized that the risks of individual assets were related, prior to modern portfolio theory they were unable to formalize how combining them into a portfolio impacted the risk at the entire portfolio level or how the addition of a new asset would change the return/risk characteristics of the portfolio. This is because practitioners were unable to quantify the returns and risks of their investments. Furthermore, in the context of the entire portfolio, they were also unable to formalize the interaction of the returns and risks across asset classes and individual assets. The failure to quantify these important measures and formalize these important relationships made the goal of constructing an optimal portfolio highly subjective and provided no insight into the return investors could expect and the risk they were undertaking. The other drawback, before the advent of the theory of portfolio selection and asset pricing theory, was that there was no measurement tool available to investors for judging the performance of their investment managers.

The theory of portfolio selection set forth by Markowitz was based on the assumption that asset returns are normally distributed. As a result, Markowitz suggested that the appropriate risk measure is the variance of the portfolio's return and portfolio selection involved only two parameters of the asset return distribution: mean and variance. Hence, the approach to portfolio selection he proposed is popularly referred to as *mean-variance analysis*.

Markowitz recognized that an alternative to the variance is the *semivariance*. The semivariance is similar to the variance except that, in the calculation, no consideration is given to returns above the expected return. Portfolio selection could be recast in terms of mean-semivariance. However, if the return distribution is symmetric, Markowitz (1959, p. 190) notes that "an analysis based on (expected return) and (standard deviation) would consider these ... (assets) as equally desirable." He rejected the semivariance noting that the variance "is superior with respect to cost, convenience, and familiarity" and when the asset return distribution is symmetric, either measure "will produce the same set of efficient portfolios." (Markowitz 1959, 193–194).[4]

---

[4] The mean-semivariance approach was revisited by Stefani and Szegö (1976).

There is a heated debate on risk measures used for valuing and optimizing the investor's risk portfolio. In this section and the one to follow, we describe the various portfolio risk measures proposed in the literature and more carefully look at the properties of portfolio risk measures.

Dispersion Measures and Safety-First Measures

According to the literature on portfolio theory, two disjointed categories of risk measures can be defined: dispersion measures and safety-risk measures. In the remainder of this chapter, we review some of the most well-known dispersion measures and safety-first measures along with their properties.

In the following, we consider a portfolio of N assets whose individual returns are given by r_1, ..., r_N. The relative weights of the portfolio are denoted as x_1, ... x_n and, therefore, the portfolio return r_p can be expressed as

$$r_p = x_1 \cdot r_1 + \dots + x_N \cdot r_N = \sum_{i=1}^{N} x_i \cdot r_i$$

We also provide a sample version of the discussed risk measures. The sample version will be based on a sample of length T of independent and identically distributed observations $r_p^{(k)}$, $k = 1, ..., T$ of the portfolio return r_p. These observations can be obtained from a corresponding sample of the individual assets.

Dispersion Measures

Several portfolio mean dispersion approaches have been proposed in the last few decades. The most significant ones are discussed below, and we provide for each measure an example to illustrate the calculation.

Mean Standard Deviation   In the *mean standard deviation* (MV) approach the dispersion measure is the standard deviation of the portfolio return r_p:[5]

$$\sigma(r_p) = \sqrt{E(r_p - E(r_p))^2} \tag{12.1}$$

The standard deviation is a special case of the mean absolute moment discussed below. The sample version can be obtained from the general case by setting $p = 2$.

---

[5] See Markowitz (1959) and Tobin (1958).

Mean Absolute Deviation   In the *mean absolute deviation* (MAD) approach,[6] the dispersion measure is based on the absolution deviations from the mean rather than the squared deviations as in the case of the standard deviation.[7] The MAD is more robust with respect to outliers. The MAD for the portfolio return r_p is defined as

$$\text{MAD}(r_p) = E(|r_p - E(r_p)|) \tag{12.2}$$

Mean Absolute Moment   The *mean absolute moment* (MAM(q)) approach is the logical generalization of the MQ approach. Under this approach the dispersion measure is defined as

$$\text{MAM}(r_p, q) = (E(|r_p - E(r_p)|^q))^{1/q} \ , \quad q \geq 1 \tag{12.3}$$

Note that the mean absolute moment for $q = 2$ coincides with the standard deviation and for $q = 1$ the mean absolute moment reduces to the mean absolute deviation. One possible sample version of (12.3) is given by

$$\text{MAM}(r_p, q) \approx \sqrt[q]{\frac{1}{T} \sum_{k=1}^{T} \left| r_p^{(k)} - \bar{r}_p \right|^q}$$

where

$$\bar{r} = \frac{1}{T} \sum_{k=1}^{T} r_p^{(k)}$$

denotes the sample mean of the portfolio return.

Gini Index of Dissimilarity   The Index of Dissimilarity is based on the measure introduced by Gini (1912, 1921).[8] Gini objected to the use of the variance or the MAD because they measure deviations of individuals

---

[6] See Konno and Yamazaki (1991), Zenios and Kang (1993), Speranza (1993), and Ogryczak and Ruszczynski (2001).

[7] The *asymptotic mean dispersion* (MQ) approach is a special variant of the classical mean absolute deviation approach. It assumes that the returns are jointly α-stable sub-Gaussian distributed with α > 1. See Rachev and Mittnik (2000, 424–464), Rachev, Ortobelli, and Schwartz (2004), Ortobelli, Huber, and Schwartz (2002), and Ortobelli, Huber, Rachev, and Schwartz (2003).

[8] For a further discussion of this index, see Rachev (1991).

from the individual observations of the mean or location of a distribution. Consequently, these measures linked location with variability, two properties that Gini argued were distinct and do not depend on each other. He then proposed the pairwise deviations between all observations as a measure of dispersion, which is now referred to as the *Gini measure*.

While this measure has been used for the past 80 years as a measure of social and economic conditions, its interest as a measure of risk in the theory of portfolio selection is relatively recent. Interest in a Gini-type risk measure has been fostered by Rachev (1991) and Rachev and Gamrowski (1995). Mathematically, the Gini risk measure for the random portfolio return r_p is defined as

$$\text{GM}(r_p, r_b) = \text{Min}\{E|r_p - r_b|\} \tag{12.4}$$

where the minimum is taken over all joint distributions of (r_p, r_b) with fixed marginal distribution functions F and G:

$$F(x) = P(r_p \leq x) \text{ and } G(x) = P(r_b \leq x), \quad x \text{ real}$$

Here r_b is the benchmark return, say, the return of a market index, or just the risk-free rate (U.S. Treasury rate or LIBOR, for example). Expression (12.4) can be represented as the mean absolute deviation between the two distribution functions F and G:

$$\text{GM}(r_p, r_b) = \int_{-\infty}^{+\infty} |F(x) - G(x)| dx$$

Given a sample or a distributional assumption for the benchmark return r_b, the latter expression can be used for estimating the Gini index by calculating the area between the graphs of the empirical distribution function of r_p and the (empirical) distribution function of r_b.

Mean Entropy In the *mean entropy* (M-entropy) approach, the dispersion measure is the exponential entropy. Exponential entropy is a dispersion measure only for portfolios with continuous return distribution because the definition of entropy for discrete random variables is formally different and does not satisfy the properties of the dispersion measures (positive and positively homogeneous). The concept of entropy was introduced in the last century in the classical theory of thermodynamics. Roughly speaking, it represents the average uncertainty in a random variable.

Probably, its most important application in finance is to derive the probability density function of the asset underlying an option on the basis of the information that some option prices provide.[9] Entropy was used also in portfolio theory by Philippatos and Wilson (1972) and Philippatos and Gressis (1975) and is defined as

$$\text{Entropy} = -E(\log f(r_p))$$

where f is the density of the portfolio return. Thus, the exponential entropy is given by

$$EE(r_p) = e^{-E(\log f(r_p))} \tag{12.5}$$

The valuation of entropy can be done either by considering the empirical density of a portfolio or assuming that portfolio returns belong to a given family of continuous distributions and estimate their unknown parameters.

Mean Colog In the *mean colog* (M-colog) approach,[10] the dispersion measure is the covariance between the random variable and its logarithm. That is, the Colog of a portfolio return is defined as

$$\text{Colog}(1 + r_p) = E(r_p \log(1 + r_p)) - E(r_p)E(\log(1 + r_p)) \tag{12.6}$$

Colog can easily be estimated based on a sample of the portfolio return distribution by:

$$\text{Colog}(1 + r_p) \approx \frac{1}{T} \sum_{k=1}^{T} (r_p^{(k)} - \bar{r}_p) \cdot (\log(1 + r_p^{(k)}) - \overline{\log(1 + r_p)})$$

where

$$\overline{\log(1 + r_p)} = \frac{1}{T} \sum_{k=1}^{T} \log(1 + r_p^{(k)})$$

denotes the sample mean of the logarithm of one plus the portfolio return.

---

[9] See Buchen and Kelly (1996) and Avellaneda (1998).
[10] See Giacometti and Ortobelli (2001).

Safety-First Risk Measures

Many researchers have suggested the safety-first rules as a criterion for decision making under uncertainty.[11] In these models, a subsistence, a benchmark, or a disaster level of returns is identified. The objective is the maximization of the probability that the returns are above the benchmark. Thus, most of the safety-first risk measures proposed in the literature are linked to the benchmark-based approach.

Even if there are not apparent connections between the expected utility approach and a more appealing benchmark-based approach, Castagnoli and LiCalzi (1996) have proven that the expected utility can be reinterpreted in terms of the probability that the return is above a given benchmark. Hence, when it is assumed that investors maximize their expected utility, it is implicitly assumed that investors minimize the probability of the investment return falling below a specified risk benchmark.

Although, it is not always simple to identify the underlying benchmark, expected utility theory partially justifies the using of the benchmark-based approach. Moreover, it is possible to prove that the two approaches are in many cases equivalent even if the economic reasons and justifications are different.[12]

Some of the most well-known safety-first risk measures proposed in the literature are described in the next section.

Classical Safety First   In the classical *safety-first* (SF) portfolio choice problem,[13] the risk measure is the probability of loss or, more generally, the probability $P_\lambda = P(r_p \leq \lambda)$ of portfolio return less than λ. Generally, safety-first investors have to solve a complex, mixed integer linear programming problem to find the optimal portfolios. However, when short sales are allowed and return distributions are elliptical, depending on a dispersion matrix Q and a vector mean μ,[14] then there exists a closed-form solution to the investor's portfolio selection problem:

Minimize: $P(r_p \leq \lambda)$

Subject to: $\displaystyle\sum_{i=1}^{N} x_i = 1, x_i \geq 0$

---

[11] See, among others, Roy (1952), Tesler (1955/6), and Bawa (1976, 1978).
[12] See Castagnoli and LiCalzi (1996, 1999), Bordley and LiCalzi (2000), Ortobelli and Rachev (2001), Rachev and Mittnik (2000, 424–464), and Rachev, Ortobelli, and Schwartz (2004).
[13] See Roy (1952).
[14] The family of elliptical distributions is described in Chapter 5.

The interesting property of this optimization problem is that we are able to express the set of optimal portfolios explicitly as a function of the shortfall barrier λ, the mean vector μ, and the dispersion matrix Q.[15] The mean m and the dispersion σ^2 of these optimal portfolios can again be expressed as a function of the threshold λ, the mean vector μ, and the dispersion matrix Q.[16] In the case where the elliptical family has finite variance (as, for example, the normal distribution), then the dispersion σ^2 corresponds to the variance.

As the risk measure consists of the probability that the return falls below a given barrier λ, we can estimate the risk measure by the ratio between the number of observations being smaller than λ and the total number of observations in the sample.

Value-at-Risk   *Value-at-risk* ($VaR_{1-\alpha}$) is a closely related possible safety-first measure of risk defined by the following equality:

$$VaR_{1-\alpha}(r_p) = -\min\{z|(P(r_p \leq z) > \alpha)\} \qquad (12.7)$$

Here, $1 - \alpha$ is denoted as the confidence level and α usually takes values like 1% or 5%. Theoretically, the VaR figure defined by equation (12.7) can admit negative values. In reality, however, it is likely and often implicitly assumed that the VaR is positive, and it can be interpreted as the level at which the losses will not exceed with a probability of $1 - \alpha\%$. Sometimes VaR is, therefore, defined as the maximum of zero and the expression defined in equation (12.7) to guarantee a positive value for VaR.

As we will see in Chapter 13, Value-at-Risk can be used as a risk measure to determine reward-risk optimal portfolios. On the other hand, as explained in Chapter 14, this simple risk measure can also be used by financial institutions to evaluate the market risk exposure of their trading portfolios. The main characteristic of VaR is that of synthesizing in a single value the possible losses which could occur with a given probability in a given temporal horizon. This feature, together with the (very intuitive) concept of maximum probable loss, allows the nonexpert investor to figure out how risky his position is and the correcting strategies to adopt. Based on a sample of return observations,

---

[15] $x(\lambda) = \dfrac{\lambda Q^{-1} e - Q^{-1}\mu}{\lambda C - B}$ for $\lambda < \dfrac{B}{C}$, where $e' = [1,1,...,1]$ $B = e'Q^{-1}\mu$ and $C = e'Q^{-1}e$.

[16] $\sigma^2 = \dfrac{\lambda^2 C - 2\lambda B + A}{(\lambda C - B)^2}$ and $m = \dfrac{\lambda B - A}{\lambda C - B}$ where $A = \mu'Q^{-1}\mu$.

VaR estimates coincide with the empirical alphaquantile.[17] We will discuss VaR and different more sophisticated methodologies for estimating VaR in further detail in Chapter 14.

Conditional Value at Risk/Expected Tail Loss The *conditional Value-at-Risk* ($CVaR_{1-\alpha}$) or expected tail loss (ETL)[18] is defined as:

$$CVaR_{1-\alpha}(r_p) = E(\max(-r_p, 0) \mid -r_p \geq VaR_{1-\alpha}(r_p)) \qquad (12.8)$$

where $VaR_{1-\alpha}(X)$ is defined in equation (12.7). From this definition we observe that the CVaR can be seen as the expected shortfall assuming the $VaR_{1-\alpha}(X)$ as the benchmark. In the next chapter we present a comparison between the qualitative and quantitative properties of VaR and CVaR optimal portfolios for different distributional assumptions.

A sophisticated estimation of CVaR depends strongly on the estimation of VaR; therefore, we postpone discussion of calculating CVaR to Chapter 14. Based on a large sample of observations, a natural estimate for CVaR can be obtained by averaging all observations in the sample which are smaller than the corresponding VaR estimate.

MiniMax An alternative way to derive some safety-first optimal portfolios is minimizing the *MiniMax* (MM) risk measure.[19] The MiniMax of a portfolio return is given by:

$$MM(r_p) = -\sup\{c \mid P(r_p \leq c) = 0\} \qquad (12.9)$$

This risk measure can be seen as an extreme case of CVaR.

Lower Partial Moment A natural extension of semivariance is the lower *partial moment* risk measure (see Bawa (1976) and Fishburn (1977)) also called *downside risk* or *probability weighted function of deviations below a specified target return*. This risk measure depends on two parameters:

1. A *power index* that is a proxy for the investor's degree of risk aversion
2. The *target rate of return* that is the minimum return that must be earned to accomplish the goal of funding the plan within a cost constraint.

---

[17] See the example in Chapter 8.
[18] See Bawa (1978), Uryasev (2000), and Martin, Rachev, and Siboulet (2003).
[19] See Young (1998).

The lower partial moment of a portfolio r_p bounded from below is given by

$$\text{LPM}(r_p, q) = \sqrt[q]{E(\max(t - r_p, 0)^q)} \tag{12.10}$$

where q is the power index and t is the target rate of return.

Given a sample of return observations, we can approximate equation (12.10) as follows:

$$\text{LPM}(r_p, q) \approx \sqrt[q]{\frac{1}{T} \sum_{k=1}^{T} \max(r_p^{(k)} - \bar{r}_p, 0)^q}$$

where as before

$$\bar{r} = \frac{1}{T} \sum_{k=1}^{T} r_p^{(k)}$$

denotes the sample mean of the portfolio return.

Power Conditional Value at Risk The *power conditional Value-at-Risk* measure is the CVaR of the lower partial moment of the return.[20] It depends on a *power index* that varies with respect to an investor's degree of risk aversion. Power CVaR generalizes the concept of CVaR and is defined as

$$\text{CVaR}_{q, 1-\alpha}(r_p) = E(\max(-r_p, 0)^q \mid -r_p \geq \text{VaR}_{1-\alpha}(r_p)) \tag{12.11}$$

A sample version of power CVaR can be obtained in the same way as sample version for the regular CVaR, that is, one calculates the q-th sample moment of all observations in the sample which are smaller than the corresponding VaR estimate.

REFERENCES

Artzner, P., F. Delbaen, J-M. Eber, and D. Heath. 2000. "Coherent Measures of Risk." *Mathematical Finance* 9: 203–228.

Artzner, P., F. Delbaen, J-M. Eber, D. Heath, and H. Ku. 2003. "Coherent Multiperiod Measures of Risk." Unpublished paper.

---

[20] This risk measure is introduced in Rachev, Jasic, Biglova, and Fabozzi (2005).

Avellaneda, M. 1998. "Minimum Entropy Calibration of Asset Pricing Models." *International Journal of Theoretical and Applied Finance* 1: 447–472.

Balzer, L. A. 2001. "Investment Risk: A Unified Approach to Upside and Downside Returns." In *Managing Downside Risk in Financial Markets: Theory Practice and Implementation*, ed. F. A. Sortino and S. E. Satchell, 103–155. Oxford: Butterworth-Heinemann.

Bawa, V. S. 1976. "Admissible Portfolio for All Individuals," *Journal of Finance* 31: 1169–1183

Bawa, V. S. 1978. "Safety-First Stochastic Dominance and Optimal Portfolio Choice." *Journal of Financial and Quantitative Analysis* 13: 255–271.

Bordley, R. and M. LiCalzi. 2000. "Decision Analysis Using Targets Instead of Utility Functions." *Decision in Economics and Finance* 23: 53–74.

Buchen, P. W., and M. Kelly. 1996. "The Maximum Entropy Distribution of an Asset Inferred from Option Prices." *Journal of Financial and Quantitative Analysis* 31: 143–159.

Castagnoli, E., and M. LiCalzi. 1996. "Expected Utility Without Utility." *Theory and Decision* 41: 281–301

Castagnoli, E., and M. LiCalzi. 1999. "Non-Expected Utility Theories and Benchmarking under Risk." *SZIGMA* 29: 199–211.

Dowd, K. 2002. *Measuring Market Risk*. Chichester: John Wiley & Sons.

Engle, R. F. 1982. "Autoregressive Conditional Heteroskedasticity with Estimates of the Variance of U.K. Inflation." *Econometrica*, 50: 987–1008.

Engle, R. F., and C. W. J. Granger. 1987 "Cointegration and Error Correction: Represenatation, Estimation, and Testing." *Econometrica* 55: 251–276

Fishburn, P. C. 1977. "Mean-Risk Analysis with Risk Associated with Below-Target Returns." *American Economic Review* 67: 116–126.

Fritelli, M., and E. Rosazza Gianin. 2004. "Dynamic Convex Risk Measures." In *Risk Measures for the 21st Century*, ed. G. Szegö, 227–249. Chichester: John Wiley & Sons.

Giacometti, R., and S. Ortobelli . 2004. "Risk Measures for Asset Allocation Models." In *Risk Measures for the 21st Century*, ed. G. Szegö, 69–87. Chichester: John Wiley & Sons.

Gini, C. (1921). "Measurement of Inequality of Incomes." *The Economic Journal* 31: 124–126.

Gini, C. 1965. "La Dissomiglianza." *Metron* 24: 309–331.

Granger, C. W. J. 1981. "Some Properties of Time series and Their Use in Econometric Model Specification." *Journal of Econometrics* 16: 121–130.

Konno, H., and H. Yamazaki. 1991. "Mean-Absolute Deviation Portfolio Optimization Model and its Application to Tokyo Stock Market." *Management Science* 37: 519–531.

Markowitz, H. M. 1952. "Portfolio Selection." *Journal of Finance* 7: 77–91.

Markowitz, H. M. 1959. *Portfolio Selection: Efficient Diversification of Investment.* New York: John Wiley & Sons.

Martin, D., S.T. Rachev, and F. Siboulet. 2003. "Phi-Alpha Optimal Portfolios and Extreme Risk Management." *Willmot Magazine of Finance*, November: 70–83.

Ogryczak, W., and A. Ruszczynski. 2001. "On Consistency of Stochastic Dominance and Mean-Semideviation Models," *Mathematical Programming* 89: 217–232.

Olsen, R. A. 1997. "Investment Risk: The Experts' Perspective." *Financial Analysts Journal*, March/April: 62–66.

Ortobelli, S. 2001. "The Classification of Parametric Choices under Uncertainty: Analysis of the Portfolio Choice Problem." *Theory and Decision* 51: 297–327.

Ortobelli, S., and S. T. Rachev. 2001. "Safety First Analysis and Stable Paretian Approach." *Mathematical and Computer Modelling* 34: 1037–1072.

Ortobelli, S., I. Huber, and E. Schwartz. 2002. "Portfolio Selection with Stable Distributed Returns." *Mathematical Methods of Operations Research* 55: 265–300.

Ortobelli, S., I. Huber, S. T. Rachev, and E. Schwartz. 2003. "Portfolio Choice Theory with Non-gaussian Distributed Returns." In *Handbook of Heavy Tailed Distributions in Finance*, ed. S.T. Rachev, 547–594. Amsterdan: North Holland Handbooks of Finance.

Philippatos, G. C., and C. J. Wilson. 1972. "Entropy, Market Risk and the Selection of Efficient Portfolio." *Applied Economics* 4: 209–220.

Philippatos, G. C., and N. Gressis. 1975. "Conditions of Equivalence among E-V,SSD and E-H Portfolio Selection Criteria: the Case for Uniform, Normal and Lognormal Distributions." *Management Science* 21: 617–625.

Rachev, S. T. 1991. *Probability Metrics and the Stability of Stochastic Models.* New York: John Wiley & Sons.

Rachev, S. T., and A. Gamrowski. 1995. "Financial Models Using Stable Laws." in *Probability Theory and its Application in Applied and Industrial Mathematics, Vol. 2*, ed. Yu V. Prohorov, 556–604. New York: Springer Verlag.

Rachev, S. T., T. Jasic, A. Biglova, and F. J. Fabozzi. 2005. "Risk and Return in Momentum Strategies: Profitability from Portfolios Based on Risk-Adjusted Stock Ranking Criteria." Technical report, Chair of Econometrics, Statistics and Mathematical Finance, School of Economics, University of Karlsruhe, Postfach 6980, D-76128, Karlsruhe, Germany and Technical Report, Department of Statistics and Applied Probability, UCSB, CA 93106, USA.

Rachev, S. T., and S. Mittnik. 2000. *Stable Paretian Model in Finance*. Chichester: John Wiley & Sons.

Rachev, S., S. Ortobelli, and E.Schwartz. 2004. "The Problem of Optimal Asset Allocation with Stable Distributed Returns." In *Stochastic Processes and Functional Analysis: A Dekker Series of Lecture Notes in Pure and Applied Mathematics*, eds. A. Krinik and R. J. Swift, 295–361. New York: Dekker.

Roy, A. D. 1952. "Safety-First and the Holding of Assets." *Econometrica* 20: 431–449.

Ryan, R., and F. J. Fabozzi. 2002. "Rethinking Pension Liabilities and Asset Allocation." *Journal of Portfolio Management*: 7–15.

Shalit, H., and S. Yitzhaki. 1984. "Mean-Gini, Portfolio Theory, and the Pricing of Risky Assets." *Journal of Finance* 39: 1449–1468.

Sortino, F. A., and S. E. Satchell. 2001. *Managing Downside Risk in Financial Markets: Theory Practice and Implementation*. Oxford: Butterworth-Heinemann.

Speranza, M. G. 1993. "Linear Programming Models for Portfolio Optimization." *Finance* 14: 107–123.

Stefani, S., and G. Szegö. 1976. "Formulazione Analitica Della Funzione Utilità Dipendente da Media e Semivarianza Mediante Il Principio Dell'utilità Attesa." *Bollettino UMI 13A*: 157–162.

Szegö, G. 2004. "On the (Non)Acceptance of Innovations." In *Risk Measures for the 21st Century*, G. Szegö (ed.), 1–10. Chichester: John Wiley & Sons.

Tesler, L. G. 1955/6. "Safety First and Hedging." *Review of Economic Studies* 23: 1–16.

Tobin, J. 1958. "Liquidity Preference as Behavior Toward Risk." *Review of Economic Studies* 25: 65–86.

Uryasev, S. P. 2000. *Probabilistic Constrained Optimization Methodology and Applications.* Dordrecht: Kluwer Academic Publishers.

Von Neumann, J. and O. Morgenstern. 1953. *Theory of Games and Economic Behavior.* Princeton, NJ: Princeton University Press.

Young, M. R. 1998. "A MiniMax Portfolio Selection Rule with Linear Programming Solution." *Management Science* 44: 673–683.

Zenios, S. A., and P. Kang. 1993. "Mean Absolute Deviation Portfolio Optimization for Mortgage-backed Securities," *Annals of Operations Research* 45: 433–450.

CHAPTER 13

Risk Measures in Portfolio Optimization and Performance Measures

There are two basic approaches to the problem of portfolio selection under uncertainty. One approach is based on the concept of *utility theory*. This approach offers a mathematically rigorous treatment of the portfolio selection problem, but appears sometimes detached from the world. It is not popular among asset managers to specify first their utility function and choose a distributional assumption for the returns—both needed for the utility maximization approach—before deciding on their investment strategy. The other is the reward-risk analysis. According to it, the portfolio choice is made with respect to two criteria: the expected portfolio return and portfolio risk. A portfolio is preferred to another one if it has higher expected return and lower risk. There are convenient computational recipes and geometric interpretations of the trade-off between the two criteria. A disadvantage of the latter approach is that it cannot capture the richness of the former.[1]

Related to the reward-risk analysis is the reward-risk ratio optimization. Since the publication of the Sharpe ratio (see Sharpe 1966), which is based on the mean-variance analysis, some new performance measures such as the STARR ratio, the MiniMax measure, Sortino-Satchell ratio, Farinelli-Tibiletti ratio, the Rachev ratio, and the Rachev Generalized ratio have been proposed. The new ratios take into account empirically

---

[1] As a matter of fact, the relationship between the two approaches is still a research topic. (See Ogryczak and Ruszczynski (2001) and the references therein.)

observed phenomena, that assets returns distributions are fat tailed and skewed, by incorporating proper reward and risk measures.

In this chapter, we explain how to determine the optimal portfolio choice for an investor under very weak distributional assumptions. We then provide a portfolio optimization using as the risk measure conditional Value-at-Risk. In the final section of this chapter, we describe the performance measures for portfolio selection mentioned previously.[2]

EFFICIENT FRONTIERS AND RETURN DISTRIBUTION ASSUMPTION

From the analysis of risk measure properties discussed in the previous chapter, we cannot deduce if there exists "the best" risk measure. The most widely used risk measure in portfolio optimization, the variance, is in reality a measure of uncertainty. A comparison among several allocation problems that assumes various risk measures has shown that there exist significant differences in the portfolio choices.[3] This means that, from a practical perspective, if portfolio return distributions depend on more than two parameters, as suggested by the empirical evidence (heavy tails and asymmetry), optimal choices cannot be determined only by the mean and a risk measure.

To take into account the distributional anomalies of asset returns, we need to measure the skewness and kurtosis of portfolio returns. In order to do this, statisticians typically use the so-called Pearson-Fisher skewness and kurtosis indexes, which provide a measure of the departure of the empirical series from the normal distribution. A positive (negative) index of asymmetry denotes that the right (left) tail of the distribution is more elongated than that implied by the normal distribution.

The Pearson-Fisher coefficient of skewness[4] is given by

$$\gamma_1(r_p) = \frac{E((r_p - E(r_p))^3)}{(E((r_p - E(r_p))^2))^{3/2}}$$

[2] Stoyanov, Rachev, and Fabozzi (2005) show how some performance ratio optimization problems reduce to more simple ones.
[3] See Rachev and Mittnik (2000, 424–464), Rachev, Ortobelli, and Schwartz (2004), and Giacometti and Ortobelli (2004).
[4] In Chapter 4, the general formula for skewness and kurtosis was presented in Exhibit 4.2. Panel b of Exhibit 4.3 provides formulas for the skewness of some popular distribution families.

The Pearson-Fisher kurtosis coefficient for a normal distribution is equal to 3. As explained in Chapter 4, distributions whose kurtosis is greater (smaller) than 3 are defined as leptokurtic (platykurtic) and are characterized by fat tails (thin tails). The Pearson-Fisher kurtosis coefficient is given by

$$\gamma_2(r_p) = \frac{E((r_p - E(r_p))^4)}{(E((r_p - E(r_p))^2))^2}$$

Let us assume that the distribution of the gross return of all admissible portfolios is uniquely determined from the first k moments. If we assume that institutional constraints imply the usual assumption about limited short selling, then we can define the following optimization problem to determine optimal portfolios for risk-averse investors with a certain risk profile:

Minimize: $\sigma(r_p)$

Subject to: $\displaystyle\sum_{i=1}^{N} x_i E(r_i) = m$ $\qquad\qquad$ (13.1)

$$\frac{E((r_p - E(r_p))^j)}{\sigma(r_p)^{j/2}} = q_j; \quad j = 3, ..., k$$

$$\sum_{i=1}^{N} x_i = 1; \ l_i \le x_i \le u_i \quad i = 1, ..., N$$

Here $\sigma(r_p)$ denotes the standard deviation of the portfolio return, m the target mean return, and q_j the target values for the higher moment for $j = 3, ..., k$. The values l_i and $u_i,\ i = 1, ..., N$ denote the lower and upper constraints for the portfolio weights x_i. If we choose $l_i = 0,\ i = 1, ..., N$, then we have the situation where no short selling is allowed.

If we assume the variance as the risk measure, we find that the Markowitz mean-variance frontier is contained in the set of the solutions to problem (13.1) obtained by varying the parameters m and q_j. Thus, this analysis is substantially a generalization of the Markowitz analysis that permits one to determine the asymmetric aspect of the risk. For this reason, we continue to call the *efficient frontier* (for a given category of investors) the whole set of optimal choices (of that category of investors). Once we have determined the class of the optimal choices, any portfolio manager could try to understand the risk attitude of his clients (with some opportune questionnaire) in order to determine the investor-specific portfolio among the optimal ones. The main difficulties of applying the above multiparameter analysis are:

1. We do not know how many parameters are necessary to identify the multiparameter efficient frontier. However, this is a common problem for every multiparameter analysis proposed in the literature.

2. Estimates of higher moments tend to be quite unstable, thus rather large samples are needed in order to estimate higher moments with reasonable accuracy.

3. Even if the above optimization problems determine the whole class of the investor's optimal choices, those problems are computationally too complex to solve for large portfolios. Thus, we need to simplify the portfolio problem by reducing the number of parameter dependence. When we simplify the optimization problem, for every risk measure we find only some among all optimal portfolios. Hence, we need to determine the risk measure that better characterizes and captures the investor's attitude.

For these reasons, it is common practice to adapt optimization problem (13.1) such that the computations remain manageable. The idea is to remove the restrictions in problem (13.1) and to capture investor preferences by an appropriately chosen risk measure ρ. The adapted optimization problem (13.1) has the form:

$$\textit{Minimize:} \quad \rho(r_p)$$

$$\textit{Subject to:} \quad E(r_p) = m \tag{13.2}$$

$$\sum_{i=1}^{N} x_i = 1; \, l_i \leq x_i \leq u_i \quad i = 1, ..., N$$

where ρ is the risk measure reflecting investors' preferences and m the target return. An alternative but equivalent formulation of equation (13.2) is the following:

Maximize: $E(r_p) - \lambda\rho(r_p)$

$$(13.3)$$

Subject to: $\sum_{i=1}^{N} x_i = 1; \ l_i \le x_i \le u_i \quad i = 1, ..., N$

where λ denotes an investor-specific parameter which can be interpreted as a risk-aversion coefficient. The most prominent choice for ρ—also suggested by regulators—is Value-at-Risk (VaR). For computational as well as theoretical reasons, it seems at least equally sensible to replace the VaR by the CVaR. The latter measure does not only tell us what happens if things do well, but also what we have to expect if things go bad. The following section compares these two measures.

PORTFOLIO OPTIMIZATION AND CONDITIONAL VALUE-AT-RISK VERSUS VALUE-AT-RISK

Let us take a look at portfolio optimization with two different risk measures: Value-at-Risk (VaR) and conditional Value-at-Risk (CVaR). Both measures were described in the Chapter 12. In Chapter 14, we discuss the limitations of VaR, a measured endorsed by regulators of financial institutions. From a portfolio optimization perspective, an intrinsic limitation of VaR is that VaR portfolio optimization is a nonconvex, nonsmooth problem with multiple local minima that can result in portfolio composition discontinuities. Furthermore, it requires complex calculation techniques such as integer programming. In contrast, portfolio optimization with CVaR turns out to be a smooth, convex problem with a unique solution.

Conditional VaR optimal portfolio (CVaROP) techniques,[5] combined with multivariate stable distribution modeling, can lead to significant improvements in risk-adjusted return as compared to optimal risk adjusted-return portfolios, which are based on the normal distribution assumption or on alternative risk measures such as standard deviation or VaR. Especially, the VaR optimal portfolio (VaROP) is difficult to compute accurately with more than two or three assets.

---

[5] The problem of finding a CVaROP can be expressed in the form of some optimization problem which has very appealing properties. For an explanation of the problem, see Rockafellar and Uryasev (2000, 2001). They show that the CVaROP weight vector can be obtained based on historical (or scenario) returns data by minimizing a relatively simple convex function. The authors further show that this optimization problem can be cast as a linear programming problem, solvable using any high-quality software.

The following illustration supports the claim that stable CVaROP produces consistently better risk-adjusted returns. Exhibits 13.1 and 13.2 report the risk-adjusted return μ/VaR (mean return divided by VaR) and μ/CVaR (mean return divided by CVaR) for 1% VaROP and CVaROP, respectively, and using a multiperiod, fixed-mix optimization in all cases.

In this simple example, the portfolio to be optimized consists of two assets, cash and the S&P 500. The example is based on monthly data from February 1965 to December 1999.[6] In this example the optimizer is maximizing $\mu - c \cdot \rho$, where c is the risk aversion (parameter), and with ρ = VaR or ρ = CVaR as the penalty function.

EXHIBIT 13.1   Stable versus Normal CVaR Optimal Portfolios

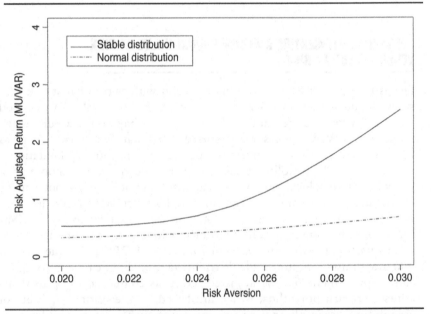

Note: The optimal portfolios were derived using the Cognity system of FinAnalytica Inc. [Cognity Integrated Risk Management System is a commercial software for financial risk analysis and portfolio optimization with stable distributed returns and CVaR and VaR as risk measures and is distributed by FinAnalytica Inc. (www.finanalytica.com)]
Source: Martin, Rachev, and Siboulet (2003).

---

[6] Since we assume full investment, the VaROP depends only on a single portfolio weight and the optimal weight(s) is found by a simple grid search on the interval 0 to 1. The use of a grid search technique overcomes the problems with nonconvex and nonsmooth VaR optimization.

EXHIBIT 13.2   Stable versus Normal CVaR Optimal Portfolios

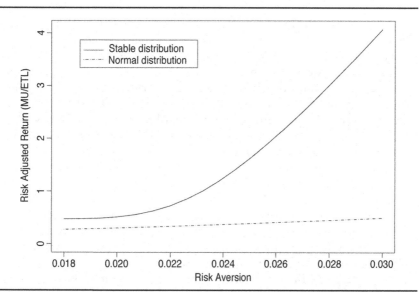

Note: The optimal portfolios were derived using the Cognity system of FinAnalytica Inc. Cognity Integrated Risk Management System is a commercial software for financial risk analysis and portfolio optimization with stable distributed returns and CVaR and VaR as risk measures and is distributed by FinAnalytica Inc. (www.finanalytica.com).
Source: Martin, Rachev, and Siboulet (2003).

Exhibit 13.1 shows that even using VaROP, one gets a significant relative gain in risk-adjusted return using stable scenarios when compared to normal scenarios, and with the relative gain increasing with increasing risk aversion. The reason for the latter behavior is that with stable distributions, the optimization pays more attention to the tails of the S&P 500 return's distribution, and allocates less investment to the S&P under stable distributions than under normal distribution assumption as risk aversion increases.

Exhibit 13.2 shows that the risk-adjusted return for the CVaROP has the same vertical axis range as the plot for VaROP in Exhibit 13.1. Exhibit 13.2 shows that the use of CVaR results in a much greater gain under the stable distribution relative to the normal distribution than in the case of VaROP.

At every level of risk aversion, the investment in the S&P 500 is even less in CVaROP than in the case of the VaROP. This behavior is to be expected because the CVaR approach pays attention to the losses beyond VaR (the expected value of the extreme loss), and which in the stable distribution case are much greater than in the normal distribution case.

PERFORMANCE MEASURES

In a mean-risk world, we can describe the uncertainty of future wealth with two summary statistics: a risk measure and the mean representing reward. Sharpe (1966) developed a measure, originally termed *reward-to-variability*, for evaluating the performance of mutual fund managers. Subsequently, under the name of the *Sharpe ratio*, it has become one of the most popular performance measures used in practical applications. Although the Sharpe ratio is fully compatible with normally distributed returns (or, in general, with elliptical returns), it will lead to incorrect investment decisions when returns present kurtosis and/or skewness.[7]

Several alternatives to the Sharpe ratio for optimal portfolio selection have been proposed. In this section, we will describe these performance measures. They differ in the risk measure used. As explained in the previous chapter, we can distinguish between two disjoint categories of risk measures used in portfolio theory: dispersion measures and safety-first risk measures. For each risk measure, there exists a performance measure to identify superior, ordinary, and inferior performance.

In particular, the ratio between the "expected excess return" and the relative risk measure is a performance measure $\rho(\cdot)$ that investors wish to maximize. The maximization of the performance measure $\rho(\cdot)$ determines the so called "market portfolio" because it represents the benchmark for the market. Therefore, the market portfolio found for each performance measure $\rho(\cdot)$ is based on a diverse risk perception and sometimes on a different reward perception.

Even if most of the attention of researchers has been devoted to finding the "right risk measure," the "right reward" perception is also crucial to determine a desirable risky investment strategy. In order to avoid ambiguities, we do not believe that there exists the "perfect performance measure," because a performance measure depends only on two parameters which summarize the complexity of all admissible choices. However, we believe that some performance measures take into account commonly held investors' opinions better than others. As a matter of fact, most decision makers have some common beliefs. For example, they prefer more than less and are generally risk averse. Thus, by minimizing a given risk measure for a fixed expected return level, we would find a portfolio that is optimal for some investors. This does not mean that this portfolio is the best choice for all decision makers that want a return with the same mean. Similarly, when we maximize a performance measure, we

---

[7] See, among others, Leland (1999), Bernardo and Ledoit (2000), Rachev and Mittnik (2000, pp. 424–464), Rachev, Ortobelli, and Schwartz (2004), and Ortobelli et al. (2003).

determine the market portfolio, which better represents a predisposition to risk and to invest for a given category of investors. These investors do not necessarily represent all the agents in the market.

Exhibit 13.3 lists performance measures proposed in the literature where the numerator for the ratio (i.e., the reward) is measured as the expected portfolio return less the risk-free rate and the risk measure is described in the previous chapter. In addition to the performance measures shown in Exhibit 13.3, we describe the following ratios below: the stable ratio, Farinelli-Tibiletti ratio, Sortino-Satchell ratio, Rachev ratio, and Rachev Generalized ratio. In the remainder of this chapter, we use the following notation: We consider a portfolio of N assets whose individual returns are given by r_1, ..., r_N. The relative weights of the portfolio are denoted as x_1, ... x_n and hence the portfolio return r_p can be expressed as

$$r_p = x_1 \cdot r_1 + \ldots + x_N \cdot r_N = \sum_{i=1}^{N} x_i \cdot r_i$$

The risk-free interest rate is denoted as r_f and the symbols t, t_1 and t_2 are used for investor specific thresholds reflecting investors' preferences. By $r_p^{(k)}$, $k = 1, \ldots T$ we denote a sample of size T of portfolio return observations which are assumed to be independent and identically distributed. The observations of the portfolio return can be gained from a sample of the underlying individual assets which the portfolio consists of.

EXHIBIT 13.3 Alternative Risk Measures where Reward is the Difference Between the Expected Portfolio Return and Risk-Free

Performance Measure	Risk Measure	Citation
Sharpe ratio	Variance (standard deviation)	Sharpe (1966, 1994)
MiniMax ratio	MiniMax	Young (1998)
MAD ratio	Mean absolute deviation	Konno and Yamazaki (1991)
$\text{VaR}_{1-\alpha}$ ratio	Value at risk	Favre and Galeano (2002); Rachev, Martin, and Siboulet (2003)
$\text{CVaR}_{1-\alpha}$ ratio[a]	Conditional value at risk[b]	Rachev, Martin, and Siboulet 2003)

[a] Also called the *STARR ratio*.
[b] Also called the *Expected Tail Loss*.
Source: Martin, Rachev, and Siboulet (2003).

Stable Ratio

The stable ratio (see Rachev and Mittnik 2000) is

$$\rho(r_p) = \frac{E(r_p - r_f)}{\sigma_{r_p}}$$

where σ_{r_p} is the dispersion parameter of the portfolio return. In this approach, it is implicitly assumed, that the vector of returns follows a multivariate sub-Gaussian stable distribution. The latter means that the return vector r can be represented as a product of two independent random variables where the first is the square root of a totally right skewed $\alpha/2$-stable random variable and the second is a zero mean multivariate normal random vector with variance-covariance matrix Q. The dispersion parameter of the portfolio return can in this case be obtained by the following formula:

$$\sigma_{r_p} = \sqrt{x'Qx}$$

Farinelli-Tibiletti Ratio

The Farinelli-Tibiletti Ratio (see Farinelli and Tibiletti 2003a, 2003b) is

$$\rho(r_p) = \frac{\sqrt[\gamma]{E(\max(r_p - t_1, 0)^{\gamma})}}{\sqrt[\delta]{E(\max(t_2 - r_p, 0)^{\delta})}} \tag{13.4}$$

A possible sample version of (13.4) can be expressed as

$$\sqrt[\gamma]{E(\max(r_p - t_1, 0)^{\gamma})} \approx \left(\frac{1}{T}\sum_{k=1}^{T} (r_p^{(k)} - t_1)_+^{\gamma}\right)^{1/\gamma}$$

where we have used the notation

$$(r_p^{(k)} - t_1)_+ = (\max(r_p^{(k)} - t_1, 0))$$

and

$$\sqrt[\delta]{E(\max(t_2 - r_p, 0)^{\delta})} \approx \left(\frac{1}{T}\sum_{k=1}^{T} (r_p^{(k)} - t_2)_-^{1/\delta}\right)$$

where similarly we have used the notation

$$(r_p^{(k)} - t_2)_- = (\max(t_2 - r_p^{(k)}, 0))$$

Sortino-Satchell Ratio

The Sortino-Satchell ratio (see Sortino 2000; and Pedersen and Satchell 2002) is

$$\rho(r_p) = \frac{E(r_p - r_f)}{\sigma_{r_p}(t)} \tag{13.5}$$

where

$$\sigma_{r_p}(t) = \sqrt[\gamma]{E(\max(t - r_p, 0)^\gamma)}$$

A possible sample version of (13.5) can be obtained from the sample version of (13.4). Note that the denominator of the Farinelli-Tibiletti ratio equals the one of the Sortino-Satchel ratio.

Rachev Ratio

The Rachev ratio is the ratio between the CVaR of the opposite of the excess return at a given confidence level and the CVaR of the excess return at another confidence level. That is,

$$\rho(r_p) = \frac{\text{CVaR}_{1-\alpha}(r_f - r_p)}{\text{CVaR}_{1-\beta}(r_p - r_f)} \tag{13.6}$$

where α and β are in $(0,1)$.

The Rachev ratio is a very flexible performance measure that generalizes the STARR ratio. In particular, we could observe that in many cases the versatile valuation of reward permits the correct assessment of the investor's performance. These characteristics represent the principal theoretical advantages of the Rachev ratio relative to the other performance measures proposed in the literature. There exists a lot of theory as to how to obtain estimates CVaR and therefore how to obtain sample version of the Rachev ratio (13.6). It turns out that the main task in determining CVaR is the estimation of the corresponding VaR figure. (See Chapter 14 where several possibilities to measure VaR are discussed.)

Rachev Generalized Ratio

The Rachev Generalized ratio is the ratio between the power CVaR of the opposite of the excess return at a given confidence level and the power CVaR of the excess return at another confidence level. That is,

$$\rho(r_p) = \frac{\text{CVaR}_{\gamma, 1-\alpha}(r_f - r_p)}{\text{CVaR}_{\delta, 1-\beta}(r_p - r_f)} \tag{13.7}$$

where

$$\text{CVaR}_{q, 1-\alpha}(X) = E(\max(-X, 0)^q \mid -X \geq \text{VaR}_{1-\alpha}(X))$$

is the Power CVaR as introduced in equation (12.11) in Chapter 12 and q is a positive constant.

The main advantage of Rachev Generalized ratio relative to the Rachev ratio is given by the power indexes γ and δ that characterize the investors' aversion to risk. Again, for the estimation of Power CVaR mainly reduces to an appropriate estimation of VaR. Several methodologies for the latter task will be discussed in Chapter 14.

REFERENCES

Bernardo, A., and O. Ledoit. 2000. "Gain, Loss and Asset Pricing," *Journal of Political Economy* 108: 144–172.

Bookstaber, R., and R. Clarke. 1985. "Problems in Evaluating the Performance of Portfolios with Options." *Financial Analysts Journal*, January–February: 70–80.

Farinelli, S., and L. Tibiletti. 2003a. "Sharpe Thinking with Asymmetrical Preferences." Technical report, University of Torino, presented at European Bond Commission, Winter Meeting, Borse Frankfurt.

Farinelli, S., and L. Tibiletti. 2003b. "Upside and Downside Risk with a Benchmark." *Atlantic Economic Journal* 31 (4): 387.

Favre, L., and J. A. Galeano. 2002. "Mean-Modified Value at Risk Optimization with Hedge Funds." *Journal of Alternative Investments* 5: 21–25.

Giacometti, R., and S. Ortobelli. 2004. "Risk Measures for Asset Allocation Models." In *Risk Measures for the 21st Century*, ed. G. Szegö, 69–86. Chichester: John Wiley & Sons.

Konno, H., and H. Yamazaki. 1991. "Mean-Absolute Deviation Portfolio Optimization Model and its Application to Tokyo Stock Market." *Management Science* 37: 519–531.

Leland, H. E. 1999. "Beyond Mean-Variance: Performance Measurement in a Nonsymmetrical World." *Financial Analyst Journal* 55: 27–35.

Martin, D., S. T. Rachev, and F. Siboulet. 2003. "Phi-Alpha Optimal Portfolios and Extreme Risk Management." *Wilmott Magazine of Finance*, November: 70–83.

Ogryczak, W., and A. Ruszczynski. 2001. "On Consistency of Stochastic Dominance and Mean-Semideviation Models." *Mathematical Programming* 89: 217–232.

Ortobelli, S., I. Huber, S. T. Rachev, and E. Schwartz. 2003. "Portfolio Choice Theory with Non-Gaussian Distributed Returns." In *Handbook of Heavy Tailed Distributions in Finance*, ed. S. T. Rachev, 547–594. Amsterdam: North Holland Handbooks.

Pedersen, C., and S. E. Satchell. 2002. "On the Foundation of Performance Measures under Asymmetric Returns." Technical report, Cambridge University.

Rachev, S. T., and S. Mittnik. 2000. *Stable Paretian Models in Finance*. Chichester: John Wiley & Sons.

Rachev, S. T., S. Ortobelli, and E. Schwartz. 2004. "The Problem of Optimal Asset Allocation with Stable Distributed Returns." In *Stochastic Processes and Functional Analysis: Dekker Series of Lecture Notes in Pure and Applied Mathematics*, ed. A. Krinik and R. J. Swift, 295–361. New York: Dekker.

Rockafellar, R. T., and S. Uryasev. 2000. "Optimization of Conditional Value-at-Risk." *Journal of Risk* 2: 21–41.

Rockafellar, R. T., and S. Uryasev. 2001. "Conditional Value-at-Risk for General Loss Distributions." Research Report 2001-5. ISE Dept., University of Florida, April.

Rockafellar, R. T., S. Uryasev, and M. Zabarankin. 2002. "Deviation Measures in Risk Analysis and Optimization." Research Report, 2002-7, University of Florida.

Rockafellar, R. T., S. Uryasev, and M. Zabarankin, 2003. "Portfolio Analysis with General Deviation Measures." Research Report, 2003-8, University of Florida.

Shalit, H., and S. Yitzhaki. 1984. "Mean-Gini, Portfolio Theory, and the Pricing of Risky Assets." *Journal of Finance* 39: 1449–1468

Sharpe, W. F. 1966. "Mutual Funds Performance." *Journal of Business*, January: 119–138.

Sharpe, W. F. 1994. "The Sharpe Ratio." *Journal of Portfolio Management*, Fall: 45–58.

Sortino, F. A. 2000. "Upside-Potential Ratios Vary by Investment Style." *Pensions and Investments* 28: 30–35.

Yitzhaki, S. 1982. "Stochastic Dominance, Mean Variance and Gini's Mean Difference." *American Economic Review* 72: 178–185.

Young, M. R. 1998. "A MiniMax Portfolio Selection Rule with Linear Programming Solution." *Management Science* 44: 673–683.

PART Four

Risk Management

CHAPTER 14

Market Risk

One of the most important tasks of financial institutions is evaluating and controlling exposure to risk. This task is called *risk management*. Risk is categorized as market risk, credit risk, and operational risk. Market risk arises from variations in equity prices, interest rates, exchange rates, and commodity prices. The exposure to market risk can be measured by changes in the portfolio value, or by profits and losses.

A commonly used methodology for estimation of market risk is *Value-at-Risk* (VaR), a measure we discussed already in earlier chapters. Regulators and the financial industry advisory committees recommend VaR as a way of measuring risk. Our focus in this chapter is on this measure of market risk.[1] In the next two chapters, we look at credit risk and operational risk. In addition, we discuss integrated risk management.

The chapter is organized as follows. After reviewing the adoptions of VaR for measuring market risk, we explain the employment of VaR for measuring market risk-based capital requirements. In this discussion, we provide the definition of VaR and the various methodologies for measuring it. We then discuss the stable VaR approach (i.e., VaR based on the stable distribution) and present empirical evidence comparing VaR modeling based on the normal distribution ("normal model") with that of the stable distribution ("stable model"). In the last section, we explain an alternative market risk measure to VaR, Expected Tail Loss, that we already described in earlier chapters.

---

[1] A more technical discussion of market risk can be found in Khindanova and Rachev (2000), Khindanova, Rachev, and Schwartz (2001), and Gamrowski and Rachev (1996).

ADOPTION OF VaR FOR MEASURING MARKET RISK

The capital structure of banks, like that of all corporations, consists of equity and debt (i.e., borrowed funds). Banks are highly leveraged institutions. That is, the ratio of equity capital to total assets is low, typically less than 8% in the case of banks. This level gives rise to regulatory concern about potential insolvency resulting from the low level of capital provided by the owners. An additional concern is that the amount of equity capital is even less adequate because of potential liabilities that do not appear on the bank's balance sheet. These so-called "off-balance sheet" obligations include commitments such as letters of credit and obligations on customized interest rate agreements (e.g., swaps, caps, and floors).

In the United States, for example, prior to 1989, capital requirements for banks were based solely on its total assets. No consideration was given to the types of assets. In January 1989, the Federal Reserve adopted guidelines for capital adequacy based on the credit risk of assets held by the bank. These guidelines are referred to as *risk-based capital requirements*. The guidelines are based on a framework adopted in July 1988 by the Basel Committee on Banking Supervision, which consists of the central banks and senior supervisory authorities of major industrialized countries.[2] The framework issued is known as the *1988 Basel Capital Accord*. The two principal objectives of the guidelines are as follows. First, regulators throughout the world sought greater consistency in the evaluation of the capital adequacy of banks. Second, regulators tried to establish capital adequacy standards that take into consideration the risk profile of the bank.

The capital adequacy standards initially implemented by regulators focused on credit risk. The standards did not take into account a bank's market risk. In July 1993, the Group of Thirty[3] first advocated the VaR approach in its study, "Derivatives: Practices and Principles." In 1993, the European Union mandated setting capital reserves to balance market risks in the Capital Adequacy Directive "EEC 6-93," which became effective January 1996.

In 1994, the Eurocurrency Standing Committee of the Bank of International Settlements published a discussion paper on public disclosure of market and credit risks by financial intermediaries. The paper

---

[2] The committee meets quarterly at the Bank for International Settlement in Basel.

[3] The Group of Thirty is a private, nonprofit, international organization composed of senior representatives of the private and public sectors. The aim of the organization is to "deepen understanding of international economic and financial issues, to explore the international repercussions of decisions taken in the public and private sectors, and to examine the choices available to market practitioners and policymakers."

(popularly known as the "Fisher Report") recommended disclosure of VaR values.

In April 1995, the Basel Committee on Banking Supervision proposed that in measuring market risk banks be allowed to use proprietary in-house models as an alternative to a standardized measurement framework that had previously been required. In the Amendment to the Basel Capital Accord released in January 1996, two approaches to calculate capital reserves for market risks were proposed: "standardized" and "internal models." A number of quantitative and qualitative criteria for those banks which wish to use proprietary models were provided. The amendment also specified the use of VaR for measuring market risk. Thus, banks could use their internal models of VaR estimations as the basis for calculation of capital requirements.

According to the internal or in-house models approach, capital requirements are computed by multiplying a bank's VaR values by a factor between 3 and 4. In August 1996, U.S. bank regulators endorsed the Basel Committee amendment and it became effective January 1998. The U.S. Securities and Exchange suggested that VaR be applied to enhance transparency in derivatives activity. The Derivatives Policy Group also recommended VaR techniques for quantifying market risks.[4]

In mid 2004, the Basel Committee released *The New Basel Accord*, popularly referred to as *Basel II*. The rationale for Basel II was that it provided for more flexibility and risk sensitivity measures. Prior to Basel II, the focus was on a single risk measure. Under Basel II, there is more emphasis on internal models of banks. Rather than one approach to fit all banks, there was flexibility, a menu of approaches, and incentives for better risk management.

The use of VaR models has rapidly expanded. Financial institutions with significant trading and investment volumes employ the VaR methodology in their risk management operations.[5] Corporations use VaR numbers for risk reporting to management, shareholders, and investors because VaR measures seem to allow one to aggregate exposures to market risks into one number in money terms. It is possible to calculate VaR for different market segments and to identify the most risky positions. The VaR estimations can complement allocation of capital resources, setting position limits, and performance evaluation.[6]

In many banks, the evaluation and compensation of traders is derived from returns per unit VaR. Institutional investors, for instance, pension funds, use VaR for quantifying market risks.

---

[4] See Kupiec (1995).
[5] See Heron and Irving (1997).
[6] See Liu (1996) and Jorion (1996a, b).

VaR AND BANK CAPITAL REQUIREMENTS

The principal application of VaR today has been the mandated use for a determining market risk-based capital requirements for banks. Consequently, we discuss this application in this section.

Standardized Method versus Internal Model Method

Bank regulators permit the calculation of capital reserves due to market risk exposure to be based on either a standardized method or an internal model method. The *standardized method* computes capital charges separately for each market (country), assigning percentage provisions for different exposures to equity, interest rate, and currency risks. The total capital charge equals the sum of the market capital requirements. The main drawback of the standardized method is that it does not take into consideration global diversification effects. That is, it ignores correlations across markets in different countries.[7]

The internal model method determines capital reserves based on in-house VaR models. The VaR values should be computed with a 10-day time horizon at a 99% confidence level using at least one year of data. The exact definition of VaR is provided later in this chapter.

Capital Requirements for General and Specific Market Risks

The market-risk based capital requirements classify market risk as general market risk and specific risk. *General market risk* is the risk attributable to changes in the overall level of interest rates, equity and commodity prices, and exchange rates. *Specific market risk* is the risk attributable to changes in prices of a financial instrument because of reasons associated with the issuer of the financial instrument.

The capital requirement for general market risk is equal to the maximum of:

1. The *current VaR* (VaR_t) number
2. The *average VaR* over the previous 60 days (denoted by AVaR_{60})

multiplied by a factor between 3 and 4.

The capital charges for specific market risk cover debt and equity positions. The specific market risk estimates obtained from the VaR models should be multiplied by a factor of 4. Thus, a market risk capital requirement at time t, C_t, is

$$C_t = A_t \cdot \max(\text{VaR}_t, \text{AVaR}_{60}) + s_t \tag{14.1}$$

---

[7] See Jackson, Maude, and Perraudin (1997) and Liu (1996).

where A_t is a multiplication factor between 3 and 4 and s_t is the capital charge for specific risk.

In equation (14.1), we have implicitly assumed that the VaR number is calculated from the distribution of the portfolio losses. This is the classical way to define VaR for measuring market risk and determining capital requirements. Nevertheless, it is sometimes more convenient to calculate the VaR number not from the distribution of the future value of the investment but from the distribution of the portfolio's return. This approach was discussed in Chapter 12, where we explained using VaR as a portfolio risk measure, and in the illustration in Chapter 13, where we illustrated the use of a VaR optimal portfolio. When we formalize our definition of VaR to measure market risk, we will adopt the previous approach and define it for returns. In this case, equation (14.1) must be adjusted to

$$C_t = A_t \cdot S(t) \cdot \max(\text{VaR}_t^*, \text{AVaR}_{60}^*) + s_t \qquad (14.2)$$

where $S(t)$ denotes the current value of the portfolio and VaR_t^* and AVaR_{60}^* denote the VaR and average VaR numbers for the return distribution. The connection between the VaR_t for the losses and the VaR_t^* for the return distribution will be discussed below when we formally introduce VaR.

Finally we have to discuss the meaning of the constant A_t in equations (14.1) and (14.2), respectively. The value for A_t depends on the accuracy of the VaR model in previous periods.[8] Accuracy is measured in terms of the number of times when daily actual losses exceeded the predicted VaR values over the last year, or the last 250 trading days.[9] Denoting this measure by K, regulators split the range of values of K into three zones: (1) green zone ($K \leq 4$), (2) the yellow zone ($5 \leq K \leq 9$), and (3) the red zone ($K \geq 10$).[10] The following values are assigned for A_t depending on the zone:

Zone	Range for K	Value for A_t
Green	$K \leq 4$	3
Yellow	$5 \leq K \leq 9$	$3 < A_t < 4$
Red	$K \geq 10$	4

---

[8] Regulators recommend using a time horizon of 10 days (two weeks) in VaR estimations. For backtesting, regulators use 1 day.

[9] A more detailed explanation of the time horizon and the window length is provided later in this chapter.

[10] Denote by $\bar{K}$ the fraction of days when the observed losses exceeded the VaR estimate. If $K = 10$, then $\bar{K}$ is 10/250 = 0.04. However, the 99% confidence level implies a probability of 0.01 for exceeding the VaR estimate of daily losses.

There were a significant number of respondents who questioned the multiplication factor when it was proposed in April 1995. Some respondents argued that a factor was unnecessary because models employed by banks measured risk with a high degree of precision. While the Basel Committee agreed that the internal models of banks provide a valuable point of departure for measuring the riskiness of a the trading portfolio of a bank, the daily VaR estimate then has to be converted into a capital charge that provides a sufficient cushion for cumulative losses that may arise from adverse market conditions over an extended period of time. The other reason for the multiplication factor is to account for potential weaknesses in the modeling process. In a paper published by the Basel Committee ("Overview of the Amendment to the Capital Accord to Incorporate Market Risks," 3), the weaknesses were identified as being the result of:

- ▪ Market price movements often display patterns (such as "fat tails") that differ from the statistical simplifications used in modelling (such as the assumption of a "normal distribution");

- ▪ The past is not always a good approximation of the future (for example volatilities and correlations can change abruptly);

- ▪ Value-at-risk estimates are typically based on end-of-day positions and generally do not take account of intra-day trading risk;

- ▪ Models cannot adequately capture event risk arising from exceptional market circumstances;

- ▪ Many models rely on simplifying assumptions to value the positions in the portfolio, particularly in the case of complex instruments such as options.

The Basel Committee stated that "When seen in the context of the other quantitative parameters, the Committee has concluded that a multiplication factor of 3 provides an appropriate and reasonable level of capital coverage to address these prudential concerns."

Definition of VaR Measure

A *VaR measure* is the highest possible loss over a certain period of time at a given confidence level. The loss can be measured by the distribution of the future dollar loss or by the distribution of the return. Formally,

VaR = $\text{VaR}_{t,\tau}$ for the return distribution is defined as the upper limit of the one-sided confidence interval:[11]

$$\text{VaR} = -\min\{c \mid P(\Delta P(\tau) \le c) > \alpha\}$$

where $1 - \alpha$ is the confidence level and $\Delta P(\tau) = \Delta P_t(\tau)$ is the *relative change* (*return*) in the portfolio value (portfolio return) over the time horizon τ.

$$\Delta P_t(\tau) = P(t + \tau) - P(\tau)$$

where

$P(t + \tau)$ = $\log S(t + \tau)$ is the logarithm of the spot value at $t + \tau$
$P(t)$ = $\log S(t)$
$S(t)$ = portfolio value at t

The time period is $[t, T]$, with $T - t = \tau$, and t is the current time.

The time horizon, or the holding period, should be determined from the liquidity of the assets and the trading activity. The confidence level should be chosen to provide a rarely exceeded VaR value.

The

$$\text{VaR}^L = \text{VaR}^L_{t,\tau}$$

for the loss distribution is defined analogously and equals the corresponding quantile of the loss distribution:

$$\text{VaR}^L = -\min\{c \mid P(S(T) - S(t) \le c) > \alpha\}$$

Here we have used the superscript L to distinguish between the VaR defined for returns and the VaR defined for losses. The conversion between VaR^L and VaR is given by the following two formulas:

$$\text{VaR}^L = S(t) \cdot (1 - e^{-\text{VaR}}) \quad \text{and} \quad \text{VaR} = \log \frac{S(t)}{S(t) - \text{VaR}^L}$$

For several reasons including, for example, the problems arising from calculating VaR^L when returns are modeled by a stable distribution, we

---

[11] This definition coincides with the one given in equation (12.7) in Chapter 12. In this definition, we use the current time t and the length of the time interval τ as parameters rather than the confidence level as in Chapter 12 because the latter is canonically assumed to equal 99% in most cases.

restrict ourselves in the following discussion to the case where VaR is defined and calculated for return distributions. Nevertheless, we mention the fact that there are also theoretically founded arguments why one should define VaR for the loss distribution. These arguments are connected to the concept of coherent risk measures and are explained in the appendix to this chapter.

COMPUTATION OF VaR

From the definition of VaR $= \text{VaR}_{t,\tau}$ given above, the VaR values are obtained from the assumed probability distribution of portfolio value returns. As explained in Chapter 3, this is found by integrating the probability density function over the relevant range. If the probability density function does not exist, then VaR can be obtained from the cumulative distribution function.

The VaR methodologies mainly differ in ways of constructing the probability density function. The traditional techniques of approximating the distribution of ΔP are:

- *Parametric method* (analytic or models-based)
- *Historical simulation* (nonparametric or empirical-based)
- *Monte Carlo simulation* (stochastic simulation)
- *Stress-testing* (scenario analysis)[12]

Parametric Method

If the changes in the portfolio value are characterized by a parametric distribution, VaR can be found as a function of distribution parameters. There are two approaches that are commonly used:

- Applications of two parametric distributions: normal and gamma
- Linear and quadratic approximations to price movements

To understand the first approach, assume that a portfolio consists of a single asset, which depends only on one risk factor. Traditionally, in this setting, the distribution of asset return is assumed to be the univariate normal distribution, identified by two parameters: the mean (μ) and the standard deviation (σ). The problem of calculating VaR is then reduced to finding the α-*th* percentile of the *standard* normal distribution.

---

[12] See JPMorgan (1995), Phelan (1995), Mahoney (1996), Jorion (1996a), Dowd (2002), Simons (1996), Fallon (1996), Linsmeier and Pearson (1996), Hopper (1996), Dave and Stahl (1997), Gamrowski and Rachev (1996), Duffie and Pan (1997), Fong and Vasicek (1997), and Pritsker (1996).

Investors in many applications assume that the expected return (mean) equals 0. This assumption is based on the conjecture that the magnitude of μ is substantially smaller than the magnitude of the standard deviation σ and, therefore, can be ignored.

If a portfolio consists of many assets, the computation of VaR is performed in several steps. Portfolio assets are decomposed into "building blocks," which depend on a finite number of risk factors. Exposures of the portfolio financial instruments are combined into risk categories. The total portfolio risk is constructed based on aggregated risk factors and their correlations.

If the return-vector of the assets included in the portfolio is *multivariate normally distributed*, the portfolio return, as a linear combination of jointly normal variables, is also normally distributed and risk can be represented by a combination of linear exposures to normally distributed factors. In this class of parametric models, to estimate risk, it is sufficient to evaluate the covariance matrix of portfolio risk factors (in the simplest case, individual asset returns). The estimation of the covariance matrix is based on *historical data* or on implied data from asset pricing models.

If portfolios contain zero-coupon bonds, stocks, commodities, and currencies, VaR can be computed from correlations of these basic risk factors and the asset weights. If portfolios include more complex securities, then the securities are decomposed into building blocks.

The portfolio returns are often assumed to be normally distributed.[13] One of the methods employing the normality assumption for returns is the delta method (the *delta-normal* or the *variance-covariance method*). The *delta method* estimates changes in prices of financial instruments using their "deltas" (with respect to basic risk factors).

Since the normal model for factor distributions is overly simplistic, Fong and Vasicek (1997) suggest estimating the probability distribution of the portfolio value changes by another type of the parametric distribution, the *gamma distribution*. We described this distribution in Chapter 3. They also assume that the basic risk factors are jointly normally distributed. However, Fong and Vasicek propose a *quadratic gamma* or *delta-gamma approximation* to the individual asset price changes.

It turns out that ΔP is a quadratic function of normal variables. This distribution of ΔP is, in general, nonsymmetric. However, one can approximate the quantile by the skewness parameter and the standard deviation. In fact, Fong and Vasicek used the approximation for the portfolio VaR value based on a generalized gamma distribution. The gamma distribution takes into consideration the skewness of the ΔP distribution, whereas the normal distribution is symmetric and does not reflect the skewness.

---

[13] See JPMorgan (1995) and Phelan (1995).

Historical Simulation

The *historical simulation approach* constructs the distribution of the portfolio value changes ΔP from historical data without imposing distribution assumptions and estimating parameters. Hence, sometimes the historical simulation method is referred to as a *nonparametric approach*. The method assumes that trends of past price changes will continue in the future. Hypothetical future prices over time are obtained by applying historical price movements to the current (log) prices. A portfolio value is then computed using the hypothetical (log) prices and the current portfolio composition.

The portfolio VaR is obtained from the distribution of computed hypothetical returns. Formally, VaR = $VaR_{t,\tau}$ is estimated by the negative of the α-*th* quantile of the empirical distribution function.

Monte Carlo Simulation

The *Monte Carlo method* specifies statistical models for basic risk factors and underlying assets. The method simulates the behavior of risk factors and asset prices by generating random price paths.

Monte Carlo simulations provide possible portfolio values on a given date T after the present time t, $T > t$. The VaR ($VaR_{t,T-t}$) value can be determined from the distribution of simulated portfolio values. The Monte Carlo approach is performed according to the following algorithm:

Step 1. Specify stochastic processes and process parameters for financial variables and correlations.

Step 2. Simulate the hypothetical price trajectories for all variables of interest. The hypothetical price changes are obtained by simulations, draws from the specified distribution.

Step 3. Obtain asset prices at time T from the simulated price trajectories. Compute the portfolio value.

Step 4. Repeat steps 2 and 3 many times to form the distribution of the portfolio return ΔP at time T.

Step 5. Measure VaR ($VaR_{t,T-t}$) as the negative of the empirical α-*th* quantile of the simulated distribution for the portfolio return at time T.

Stress Testing

The parametric, historical simulation, and Monte Carlo methods estimate the VaR (expected losses) depending on risk factors. The *stress testing* method examines the effects of large movements in key financial variables on the portfolio return. The price movements are simulated in line with certain scenarios. Scenarios include possible movements of the yield curve, changes in exchange rates, credit spreads, and the like together with estimates of the underlying probabilities.

Portfolio assets are reevaluated under each scenario. The portfolio return is then computed for each scenario. Estimating a probability for each scenario allows the construction of a distribution of portfolio returns, from which VaR can be derived.

Components of VaR Methodologies

Implementation of the VaR methodologies requires analysis of their components:

- Distribution and correlation assumptions
- Volatility and covariance models
- Weighting schemes
- The effect of the time horizon (holding period) on the VaR values
- The window length of data used for parameter estimations
- Incorporation of the mean of returns in the VaR analysis

Each component is described in the following sections.

Distribution and Correlation Assumptions

The parametric VaR methods assume that asset returns have parametric distributions. The parametric approaches are subject to "model risk": distribution assumptions might be incorrect. The frequent assumption is that asset returns have a multivariate normal distribution, despite the evidence discussed in Chapter 11. The historical simulation technique does not impose distributional assumptions; thus, it is free of model risk and "parameter estimation" risk, but future scenarios might be very different from historical evolutions of the risk factors. The Monte Carlo approach specifies the distributions of the underlying instruments that are being priced.

Volatility and Covariance Models

The VaR methods apply diverse volatility and correlation models:[14]

- Constant volatility (moving window)
- Exponential weighting
- GARCH

---

[14] See Duffie and Pan (1997), Jackson, Maude, and Perraudin (1997), JPMorgan (1995), Phelan (1995), Hopper (1996), Mahoney (1996), and Hendricks (1996).

■ EGARCH (asymmetric volatility)
■ Cross-market GARCH
■ Implied volatility
■ Subjective views

In the *constant volatility* (*equally weighted*) models, variances and covariances do not change over time. They are approximated by sample variances and covariances over the estimation "window."

Empirical financial data, however, do not exhibit constant volatility. The exponential weighting models take into account time-varying volatility and accentuate the recent observations by giving them greater weight. The weighting schemes are classified as either uniform or asset-specific schemes. Riskmetrics uses the uniform weighting scheme. Credit Suisse First Boston's PrimeRisk employs an asset-specific scheme with specific volatility models (different weighting schemes) for different equities, futures, and OTC options.

It is important to note that the uniform weighting scheme may lead to higher tail probabilities (i.e., proportions of actual observations exceeding the VaR predictions).[15]

Popular models explaining time-varying volatility are *autoregressive conditional heteroskedasticity* (ARCH) models. As explained in Chapter 9, in ARCH models the conditional variances follow a kind of autoregressive process. In the ARCH(1) model, the conditional volatility at period t depends on the volatility at the previous period $t - 1$. If volatility at time $t - 1$ was large, the volatility at time t is expected to be large as well. Observations will exhibit clustered volatilities: One can distinguish periods with high volatilities and tranquil periods.

In *generalized ARCH* (GARCH) model, the conditional variance contains both autoregressive and a kind of moving average components. The advantage of using the GARCH model follows from the fact that an autoregressive process of a high order might be represented by a more parsimonious ARMA process. Due to similar reasons, the GARCH model will have less parameters that have to be estimated than the corresponding ARCH model. The advantage of using the *exponential GARCH* (EGARCH) model[16] is that it does not impose certain restrictions on the coefficients of the model, whereas the GARCH model does. The *cross-market GARCH* allows the estimation of volatility in one market from volatilities in other markets.[17]

---

[15] See Table 4 in Jackson, Maude, and Perraudin (1997, 179).

[16] EGARCH was suggested by Nelson (1991).

[17] Duffie and Pan (1997) provide an example of cross-market GARCH, which employs the *bivariate GARCH*.

Sometimes analysts use *implied volatilities* to estimate future volatilities. Implied volatilities are volatilities derived from pricing models. For instance, implied volatilities can be obtained from the Black-Scholes option pricing model (see Chapter 18). The *implied tree* assumes implied volatilities change over time and computes them relating the modeled and observed option prices.[18] One of the methods for estimating volatility is the method of *subjective views*.[19] Analysts make predictions of volatility from their own views of market conditions.

Besides the distribution assumptions and volatility models, the VaR computations also need specification of correlation assumptions on price changes and volatilities within and across markets.[20] Beder (1995) illustrated the sensitivity of VaR results to correlation assumptions. She computed VaR using the Monte Carlo simulation method under different assumptions: (1) correlations across asset groups and (2) correlations only within asset groups. The VaR estimates obtained were lower for the first type of correlation assumptions than for the second type.

Time Horizon

The *time horizon* (the *holding period*) in the VaR computations can take any time value. In practice, it varies from one day to two weeks (10 trading days) and depends on liquidity of assets and frequency of trading transactions. It is assumed that the portfolio composition remains the same over the holding period.

This assumption constrains dynamic trading strategies. The Basel Committee recommends the use of the 10-day holding period. Practitioners argue that the time horizon of 10 days is inadequate for frequently traded instruments and is restrictive for illiquid assets. Long holding periods are usually recommended for portfolios with illiquid instruments, although many model approximations are only valid within short periods of time.

Beder (1995) analyzed the impact of the time horizon on VaR estimations. She calculated VaR for three hypothetical portfolios applying four different approaches for the time horizons of 1-day and 10-days.

Window Length

The *window length* is the length of the data subsample (the observation period) used for a VaR estimation. The window length choice is related to sampling issues and availability of databases. Regulators suggest using the 250-day (one-year) window length.

---

[18] See, for example, Derman and Kani (1994), Rubinstein (1994), and Jackwerth and Rubinstein (1995 and 1996).

[19] See Hopper (1996).

[20] See Duffie and Pan (1997), Beder (1995), and Liu (1996).

Jackson, Maude, and Perraudin (1997) computed parametric and simulation VaRs for the 1-day and 10-day time horizons using the window lengths from three to 24 months. They concluded that VaR forecasts based on longer data windows are more reliable.[21] Beder (1995) estimated VaR applying the historical simulation method for the 100-day and 250-day window lengths and showed that the VaR values increase with the expanded observation intervals.

Hendricks (1996) calculated the VaR measures using the parametric approach with equally weighted volatility models and the historical simulation approach for window lengths of 50, 125, 250, 500, and 1,250 days.[22] He reports that the VaR measures become more stable for longer observation periods.

Incorporation of the Mean of Returns

In many cases, the mean of returns is assumed to be zero. Jackson, Maude, and Perraudin (1997) analyze the effects of (1) inclusion of the mean in calculations and (2) setting the mean to zero on VaR results. Their analysis was not conclusive.[23]

EVALUATION OF VaR METHODS: STRENGTHS AND WEAKNESSES

The VaR methods provide only estimated VaR values. The important task is to evaluate accuracy of the VaR estimates. Researchers propose different performance measures.

The VaR methodologies are becoming necessary tools in risk management. It is essential to be aware of VaR strengths and weaknesses.[24] Institutions use the VaR measurements to estimate exposure to market risks and assess expected losses. Application of different VaR methods provides different VaR estimates.

The choice of methods should mostly depend on the portfolio composition. If a portfolio contains instruments with linear dependence on basic risk factors, the delta method will be satisfactory. Strength of the delta approach is that computations of VaR are relatively easy. Drawbacks of the delta-normal method are:

---

[21] See Table 5 in Jackson, Maude, and Perraudin (1997, 180).

[22] Hendricks (1996)

[23] See Table 6 in Jackson, Maude and Perraudin (1997, 181)).

[24] For a more detailed discussion, see Beder (1995), Mahoney (1996), Simons (1996), Jorion (1996a, 1996b/1997 and 1997), Hopper (1996), Shaw (1997), and *Derivatives Strategy* (1998).

1. Empirical observations on returns of financial instruments do not exhibit a normal distribution and, thus, the delta-normal technique does not fit well data with heavy tails.
2. Accuracy of VaR estimates diminishes with financial instruments where there are nonlinear payoffs such as options and option-like instruments (which we will refer to as nonlinear instruments): in their presence, VaR estimates may be understated.

For portfolios with option or option-like instruments, historical and Monte Carlo simulations are more suitable. The historical simulation method is easy to implement having a sufficient database. The advantage of using the historical simulation is that it does not impose distributional assumptions. Models based on historical data assume that the past trends will continue in the future. However, the future might encounter extreme events. The historical simulation technique is limited in forecasting the range of portfolio value changes. The stress-testing method can be applied to investigate the effects of large movements. The Monte Carlo method can incorporate nonlinear positions and non-normal distributions. It does not restrict the range of portfolio value changes. The Monte Carlo method can be used in conducting the sensitivity analysis. The main limitations in implementing the Monte Carlo methodology are: (1) it is affected by model risk; (2) computations and software are complex; and (3) it is time consuming.

VaR methodologies are subject to *implementation risk*: implementation of the same model by different users produces different VaR estimates. Marshall and Siegel (1997) conducted an innovative study of implementation risk. Comparing VaR results obtained by several risk management systems developers using one model, JPMorgan's RiskMetrics, they find that different systems do not produce the same VaR estimates for the same model and identical portfolios. The varying estimates can be explained by the sensitivity of VaR models to users' assumptions. The degree of variation in VaR numbers was associated with the portfolio composition. Dependence of implementation risk on instrument complexity can be summarized in the following relative ascending ranking: foreign exchange forwards, money market instruments, forward rate agreements, government bonds, interest rate swaps, foreign exchange options, and interest rate options index. Nonlinear instruments entail larger discrepancy in VaR results than linear securities. In order to take into account implementation risk, it is advisable to accompany VaR computations for nonlinear portfolios with sensitivity analysis to underlying assumptions.

Other VaR weaknesses are:

- Existing VaR models reflect observed risks and they are not useful in transition periods characterized by structural changes, additional risks, contracted liquidity of assets, and broken correlations across assets and across markets.
- The trading positions change over time. Therefore, extrapolation of a VaR for a certain time horizon to longer time periods might be problematic.[25]
- The VaR methodologies assume that necessary database is available. For certain securities, data over a sufficient time interval may not exist.
- If historical information on financial instruments is not available, the instruments are mapped into known instruments. Though, mapping reduces precision of VaR estimations, mapping reduces precision of VaR estimations.
- Model risks can occur if the chosen stochastic underlying processes for valuing financial instruments are incorrect.
- Since true parameters are not observable, estimates of parameters are obtained from sample data. The measurement error rises with the number of parameters in a model.
- VaR is not effective when strategic risks are significant.

STABLE MODELING OF VaR

In this section we discuss the use of stable distributions in VaR modeling. We first describe the stable VaR approach with the existing methodologies.[26]

Estimation of Stable Parameters

Where the primary concern is the tail behavior of distributions, three methods have been proposed to estimate the stable parameters and their applicability in VaR computations: (1) tail estimation, (2) entire-distribution modeling, and (3) a combination of (1) and (2). As the estimation of the tail index is a difficult task requiring a lot of observations, we focus our presentation on the second and third approach.

Using different estimation procedures of type (2) and (3), Khindanova, Rachev, and Schwartz (KRS) (2001) consider a stable VaR model which assumes that the portfolio return distribution follows a stable law. They derive "stable" VaR estimates and analyze their properties applying in-sample and forecast evaluations using "normal" VaR measurements as benchmarks for investigating characteristics of "stable" VaR measurements.

---

[25] Duffie and Pan (1997) point out that if intraperiod position size is stochastic, then the VaR measure obtained under the assumption of constant position sizes should be multiplied by a certain factor.

[26] The results of this section draw from Khindanova, Rachev, and Schwartz (2001).

KRS conducted analysis for eight financial data sets: (1) yen/British pound exchange rate, (2) British pound/U.S. dollar exchange rate, (3) Deutsche mark (DM)/British pound exchange rate, (4) S&P 500 index, (5) DAX30 index, (6) CAC40 index, (7) Nikkei 225 index, and (8) Dow Jones Commodities Price Index (DJCPI). A brief description of the data is given in Exhibit 14.1.

They evaluate stable and normal VaR models by examining distances between the VaR estimates and the empirical VaR measures. Because regulators recommend using a time horizon of one day for the purpose of testing VaR models, KRS use one day in their analysis. At each time t, an estimate VaR_t^* is obtained using lw recent observations of portfolio returns

$$VaR_t^* = VaR(r_{t-1}, r_{t-2}, ..., r_{t-lw})$$

The lw parameter is called the *window length*.

KRS report the results when VaR is estimated employing the entire sample of observations, that is, lw is equal to the sample size. They compute both the stable VaR and normal VaR measurements at the confidence level $c = 1 - \alpha$ in two steps: (1) fitting empirical data by a stable (normal) distribution and (2) calculating a VaR as the negative of the $(\alpha)th$ quantile of a fitted stable (normal) distribution.

"Stable" fitting is implemented using three methods: maximum likelihood (ML) method, Fourier Transform (FT) method, and Fourier Transform-Tail (FTT).[27] The first two methods were briefly discussed in Chapter 8, the latter is a variant of the second. The estimated parame-

EXHIBIT 14.1   Financial Data Series (Daily)

Series	Source	Number of Observations	Time Period
Yen/BP	Datastream	6,285	1.01.74–1.30.98
BP/US$	D. Hindanov	6,157	1.03.74–1.30.98
DM/BP	Datastream	6,285	1.02.74–1.30.98
S&P 500	Datastream	7,327	1.01.70–1.30.98
DAX30	Datastream	8,630	1.04.65–1.30.98
CAC40	Datastream	2,756	7.10.87–1.30.98
Nikkei 225	Datastream	4,718	1.02.80–1.30.98
DJCPI	Datastream	5,761	1.02.76–1.30.98

Source: Khindanova, Rachev, and Schwartz (2001).

---

[27] See Khindanova, Rachev, and Schwartz (2001).

ters of density functions and corresponding confidence intervals computed by KRS are reproduced in Exhibit 14.2.[28]

The empirical analysis showed that a set of 1,000 replications is: (1) satisfactory for constructing 95% confidence interval and (2) insufficient for obtaining reliable 99% confidence intervals. In their experiments, they found that sets of 1,000 replications generated 95% confidence intervals for α and σ whose bounds coincided up to two decimal points and 95% confidence intervals for μ with slightly varying bounds. For 99% confidence intervals, they report insignificant variation of left limits.

EXHIBIT 14.2 Parameters of Stable and Normal Density Functions[a]

| Series | Normal | | | Stable | | | |
	Mean	Standard Deviation	Method	α	β	μ	σ
Yen/BP	-0.012	0.648	ML	1.647	-0.170	-0.023	0.361
			FT	1.61		-0.018	0.34
				[1.57, 1.66]		[-0.095, 0.015]	[0.33, 0.36]
				[1.55, 1.68]		[-0.178, 0.025]	[0.33, 0.37]
			FTT	1.50		-0.018	0.32
				[1.46, 1.55]		[-0.131, 0.034]	[0.31, 0.34]
				[1.44, 1.64]		[-0.261, 0.070]	[0.31, 0.39]
BP/US	0.006	0.658	ML	1.582	0.038	0.007	0.349
			FT	1.57		0.006	0.33
				[1.53, 1.65]		[-0.096, 0.045]	[0.32, 0.36]
				[1.51, 1.75]		[-0.393, 0.065]	[0.32, 0.47]
			FTT	1.45		0.006	0.31
				[1.41, 1.51]		[-0.134, 0.070]	[0.30, 0.33]
				[1.40, 1.62]		[-0.388, 0.097]	[0.30, 0.47]
DM/BP	-0.012	0.489	ML	1.590	-0.195	0.018	0.256
			FT	1.60		-0.012	0.24
				[1.54, 1.75]		[-0.064, 0.013]	[0.23, 0.26]
				[1.53, 1.75]		[-0.165, 0.022]	[0.23, 0.27]
			FTT	1.45		-0.012	0.23
				[1.41, 1.55]		[-0.114, 0.038]	[0.22, 0.26]
				[1.40, 1.77]		[-0.402, 0.061]	[0.22, 0.40]

[28] In the FT and FTT fitting, KRS assume that distributions of returns are symmetric, that is, the skewness parameter β is equal to zero. Hence, no value is shown for β in the exhibit.

EXHIBIT 14.2   (Continued)

Series	Normal		Method	Stable			
	Mean	Standard Deviation		α	β	μ	σ
S&P 500	0.032	0.930	ML	1.708	0.004	0.036	0.512
			FT	1.82		0.032	0.54
				[1.78, 1.84]		[−0.013, 0.057]	[0.53, 0.54]
				[1.77, 1.84]		[−0.062, 0.067]	[0.53, 0.55]
			FTT	1.60		0.032	0.48
				[1.56, 1.65]		[−0.066, 0.078]	[0.47, 0.49]
				[1.54, 1.66]		[−0.120, 0.095]	[0.46, 0.50]
DAX 30	0.026	1.002	ML	1.823	−0.084	0.027	0.592
			FT	1.84		0.026	0.60
				[1.81, 1.88]		[−0.050, 0.088]	[0.68, 0.73]
				[1.80, 1.89]		[−0.050, 0.057]	[0.58, 0.62]
			FTT	1.73		0.026	0.57
				[1.69, 1.77]		[−0.031, 0.061]	[0.56, 0.58]
				[1.68, 1.79]		[−0.124, 0.073]	[0.56, 0.59]
CAC 40	0.028	1.198	ML	1.784	−0.153	0.027	0.698
			FT	1.79		0.028	0.70
				[1.73, 1.85]		[−0.050, 0.088]	[0.68, 0.73]
				[1.71, 1.87]		[−0.174, 0.103]	[0.67, 0.74]
			FTT	1.76		0.028	0.69
				[1.71, 1.84]		[−0.053, 0.091]	[0.61, 0.72]
				[1.69, 1.87]		[−0.394, 0.101]	[0.66, 0.77]
Nikkei 225	0.020	1.185	ML	1.444	−0.093	−0.002	0.524
			FT	1.58		0.02	0.59
				[1.53, 1.64]		[−0.127, 0.102]	[0.57, 0.62]
				[1.52, 1.67]		[−0.421, 0.130]	[0.57, 0.69]
			FTT	1.30		0.02	0.49
				[1.26, 1.47]		[−0.451, 0.316]	[0.47, 0.69]
				[1.05, 1.67]		[−1.448, 0.860]	[0.47, 1.10]
DJCPI	0.006	0.778	ML	1.569	−0.060	0.003	0.355
			FT	1.58		0.006	0.35
				[1.53, 1.66]		[−0.026, 0.100]	[0.34, 0.37]
				[1.52, 1.67]		[−0.140, 0.120]	[0.33, 0.39]
			FTT	1.49		0.006	0.33
				[1.44, 1.55]		[−0.160, 0.062]	[0.32, 0.36]
				[1.44, 1.69]		[−0.396, 0.100]	[0.32, 0.46]

[a] The confidence intervals right below the estimates are the 95% confidence intervals and the next confidence intervals are the 99% confidence intervals.
Source: Khindanova, Rachev, and Schwartz (2001).

VaR measurements were calculated at 99% and 95% confidence levels. The 99% (95%) VaR was determined as the negative of the 1% (5%) quantile. The 99% and 95% VaR estimates are reported in Exhibit 14.3 and 14.4, respectively. Biases of stable and normal VaR measurements are provided in Exhibit 14.5. Biases are computed by subtracting the empirical VaR from the model VaR estimates.

EXHIBIT 14.3 Empirical. Normal, and Stable 95% VaR Estimates[a]

Series	Empirical	Normal	Stable ML	Stable FT	Stable FTT
				95% VaR	
Yen/BP	1.103	1.086	1.033	0.968 [0.926, 1.047] [0.911, 1.186]	0.995 [0.937, 1.132] [0.911, 1.329]
BP/US$	1.038	1.077	0.981	0.944 [0.898, 1.072] [0.876, 1.599]	0.986 [0.917, 1.158] [0.895, 1.588]
DM/BP	0.806	0.816	0.772	0.687 [0.652, 0.749] [0.641, 0.894]	0.748 [0.695, 0.894] [0.678, 1.418]
S&P 500	1.384	1.497	1.309	1.308 [1.275, 1.361] [1.265, 1.411]	1.319 [1.265, 1.423] [1.246, 1.503]
DAX 30	1.508	1.623	1.449	1.451 [1.415, 1.500] [1.402, 1.533]	1.452 [1.405, 1.521] [1.395, 1.650]
CAC 40	1.819	1.943	1.756	1.734 [1.653, 1.837] [1.621, 1.944]	1.734 [1.647, 1.845] [1.616, 2.288]
Nikkei 225	1.856	1.929	1.731	1.666 [1.570, 1.839] [1.558, 2.280]	1.840 [1.582, 2.512] [1.500, 5.022]
DJCPI	1.066	1.274	1.031	0.994 [0.888, 1.047] [0.870, 1.200]	1.011 [0.944, 1.188] [0.915, 1.615]

[a] The confidence intervals right below the estimates are the 95% confidence intervals and the next confidence intervals are the 99% confidence intervals.
Source: Khindanova, Rachev, and Schwartz (2001).

EXHIBIT 14.4   Empirical. Normal, and Stable 99% VaR Estimates[a]

Series	Empirical	Normal	99% VaR		
				Stable	
			ML	FT	FTT
Yen/BP	1.979	1.528	2.247	2.212 [1.968, 2.252] [1.919, 2.415]	2.494 [2.276, 2.736] [2.230, 2.836]
BP/US$	1.774	1.526	2.221	2.200 [2.014, 2.412] [1.956, 2.593]	2.668 [2.436, 2.925] [2.358, 3.029]
DM/BP	1.489	1.149	1.819	1.520 [1.190, 1.712] [1.179, 1.742]	1.996 [1.792, 2.211] [1.700, 2.329]
S&P 500	2.293	2.131	2.559	2.200 [2.117, 2.258] [2.106, 2.470]	2.984 [2.757, 3.243] [2.700, 3.336]
DAX 30	2.564	2.306	2.464	2.375 [2.260, 2.502] [2.240, 2.569]	2.746 [2.557, 2.949] [2.523, 2.997]
CAC 40	3.068	2.760	3.195	3.019 [2.756, 3.364] [2.682, 3.520]	3.144 [2.788, 3.504] [2.700, 3.841]
Nikkei 225	3.428	2.737	4.836	3.842 [3.477, 4.254] [3.367, 4.453]	6.013 [5.190, 6.701] [4.658, 19.950]
DJCPI	2.053	1.804	2.446	2.285 [1.955, 2.423] [1.916, 2.474]	2.603 [2.382, 2.870] [2.288, 3.035]

[a] The confidence intervals right below the estimates are the 95% confidence intervals and the next confidence intervals are the 99% confidence intervals.
Source: Khindanova, Rachev, and Schwartz (2001).

EXHIBIT 14.5 Biases of Normal and Stable 99% VaR Estimates

	99% VaR$_m$ – 99% VaR$_{Empirical}$[a]			
		Stable		
Series	Normal	ML	FT	FTT
Yen/BP	−0.451	0.268	0.133	0.515
BP/US$	−0.248	0.447	0.426	0.894
DM/BP	−0.340	0.330	0.031	0.507
S&P 500	−0.162	0.266	−0.093	0.691
DAX 30	−0.258	−0.100	−0.189	0.182
CAC 40	−0.308	0.127	−0.049	0.076
Nikkei 225	−0.691	1.408	0.414	2.585
DJCPI	−0.249	0.393	0.232	0.550
Mean absolute bias	0.338	0.416	0.196	0.750

[a] Var$_m$ is obtained with the normal, stable-ML, stable-FT, and stable-FTT methods.
Source: Khindanova, Rachev, and Schwartz (2001).

In general, the stable modeling (ML, FT, and FTT) provided evaluations of the 99% VaR greater than the empirical 99% VaR (see Exhibits 14.3 and 14.5). It underestimated the sample 99% VaR in the applications of two methods: FT (for the CAC 40, S&P 500, and DAX 30) and ML (for the DAX30). Biased downwards stable VaR estimates were closer to the true VaR than the normal estimates (see Exhibit 14.5). Among the methods of stable approximation, the FT method provided more accurate VaR estimates for seven data sets (see Exhibit 14.5). For all analyzed data sets, the normal modeling underestimated the empirical 99% VaR. Stable modeling provided more accurate 99% VaR estimates: mean absolute bias under the stable (FT) method was 42% smaller than under the normal method.

At 95% confidence level, the stable VaR estimates were lower than the empirical VaR for all data sets. The normal VaR measurements exceeded the true VaR, except the yen/BP exchange rate series (see Exhibit 14.6). For the exchange rate series (yen/BP, BP/US$, and DM/BP), the normal method resulted in more exact VaR estimates. For the S&P 500, DAX 30, CAC 40, and DJCPI, stable methods underestimated VaR, though the estimates were closer to the true VaR than the normal estimates. Mean absolute biases under stable and normal modeling are of comparable magnitudes.

In-sample examination of VaR models showed:

■ The stable modeling generally results in conservative and accurate 99% VaR estimates, which is preferred by financial institutions and regulators.

EXHIBIT 14.6 Biases of Normal and Stable 95% VaR Estimates

Series	95% VaR$_m$ – 95% VaR$_{Empirical}$[a]			
		Stable		
	Normal	ML	FT	FTT
Yen/BP	–0.017	–0.070	–0.135	–0.108
BP/US$	0.039	–0.057	–0.094	–0.052
DM/BP	0.010	–0.034	–0.119	–0.058
S&P 500	0.113	–0.075	–0.076	–0.065
DAX 30	0.115	–0.059	–0.057	–0.056
CAC 40	0.124	–0.063	–0.085	–0.085
Nikkei 225	0.073	–0.125	–0.190	–0.016
DJCPI	0.208	–0.035	–0.072	–0.055
Mean absolute bias	0.087	0.065	0.104	0.070

[a] Var$_m$ is obtained with the normal, stable-ML, stable-FT, and stable-FTT methods.
Source: Khindanova, Rachev, and Schwartz (2001).

■ The normal approach leads to overly optimistic forecasts of losses in the 99% VaR estimation.
■ From a conservative point of view, the normal modeling is acceptable for the 95% VaR estimation.
■ The stable models underestimate the 95% VaR. In fact, the stable 95% VaR measurements are closer to the empirical VaR than the normal 95% VaR measurements.

Forecast-Evaluation of VaR

The next step in evaluating VaR models is analysis of their forecasting characteristics. In this section, we discuss KRS's results with respect to the forecasting properties of stable and normal VaR modeling by comparing predicted VaR with observed returns as reported by KRS for the data series in Exhibit 14.1. The testing required that KRS develop bounds of admissible VaR exceedings (denoted by E) and exceedings frequencies (denoted by E/T) for testing at different levels of significance. These bounds are reported for the 5% and 1% levels in Exhibit 14.7.[29]

In their testing procedures, KRS considered a window lengths (lw) = 260 observations (data over 1-year) and {lw} = 1,560 observations (data over 6 years). The next step in evaluating VaR models is analysis of their

---

[29] The methodology to get the confidence bounds for the number of exceedings in Exhibit 14.7 is explained in an example in Chapter 8.

EXHIBIT 14.7 Admissible VaR Exceedings and Exceeding Frequencies

VaR Confidence Level, c	Length of a Testing Interval, T	Admissible VaR Exceedings, E		Admissible VaR Frequencies, E/T	
		Significance Level, x		Significance Level, x	
		5%	1%	5%	1%
95%	500	[17, 33]	[14, 36]	[3.40%, 6.60%]	[2.80%, 7.20%]
	1,500	[61, 89]	[56, 94]	[4.07%, 5.93%]	[3.73%, 6.27%]
99%	500	[2, 8]	[0, 10]	[0.40%, 1.60%]	[0.00%, 2.00%]
	1,500	[9, 21]	[6, 23]	[0.60%, 1.40%]	[0.40%, 1.53%]

Source: Khindanova, Rachev, and Schwartz (2001).

forecasting characteristics. KRS considered lengths of testing intervals $T = 500$ days and $T = 1,500$ days.

KRS's evaluation results are reported in Exhibits 14.8 and 14.9. The numbers in bold font reported in these two exhibits indicate cases that are outside of acceptable ranges shown in Exhibit 14.7.

From Exhibit 14.8 it can be seen that normal models for the 99% VaR computations commonly produce numbers of exceedings above the acceptable range, which implies that normal modeling significantly underestimates VaR (losses). At window length of 260 observations, stable modeling is not satisfactory. It provided a permissible number of exceptions only for the BP/US$ and DJCPI series. At a sample size of 1,560, and testing interval of 500 observations, exceedings by the stable-FT method are outside of the admissible interval for the S&P 500, DAX 30, and CAC 40.

Testing on the longer interval with $T = 1,500$ showed that numbers of "stable" exceptions are within the permissible range. Exhibit 14.8 indicates that increasing the window length from 260 observations to 1,560 observations reduces the number of stable-FT exceedings. In contrast, extending the window length for normal models does not decrease exceedings; in some cases, it is even elevated. These results illustrate that stable modeling outperforms normal modeling in the 99% VaR estimations.

The 95% VaR normal estimates (except the DAX 30 series) obtained using 260 observations are within the permissible range. Increasing the window length generally worsens the normal VaR measurements. The stable-FT method provided sufficient 95% VaR estimates for the yen/BP and BP/US$ exchange rates and the CAC40 and Nikkei 225. A study of the predictive power of VaR models suggests that:

■ The normal modeling significantly underestimates 99% VaR.

EXHIBIT 14.8   99% VaR Exceedings

Series	Length of a Testing Interval, T	99% VaR Exceedings							
		Window Length = 260 obs.				Window Length = 1,560 obs.			
		Normal		FT		Normal		FT	
		E	E/T	E	E/T	E	E/T	E	E/T
Yen/BP	500	15	3.00%	13	2.60%	10	2.00%	2	0.40%
	1,500	40	1.67	34	2.27	45	3.00	21	1.40
BP/US$	500	10	2.00	5	1.00	1	0.20	0	0.00
	1,500	26	1.73	13	0.86	17	1.33	5	0.33
DM/BP	500	18	3.60	14	2.80	17	3.40	8	1.60
	1,500	45	3.00	33	2.20	50	3.33	19	1.27
S&P 500	500	17	3.40	13	2.60	25	5.00	13	2.60
	1,500	35	2.33	27	1.80	28	1.87	14	0.93
DAX 30	500	21	4.20	14	2.80	19	3.80	18	3.60
	1,500	41	2.73	29	1.93	25	1.67	20	1.33
CAC 40	500	16	3.20	14	2.80	14	2.80	13	2.60
	1,500	34	2.27	29	1.93	17	1.63	19	1.27
Nikkei 225	500	15	3.00	14	2.80	13	2.60	7	1.40
	1,500	31	2.07	23	1.53	26	1.73	10	0.67
DJCPI	500	12	2.40	7	1.40	15	3.00	10	2.00
	1,500	29	1.93	15	1.00	28	1.87	17	1.13

Source: Khindanova, Rachev, and Schwartz (2001).

- The stable method results in reasonable 99% VaR estimates.
- 95% normal measurements are in the admissible range for the window length of 260 observations; increasing window length to 1,560 observations might deteriorate the precision of the estimates.

ALTERNATIVE TO VaR: EXPECTED TAIL LOSS

There is no doubt that the popularity of VaR measures in risk management is in large part due to its simplicity and its ease of calculation for a given confidence interval. However, there is a price to be paid for the simplicity of VaR in the form of several intrinsic limitations. They include:[30]

---

[30] There is another limitation having to do with portfolio optimization explained in Chapter 13 and in Martin, Rachev, and Siboulet (2003) and the references therein.

EXHIBIT 14.9 95% VaR Exceedings

Series	Length of a Testing Interval, T	95% VaR Exceedings							
		Window Length = 260 obs.				Window Length = 1,560 obs.			
		Normal		FT		Normal		FT	
		E	E/T	E	E/T	E	E/T	E	E/T
Yen/BP	500	35	7.00%	38	7.60%	27	5.40%	31	6.2%
	1,500	94	6.27	104	6.93	109	7.27	122	8.13
BP/US$5	500	33	6.60	45	9.00	10	2.00	17	3.40
	1,500	73	4.87	96	6.40	46	3.07	57	3.80
DM/BP	500	32	6.40	38	7.60	29	5.80	37	7.40
	1,500	89	5.93	114	7.60	105	7.00	139	9.27
S&P 500	500	34	6.80	39	7.80	43	8.60	47	9.40
	1,500	79	5.27	98	6.53	62	4.13	69	4.60
DAX 30	500	47	9.40	50	10.00	42	8.40	45	9.00
	1,500	98	6.53	109	7.27	62	4.13	79	5.27
CAC 40	500	32	6.40	34	6.80	31	6.20	32	6.40
	1,500	81	5.40	87	5.80	51	4.90	82	5.47
Nikkei 225	500	37	7.40	40	8.00	28	5.60	33	6.60
	1,500	85	5.67	90	6.00	68	5.43	87	5.80
DJCPI	500	29	5.80	35	7.00	37	7.40	46	9.20
	1,500	70	4.67	93	6.20	77	5.13	108	7.20

Source: Khindanova, Rachev, and Schwartz (2001).

Limitation 1: VaR does not give any indication of the risk beyond the quantile.
Limitation 2: VaR exhibits theoretical weaknesses.
Limitation 3: VaR can be a very misleading risk indicator.

Limitation 2 means that VaR applied to the distribution of the future portfolio value fails to fulfill the requirements of a coherent risk measure. The concept of a coherent risk measure together with the defining properties is explained in the appendix to this chapter. Limitation 3 is particularly important. Examples exist where an investor, unintentionally or not, decreases portfolio VaR while simultaneously increasing the expected losses beyond the VaR, that is, by increasing the "tail risk" of the portfolio.

In addition to these three intrinsic limitations, the specific VaR implementations that we described earlier are fraught with further flaws:

■ Historical VaR limits the range of the scenarios to data values that have actually been observed, while Normal Monte Carlo tends to seriously underestimate the probability of extreme returns. In either case, the probability density functions beyond the sample range are either zero or excessively close to zero.

■ Lacking the ability to accurately model extreme returns, practitioners are forced to use stress testing as a palliative to the limitations of traditional VaR models. In doing so, they use a large degree of subjectivity in the design of the stress test and in the selection of past data to use in making a risk assessment.

■ The traditional modeling of risk factor dependencies cannot account for intraday volatility patterns, long-term volatility patterns, or more importantly unusual extreme volatility. In stressed markets, the simple linear diversification assumptions fail, and atypical short-term concentration patterns that bind all the assets in a bearish spiral emerge.

Basak and Shapiro (2001) find that when investors use VaR for their risk management, the resulting market positions that result from the optimizing behavior have exposure to extreme loss. This is due to the fact that VaR generated misleading information about the distribution's tail. Yamai and Yoshiba (2002) argue that if VaR is widely adopted for risk management, it could lead to market instability.

Given the well-documented limitations of VaR, why does it continue to be the risk of choice of regulators and many practitioners? Given the superiority of the Expected Tail Loss (ETL), why is it not used instead of VaR? The reasons are controversial. In the preface to his book on measuring market risk, Dowd (2002, xii) provides an explanation:

Part of the answer is that there will be a need to measure VaR for as long as there is a demand for VaR itself: if someone wants the number, then someone has to measure it, and whether they should want the number in the first place is another matter. ... a purist would say that VaR is inferior to ETL, but people still want VaR numbers and so the business of VaR estimation goes on. However, there is also a second, more satisfying, reason to continue to estimate VaR: we often need VaR estimates to be able to estimate ETL. We don't have many formulas for ETL and, as a result, we would often be unable to estimate ETL if we had to rely on ETL formulas alone. Fortunately, it turns out that we can always estimate the ETL if we can estimate the VaR. The reason is that the VaR is a quantile and, if we can estimate the quantile, we can easily estimate the ETL—because the ETL itself is just a quantile average.

Expected Tail Loss and Stable versus Normal Distributions[31]

As explained in Chapter 12, Expected Tail Loss (ETL) is simply the average (or expected value) loss for losses larger than VaR. (ETL is also known as Conditional Value-at-Risk (CVaR), or Expected Shortfall (ES)). In Chapter 13, we applied ETL to the portfolio selection.

Usual (1 to 5% confidence interval (CI)) normal ETL (i.e., ELT assuming a standard normal distribution) is close to normal VaR (i.e., VaR assuming a standard normal distribution):[32]

- For CI = 5%, VaR = 1.645 and ETL = 2.062
- For CI = 1%, VaR = 2.336 and ETL = 2.667

By failing to capture kurtosis and skewness, normal distributions underestimate ETL. The ubiquitous normal assumption makes ETL difficult to interpret, in spite of ETL's remarkable properties that we describe later. As explained in Chapter 7, unlike normal distributions, stable distributions capture leptokurtic tails ("fat tails"). Unlike normal ETL, stable ETL provides reliable values. Further, when stable distributions are used, ETL is generally substantially different from VaR.

Exhibit 14.10 shows the time series of daily returns for the stock of Oxford Industries (OXM) from January 2000 to December 2001. Observe the occurrences of extreme values.

EXHIBIT 14.10 Returns of Oxford Industries (OXM):
January 2000–December 2001

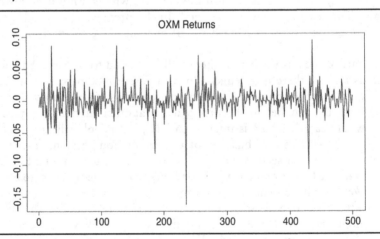

Source: Martin, Rachev, and Siboulet (2003).

---

[31] This section and all of the exhibits are drawn from Martin, Rachev, and Siboulet (2003).
[32] See Jorion (1997).

While this series also displays obvious volatility clustering that deserves to be modeled as described in Chapter 9, we shall ignore this aspect for the moment. Rather, here we provide a compelling example of the difference between ETL and VaR based on a well-fitting stable distribution as compared with a poor fitting normal distribution.

Exhibit 14.11 shows a histogram of the OXM returns with a normal density fitted using the sample mean and sample standard deviation, and a stable density fitted using maximum likelihood estimates of the stable distribution parameters. The stable density function is shown by the solid line and the normal density function is shown by the dashed line. The former is obviously a better fit than the latter when using the histogram of the data values as a reference. The estimated stable tail thickness index is $\hat{\alpha}$. The 99% VaR values for the normal and stable fitted density functions are 0.047 and 0.059, respectively, a ratio of 1.26 which reflects the heavier-tailed nature of the stable fit.

Exhibit 14.12 displays the same histogram and fitted density functions with 99% ETL values instead of the 99% VaR values. The 99% ETL values for the normal and stable fitted density functions are 0.054 and 0.174, respectively, a ratio of a little over three-to-one. This larger ratio is due to the stable density function's heavy tail contribution to ETL relative to the normal density function fit.

Unlike VaR, ETL has a number of attractive properties:

- ETL gives an informed view of losses beyond VaR.
- ETL possesses a number of theoretically appealing properties. When defined on the basis of value or loss distributions it satisfies the complete set of coherent risk measure properties discussed in the appendix to this chapter.[33]
- ETL is a form of expected loss (i.e., a conditional expected loss) and is a very convenient form for use in scenario-based portfolio optimization. It is also quite a natural risk-adjustment to expected return.

The limitations of current normal risk factor models and the absence of regulator blessing have held back the widespread use of ETL, in spite of its highly attractive properties. As Embrechts, Kluppelberg, and Mikosch (1997) note: "Expected Tail Loss gives an indication of extreme losses, should they occur. Although it has not become a standard in the financial industry, expected tail loss is likely to play a major role, as it currently does in the insurance industry."

---

[33] See Artzner, Delbaen, Eber, and Heath (1999).

EXHIBIT 14.11 99% VaR for Normal and Stable Density Functions

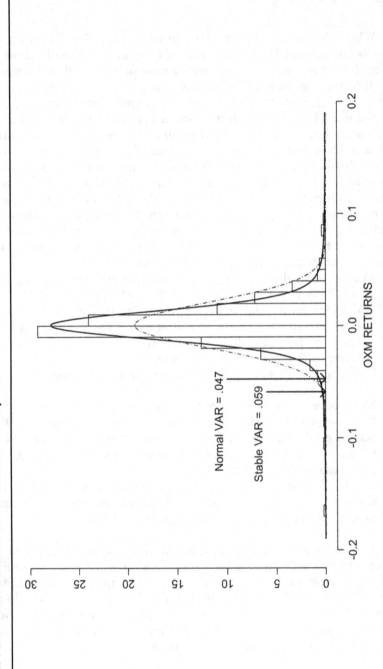

Source: Martin, Rachev, and Siboulet (2003).

EXHIBIT 14.12 99% ETL for Normal and Stable Density Functions

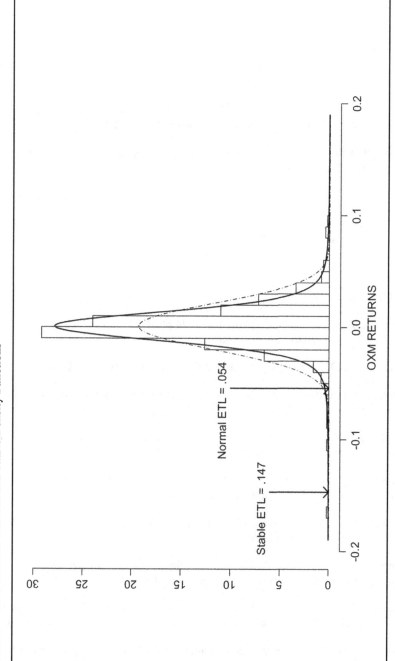

Source: Martin, Rachev, and Siboulet (2003).

REFERENCES

Artzner, P., F. Delbaen, J-M. Eber, and D. Heath. 1999. "Coherent Measures of Risk." *Mathematical Finance* 9: 203–228.

Basak, S., and A. Shapiro. 2001. "Value-at-Risk-Based Risk Management: Optimal Policies and Asset Prices." *Review of Financial Studies* 14: 371–406.

Beder, T. 1995. "VAR: "Seductive But Dangerous." *Financial Analysts Journal*, September/October: 12–24.

Bollerslev, T. 1986. "Generalized Autoregressive Conditional Heteroskedasticity." *Journal of Econometrics* 31: 307–327.

Dave, R. D., and G. Stahl. 1997. "On the Accuracy of VAR Estimates Based on the Variance-Covariance Approach." Working paper.

Derivatives Strategy. 1998. "Roundtable: The Limits of VAR." *Derivatives Strategy*, 3 (4): 14–22.

Derman, E., I. Kani, and N. Chriss. 1996. "Implied Trinomial Trees of the Volatility Smile." *Journal of Derivatives*, Summer: 7–22.

Dowd, K. 2002. *Measuring Market Risk*. Chichester: John Wiley & Sons.

Duffie, J. D., and J. Pan. 1997. "An Overview of Value at Risk." *Journal of Derivatives*, Spring: 7–49.

Embrechts, P., C. Kluppelberg, and T. Mikosch. 1997. *Modelling Extremal Events for Insurance and Finance*. Berlin: Springer.

Engle, R. F. 1982. "Autoregressive Conditional Heteroskedasticity with Estimates of the Variance of U.K. Inflation." *Econometrica* 50: 987–1008.

Fallon, W. 1996. "Calculating Value at Risk." Working paper, 96-49, Wharton Financial Institutions Center Working Paper Series

Fong, G., and O.,A. Vasicek. 1997. "A Multidimensional Framework for Risk Analysis." *Financial Analysts Journal*, July/August: 51–58.

Gamrowski, B., and S. T. Rachev. 1996. "Testing the Validity of Value-at-Risk Measures." In *Applied Probability*, ed. C. C. Heyde, et al. 307–320. Berlin: Springer.

Hendricks, D. 1996. "Evaluation of Value-at-Risk Models Using Historical Data." *Federal Reserve Bank of New York Economic Policy Review* 2 (April): 39–70.

Heron, D., and R. Irving. 1997. "Banks Grasp the VAR Nettle." In *VAR: Understanding and Applying Value-at-Risk*, ed. S. Grayling, 35–39. London: Risk.

Hopper, G. 1996. "Value at Risk: A New Methodology For Measuring Portfolio Risk." *Federal Reserve Bank of Philadelphia Business Review*, July/August: 19–30.

Jackson, P., D. Maude, and W. Perraudin. 1997. "Bank Capital and Value-at-Risk." *Journal of Derivatives* 4 (Spring): 73–90.

Jackwerth, J. C., and M. Rubinstein. 1995. "Implied Probability Distributions: Empirical Analysis." Finance Working paper, 250, Research Program in Finance Working Paper Series, Institute of Business and Economic Research, University of California at Berkeley.

Jackwerth, J. C., and M. Rubinstein. 1996. "Recovering Probability Distributions from Option Prices." *Journal of Finance* 51 (5): 1611–1631.

Jorion, P. 1996a. *Value at Risk: The New Benchmark for Controlling Market Risk.* Chicago: Irwin Professional.

Jorion, P. 1996b. "Risk2: Measuring the Risk in Value At Risk." *Financial Analysts Journal* 52 (November/December): 47–56.

Jorion, P. 1997. "In Defense of VAR." *Derivatives Strategy* 2 (April): 20–23.

JPMorgan. 1995. *RiskMetrics, Third Edition.* New York: JPMorgan.

Khindanova, I., and S. T. Rachev. 2000. "Value at Risk: Recent Advances." In *Handbook of Analytic-Computational Methods in Applied Mathematics*, ed. George Anastassiou, 801–858. Boca Raton, FL: CRC Press.

Khindanova, I., S. T. Rachev, and E. Schwartz. 2001. "Stable Modeling of Value at Risk." *Mathematical and Computer Modelling* (Special Issue on Stable Non-Gaussian Models in Finance and Econometrics) 34: 1223-1259.

Kupiec, P. 1995. "Techniques for Verifying the Accuracy of Risk Measurement Models." *Journal of Derivatives* 3 (Winter): 73–84.

Linsmeier, T., and N. Pearson. 1996. "Risk Measurement: An Introduction to Value at Risk." Department of Accountancy and Department of Finance, University of Illinois at Urbana-Champaign.

Liu, R. 1996. "VAR and VAR Derivatives." *Capital Market Strategies* 5 (September): 23–33.

Mahoney, J. 1996. "Empirical-Based Versus Model-Based Approaches to Value-at-Risk: An Examination of Foreign Exchange and Global Equity Portfolios." *Risk Measurement and Systemic Risk*, Proceedings of a Joint Central Bank Research Conference, Board of Governors of the Federal Reserve System, Washington DC: 199–217.

Marshall, C., and M. Siegel. 1997. "Value at Risk: Implementing A Risk Management Standard." *Journal of Derivatives* 4 (Spring): 91–110.

Martin, D., S. T. Rachev, and F. Siboulet. 2003. "Phi-Alpha Optimal Portfolios and Extreme Risk Management." *Wilmott Magazine of Finance*, November: 70–83.

Phelan, M. J. 1995. "Probability and Statistics Applied to the Practice of Financial Risk Management: The Case of JP Morgan's RiskMetrics." Working paper, 95–19, Wharton Financial Institutions Center Working Paper Series.

Pritsker, M. 1996. "Evaluating Value at Risk Methodologies: Accuracy versus Computational Time." Working paper, 96-48, Wharton Financial Institutions Center Working Paper Series.

Rockafellar, R. T., and S. Uryasev. 2000. "Optimization of Conditional Value-at-Risk, *Journal of Risk* 3: 21–41.

Rubinstein, M. 1994. "Implied Binomial Trees." *Journal of Finance* 69: 771–818.

Shaw, J. 1997. "Beyond VAR and Stress Testing." In *VAR: Understanding and Applying Value-at-Risk*, ed. S. Grayling, 211–223. London: Risk.

Shimko, D. 1997a. "VAR for Corporates." In *VAR: Understanding and Applying Value-at-Risk*, ed. S. Grayling, 345–347. London: Risk.

Shimko, D. 1997b. "Investors' Return on VAR." In S. Grayling (Ed.), *VAR: Understanding and Applying Value-at-Risk*, London: Risk: 349.

Simons, K. 1996. "Value at Risk—New Approaches to Risk Management." *Federal Reserve Bank of Boston New England Economic Review*, September/October: 3–13.

Yamai, Y., and T. Yoshiba. 2002. "Comparative Analyses of Expected Shortfall and Value-at-Risk (3): Their Validity under Market Stress." *Monetary and Economic Studies*, October: 181–237.

APPENDIX: COHERENT RISK MEASURES

Before Artzer, Delbaen, Eber, and Heath (1999) published their seminal paper on coherent risk measures, it was common to evaluate risk measures on an intuitive level. The ideas of Artzner et al. provided theoretically based criteria to distinguish between "good" and "bad" risk measures. They identify a minimal set of properties which very sensible risk measure should satisfy.

What is important to realize and what distinguishes the ideas of Artzner et al. from the discussion presented in Chapters 12 and 13 and the body of Chapter 14 is that they define risk or loss measures for the future outcome of investments rather than for returns. Artzner et al. model the random future wealth or in other words the random future value of a portfolio by a random variable over a probability space with a finite state space. Moreover, to the risky investments, they assume the existence of a reference (risk-free) investment instrument whose price today equals one and which pays back at the end of the period the amount r.

According to Artzner et al., a risk measure ρ is a function from the set of random variables representing the future portfolio values into the real numbers, assigning to the random future portfolio value X the risk $\rho(X)$. They provide reasons why they think that risk should be assigned to the random future value of a portfolio rather than to its return. Their reasoning is strongly inspired by the goal to connect the notions of capital charge, acceptable investment and risk: How much of riskless funds do I have to add to my risky position to turn it into an acceptable investment? This is exactly the concern of regulators who require capital charges to insure against losses in the risky investments or the idea of a margin account where an investor deposits collateral for the same reasons. These motivations are, however, distinct from the goals of portfolio optimization where the risk must depend on the relationship between the amount of invested funds and the distribution of the potential outcome—hence the return.

In this appendix, we introduce four properties—positive homogeneity, monotonicity, subadditivity, and translation invariance—that are the necessary and sufficient properties for a risk measure of future wealth to be qualified as coherent. These properties can be seen as essential for a risk measure on future wealth to make sense. Due to the differences between risk measures for returns and risk measures for wealth, there is however no reason why these properties should or should not be fulfilled by risk measures for returns as well.

Positive Homogeneity

A risk measure is said to be *positive homogeneous* if for all positive λ it satisfies the relation

$$\rho(\lambda X) = \lambda \rho(X)$$

The intuition behind this definition is quite simple: If an investor doubles the invested amount in every position of his portfolio, then he doubles his risk. More generally, if an investor multiplies every position in his portfolio by λ, then the risk he is facing is rescaled by λ, too. Obviously, it makes sense to require this property for every sensible risk measure.

Monotonicity

Another intuitive property which every risk measure should fulfill is *monotonicity*. If outcome X dominates outcome Y in every possible state, then the risk associated with outcome Y must be at least as large as the one associated with X. Formally, we have

For every pair of investments with future outcome X, Y, with $X \geq Y$, we have $\rho(X) \leq \rho(Y)$.

Subadditivity

A very important property of risk measures which incorporates the common thinking that diversification decreases risk is given by the subadditivity property. A risk measure ρ is called *subadditive* if the risk of a combination of investments is at most as large as the sum of the individual risks. Formally, we have

For every pair of investments with future outcome X, Y we have: $\rho(X_1 + X_2) \leq \rho(X_1) + \rho(X_2)$.

If the risk measure does not fulfill this basic property, then it could be optimal for a bank, for example, to split into two subsidiaries to reduce the amount of capital charge required by regulators. An example of a popular risk measure which *fails* to be subadditive is the Value at Risk measure.

Translation Invariance

The last property of risk measures we will discuss is called *translation invariance*. A risk measure $\rho(X)$ is called *translation invariant* if for all real t it satisfies the condition

$$\rho(X + \alpha r) = \rho(X) - \alpha$$

This axiom is inspired by the idea that the risk of the total position can be reduced by investing a certain additional amount in the risk-free asset. This idea is reflected in regulatory requirements such as minimum capital charge for credit or operational risks faced by the banking industry. As for a translation invariant risk measure, the equation $\rho(X + \rho(X)r) = 0$ holds always true, we can see that the risk can be reduced to zero by putting as much money into the risk-free asset as our risky position admits risk. The axiom of translation invariance has evoked a discussion as one could argue exactly in the opposite direction: Just adding a safe amount of money to a position does not change the riskiness of the position. This idea has been examined by Gaivronsky and Pflug (2001), leading to the definition of the so-called *Gaivoronsky-Pflug* (G-P) *translation invariance,* which is that the risk measure ρ satisfies, for all real t, the equation

$$\rho(X + t) = \rho(X)$$

CHAPTER 15

Credit Risk

In this chapter, we look at credit risk. We provide an overview of the credit risk framework for banks as set forth in Basel II, credit risk models, and credit risk tools. At the end of this chapter, we present a framework for integrating market and credit risk management based on two approaches for modeling credit risk. The framework provides a full picture of portfolio credit risks incorporating extreme loss dependencies.

CREDIT RISK

Credit risk includes three types of risk: default risk, credit spread risk, and downgrade risk.

Default risk is the risk that the issuer of a debt instrument or the counterparty in a borrowing arrangement will fail to satisfy the terms of the obligation with respect to the timely payment of interest and repayment of the amount borrowed. For long-term debt obligations, a credit rating is a forward-looking assessment of the probability of default and the relative magnitude of the loss should a default occur. For short-term debt obligations, a credit rating is a forward-looking assessment of the probability of default. The three major rating agencies are Moody's Investors Service, Standard & Poor's Corporation, and FitchRatings. To gauge default risk, investors rely on analysis performed by nationally recognized statistical rating organizations that perform credit analysis of issues and issuers and express their conclusions in the form of a credit rating. *Credit spread risk* is the loss or underperformance of an issue or issues due to an increase in the credit spread demanded by the market. *Downgrade risk* is the risk that an issue or issuer will be downgraded, resulting in an increase in the credit spread and, therefore, in a reduced value for the issuer's bonds.

CREDIT RISK FRAMEWORK FOR BANKS: BASEL I AND BASEL II

The 1988 Basel Accord requires internationally active banks to hold capital equal to at least 8% of a basket of assets measured in different ways according to their riskiness. The Basel Accord created capital requirements for credit risk. A portfolio approach was taken to measure the risk, with assets classified into the following four *risk buckets* according to the debtor category:

1. *0% risk weight* Generally consisting of claims on Organisation for Economic Coordination and Development (OECD) governments.
2. *20% risk weight* Generally consisting of claims on banks incorporated in OECD countries.
3. *50% risk weight* Generally consisting of residential mortgage claims.
4. *100% risk weight* Generally consisting of claims on consumers and corporates.

These risk weights multiplied by the respective exposure result in the so-called *risk-weighted assets* (RWA).

There is also a scale of charges for off-balance sheet exposures through guarantees, swaps, and so on. This requires a two-step approach. First a bank converts its off-balance-sheet positions into a credit equivalent amount through a scale of *credit conversion factors* (CCF) Then these positions are weighted according to the counterparty's risk weight. There have been several supplements to the 1988 Accord. A good number of the supplements dealt with the treatment of off-balance-sheet activities.

While the two principal purposes of the 1988 Accord have been achieved—providing an adequate level of capital in the international banking system and creating a more level playing field in competitive terms so that banks could no longer build business volume without adequate capital backing—there have been some unfavorable consequences. The capital requirement under the 1988 Accord was in conflict with the increased level of sophistication of internal measures of economic capital determined by banks. This resulted in banks moving assets off balance sheet using transactions such as securitization. Doing so has decreased the average quality of bank loans retained on a bank's loan portfolio. Moreover, the 1988 Accord did not give sufficient recognition to reduction of credit risk by standard credit risk mitigation techniques (e.g., taking collateral, taking appropriate positions in credit derivatives, obtaining guarantees, taking an offsetting position subject to a netting agreement). For these reasons, the Basel Committee for Bank Supervision began working on a more risk-sensitive framework.

In June 1999, the initial consultative proposal contained three fundamental innovations, each designed to introduce greater risk sensitivity. First, a more balanced approach to the capital assessment process was suggested. Second, banks with advanced risk management capabilities should be permitted to use their own internal systems for evaluating credit risk (known as "internal ratings") instead of standardized risk weights for each class of asset (the four risk buckets cited earlier). Finally, banks should be allowed to use gradings provided by approved external credit assessment institutions to classify their sovereign claims into five risk buckets and their claims on corporates and banks into three risk buckets. In comments to the June 1999 consultative proposal many details of the proposal were criticized. In particular, there was concern that the threshold for the use of internal ratings would be set so high as to prevent well-managed banks from employing them.

In June 2004, the Basel Committee on Bank Supervision issued *International Convergence of Capital Measurement and Capital Standards: A Revised Framework*, referred to as Basel II. In this framework, banks are permitted to select between the two broad methodologies for calculating their capital requirements for credit risk proposed in the June 1999 consultative proposal: standardized approach and *internal ratings-based* (IRB) approach. In determining the risk weights in the standardized approach, banks may use assessments by external credit assessment institutions recognized as eligible for capital purposes by regulators of banks. The use of the IRB approach allows a bank to use its internal rating systems for credit risk but its adoption is subject to the explicit approval of the bank's regulator.

When employing the IRB approach, the bank may rely on its own internal estimates of the components of credit risk for a given exposure. The risk components include (1) measures of the probability of default, (2) loss given default, (3) the exposure at default, and (4) effective maturity.[1] Under the IRB approach, banks categorize their banking-book exposures into broad classes of assets with different underlying risk characteristics. The classes of assets are (1) corporate, (2) sovereign, (3) bank, (4) retail, and (5) equity. Within each class, there are subclasses. It was felt that classification of exposures in this manner is generally consistent with established bank practice. A bank may employ different definitions in their internal risk management and measurement systems. However, a bank seeking to do so must demonstrate to regulators that

---

[1] Basel II specifies that there may be cases where banks may be required to use a supervisory specified value rather than an internal estimate for one or more of the risk components.

the methodology for assigning exposures to different classes is appropriate and consistent over time.

OVERVIEW OF CREDIT RISK MODELING

In this section, we provide a brief overview of credit risk models. There are several excellent surveys in the literature that provide an in depth mathematical treatment of the subject.[2] The discussion in this section draws from the framework in these surveys, particularly D'Souza and Racheva-Iotova (2003).

Credit risk models seek to provide answers to questions involving the measurement of credit risk and the pricing of defaultable assets. In measuring credit risk, models seek to provide an estimate of the probability an obligor or group of obligors will default and, if a default occurs, provide an estimate of the magnitude of expected losses. For a portfolio of defaultable assets, a related output of credit risk models is an estimate of the credit quality correlation among the obligors. To obtain these estimates, conditions governing default events and recovery are assumed by the model builder. These models must be consistent with financial theory, the laws governing bankruptcy, and observed credit spreads in the marketplace.

In addressing the second question, pricing of a defaultable asset, credit risk models seek to estimate credit risky cash flows obtained by modeling default probabilities and expected losses. The output of these models can be used to assess how investors are being compensated for accepting credit risk.

The two questions addressed by credit risk models are obviously linked. The management of credit risk requires the estimation of credit risk exposure and the valuation of the defaultable assets under alternative credit risk scenarios.

The two main approaches to credit risk modeling for estimating default probabilities and expected losses are *structural models* and *reduced-form models*. Funding for a firm is obtained from two sources: equity and debt. A firm's value is equal to the present value of the expected cash flows that will be generated by its assets. Because debt holders and equity holders have claims to these cash flows, the value of debt and equity at any time is then contingent on the firm's asset value.

---

[2] See Rodgers (1999), Cossing (1977), Cossin and Pirotte (2001), Anson, Fabozzi, Choudhry, and Chen (2004), Wilson (1997a, 1997b), and D'Souza and Racheva-Iotova (2003).

As explained below, structural models explicitly refer to a firm's asset value while reduced-form models implicitly refer to them.

Both approaches have been employed in credit risk analysis but both have their shortcomings. Structural models have not been successful in capturing credit spreads observed in the market. Specifically, while structural models predict that corporate credit spreads decrease to zero as the maturity decreases, even in the short term one cannot rule out the possibility that a firm's value can face a catastrophic loss. A limitation of reduced-form models is that they can have difficulties with being able to model dependency between defaults of different firms.

Structural Models

The basic idea, common to all structural-type models, is that a company defaults on its debt if the value of the assets of the company falls below a certain default point. The structural approach has its foundation in the pioneering work of option-pricing theory developed by Black and Scholes (1973) and Merton (1973). Shortly after, Merton (1974) recognized that option pricing theory could be carried over to the pricing of defaultable claims by demonstrating that the credit holder position can be interpreted as a portfolio of risk-free bonds and a put option on firm's assets.

In the structural approach, defaultable obligations and their dynamics depend upon the evolution of the firm's asset value which is used also to infer the probability that the issuer of the debt obligation will default. Typically, the evolution of the firm's value is described mathematically by a diffusion process.[3] A default event is the first time the firm's value reaches some exogenous prespecified barrier or boundary.

There are two types of structural models to value defaultable obligations: firm value models and first passage time models. *Firm value models* price defaultable obligations using option pricing theory by characterizing the firm's asset value process at a given fixed time in the future, the maturity of the defaultable obligation. *First passage time models* characterize the first time the firm's value process hits an exogenously defined boundary.

Firm Value Models

Merton (1974) extended the Black and Scholes (1973) model to value corporate bonds derived from modeling the value of a firm's assets relative to its liabilities in a contingent claim analytic framework. Equivalently, the bond holders and equity holders are entitled to the value

---

[3] Diffusions are a special subclass of stochastic processes in continuous time. One characteristic property among others is that diffusions possess continuous paths. An example of a diffusion is geometric Brownian motion discussed in Chapter 10.

generated by the firm's assets with the former claim holders legally entitled to ownership of a firm's assets if the firm fails to make required payments (interest and principal repayment) to them.

Merton's model provides an analytical framework derived directly
from the fundamentals of a firm, its asset value process. While this
model is economically intuitive with respect to the condition under
which default happens (i.e., when a firm has insufficient value to cover
its debt obligation), the oversimplified and restrictive assumptions make
it difficult to apply in practice. These assumptions include:

- A constant risk-free rate.
- Default can only occur at maturity of the discount bond.
- There is only one class of debt in the firm's capital structure.

An implication of the last assumption is when a company is liqui-
dated, creditors receive distributions based on the "absolute priority
rule" to the extent assets are available. The absolute priority rule is the
principle that senior creditors are paid in full before junior creditors are
paid anything. For secured creditors and unsecured creditors, the absolute priority rule guarantees their seniority to equityholders.

In the real world, (1) risk-free rates are stochastic, (2) a firm's value
can result in a default long before the maturity of debt, resulting in pre-
maturity default, and (3) there are many classes of debt in a firm's capital structure. Moreover, empirical evidence indicates that observed
corporate bond credit spreads are much higher than can be explained by
the Merton model for short maturity bonds.[4]

With respect to absolute priority, in liquidations the rule generally
holds. In contrast, there is a good body of literature that argues that
strict absolute priority has *not* been upheld by the courts or the U.S.
Securities and Exchange Commission.[5] Studies of actual reorganizations
under Chapter 11 have found that the violation of absolute priority is
the rule rather the exception.[6] Failure of the courts to follow strict absolute priority has implications for the capital structure decision (that is,
choice between debt and equity) of a firm. The view by financial economists that the firm is effectively owned by the creditors who have sold
the stockholders a call option on the firm's assets is not sustainable if
the stockholders are not viewed as residual claimants.

---

[4] See the results reported in Jones, Mason, and Rosenfeld (1984).
[5] See, for example, Meckling (1977), Miller (1977), Warner (1977), and Jackson
(1986).
[6] See, for example, Franks and Torous (1989), Weiss (1990), and Fabozzi, Howe,
Makabe, and Sudo (1993).

There have been extensions to Merton's model to incorporate the following modifications:

- The possibility of defaults prior to maturity
- Stochastic riskless interest rates
- Deviations from the absolute priority rule
- Application to modeling coupon bonds including bonds with callability and convertibility features

First Passage Time Models

In first passage time models, default can occur prior to a bond's maturity if the value of the firm's assets reaches a prespecified and typically time-dependent barrier. The first of these models was developed by Black and Cox (1976). For a deterministic time-dependent boundary, the recovery rate is a deterministic function of time. Alternatively, recovery can be exogenous and independent of firm value.

The impact of safety covenants, subordination arrangements, and restrictions on financing of interest and dividend payments in bond indentures on defaultable bond prices is examined by Black and Cox.

Stochastic Interest Rates Longstaff and Schwartz (1995) extend the Black and Cox model permitting stochastic interest rates. In their model (1) the riskless rate is correlated with the dynamics of the firm's value; (2) the boundary for default is constant; (3) the recovery rate is exogenous; and (4) the recovery rate is different for different classes of debt (recovery rates are higher for senior versus junior debt). Because the recovery rate in their model is exogenous, deviations from absolute priority rules are permitted. Of particular interest is that Longstaff and Schwartz find that variations in credit spreads across industries and sectors seem to be linked to correlations between equity returns and changes in the riskless interest rate. Their finding that investment-grade bond credit spreads and changes in firm value are affected by changes in the interest rates is evidence of the dependence between market and credit risk. Consequently, as explained later in this chapter, in valuing corporate bonds it is important to model the dependence between market and credit risk.

Kim, Ramaswamy, and Sundaresan (1993) modify the Black and Cox model by incorporating stochastic interest rates. The default boundary in their model is constant and depends on the level of coupon payments to the bondholders. If that boundary is not reached during the bond's lifetime, bondholders receive the minimum of the value of the firm and the face value of the bond. If the boundary is reached, the firm defaults and bondholders receive the minimum of the value of the firm and the write down of a default-free bond. In the Kim-Ramaswamy-Sundaresan model, stochastic interest rates produce credit spreads that increase compared to deterministic models for interest rates. Because the recovery rate is constant at default, the model proposed by Kim, Ramaswamy, and Sundaresan differs from the model proposed by Longstaff and Schwartz.

Nielsen et al. (1993) extend first passage time models further by assuming both a stochastic default barrier and stochastic interest rates. They assume recovery is a constant fraction of an equivalent default-free bond.

Briys and de Varenne (1997) suggest a default threshold and recovery rate where the firm cannot pay out more than its assets are worth. This payout restriction is not assured in the models proposed by Longstaff and Schwartz and Nielsen et al. In the Briys and de Varenne model, different recovery rates for a firm that defaults prior to or at maturity are assumed.

Jump-Diffusion Models   Mason and Bhattacharya (1981) extend the first passage time model of Black and Cox by incorporating an additional jump process. Because the firm value process is a continuous diffusion process in the Black and Cox model, the time of default is not deterministic. Incorporating a jump process for the firm's value randomizes the default time.

Zhou (1997) generalizes the jump-diffusion model of Mason and Bhattacharya, providing a framework that incorporates both market and credit risk for corporate bond valuation. His model can explain some of the empirical regularities observed in default probabilities, recovery rates, and credit spreads that are not captured by the other traditional diffusion-type models.

Schonbucher (1996) also attempts to deal with the low credit spreads generated from traditional diffusion-type models by introducing a jump-diffusion model for the firm's value process.

Some Final Thoughts on Structural Models

Structural models have many advantages. First, they model default on the very reasonable assumption that it is a result of the value of the firm's assets falling below the value of its debt. The outputs of the model show how the credit risk of a corporate debt is a function of the leverage and the asset volatility of the issuer. The term structure of spreads also appear realistic and empirical evidence argues for and against their shape. However, structural models are difficult to calibrate and so are not suitable for the frequent marking to market of credit contingent securities. An estimation of the model parameters, based on historical observations, is problematic as the asset value process is not directly observable. Structural models are also computationally burdensome. For instance, the pricing of a defaultable zero-coupon bond is as difficult as pricing an option. Just adding coupons transforms the problem into the equivalent of pricing a compound option. Pricing any subordinated debt requires the simultaneous valuation of all of the more senior debt. Consequently, structural models are not used where there is a need for rapid and accurate pricing of many credit-related securities.

Instead, the main application of structural models is in the areas of credit risk analysis and corporate structure analysis. A structural model is more likely to be able to predict the credit quality of a corporate security than a reduced form model. It is therefore a useful tool in the analysis of counterparty risk for banks when establishing credit lines with companies and a useful tool in the risk analysis of portfolios of securities. Corporate analysts might also use structural models as a tool for analyzing the best way to structure the debt and equity of a company.

Reduced-Form Models

In *reduced-form models*, also referred to as *intensity-based models* or *stochastic default rate models*, there is no explicit relationship between the default event and the firm's value process. That is, in contrast to structural models where the default process and recovery rates should a bankruptcy occur depend on the corporation's structural characteristics, reduced-form models do not look "inside the firm," but instead model directly the probability of default or downgrade. The default process and the recovery process are (1) modeled independently of the corporation's structural features and (2) are independent of each other. In reduced-form models, corporate bond valuation can be done without estimating the firm's asset value process. This is the principal advantage of reduced-form models over structural models.

Default is treated as an unpredictable exogenous event that is modeled by a hazard rate function. As explained in Chapter 3, the hazard rate is simply the conditional probability of default per unit time given that the company has not previously defaulted. The hazard rate function can be deterministic or stochastic. In the latter case, it depends on some exogenously specified state variables. In reduced-form models, the time of default is the first time the process jumps. When the hazard rate is stochastic, the jump arrival time becomes a totally inaccessible stopping time.

Differences in the reduced-form models proposed in the literature are due to when and how recovery is modeled. The key elements in these models are the (1) default-free interest rate, (2) default-time, and (3) recovery rate process. Those who have proposed reduced-form models have been able to obtain closed-form solutions under very restrictive assumptions about the dynamics of these processes.[7]

In many reduced-form models, default is modeled with stochastic hazard rate processes that depend upon state variables. For example, the default process can be correlated with the default-free interest rate processes. In Lando (1994), the default process is modeled with a Cox process.[8] Duffie and Singleton (1999) consider a defaultable claim that pays a random amount, an intuitive representation for the value of this claim when the recovery of the claim in the event of default is some fraction of the claim just prior to default.

In the literature, there are three main recovery models. They are referred to as the *recovery of market value, recovery of face value and accrued interest,* and the *recovery of Treasury value.*[9] Any recovery model must recognize the trade-off between analytic tractability and practical applicability because of the difficulty of accurately modeling the bankruptcy recovery process.

As noted earlier, the principal advantage of reduced-form models is that they do not require the estimation of unobservable firm value in order to value defaultable obligations. The predictions regarding corporate credit spreads from reduced-form models are consistent with observed credit spreads. This is in stark contrast to structural models which predict that a firm has constant value upon default, a finding that is not consistent with what is observed empirically in the corporate bond market. Actual credit spreads on corporate bonds are too high to be matched by the credit spreads implied by structural models.[10] That is, structural models do not allow for the variation in the recovery rate to depend on the remaining value of the firm at default. To address these problems, the jump diffusion model was developed, thereby facilitating the flexibility of fitting credit spreads.

---

[7] In the academic literature, papers by Artzner and Delbaen (1992, 1994), Jarrow and Turnbull (1995), Lando (1994, 1998), Jarrow, Lando, and Turnbull (1997), Madan and Unal (1998), Flesaker et al. (1994), Duffie and Singleton (1997 and 1999), Duffie, Schröder, and Skiadas (1996), Duffie and Huang (1996), and Duffie (1994), among others, represent the reduced-form approach.

[8] As explained in Chapter 10, a Cox process (or doubly stochastic Poisson process) is a generalization of an inhomogeneous Poisson process, where the intensity is modeled by its own stochastic process.

[9] Duffie and Singleton (1999) discuss the relative merits of each recovery specification.

[10] See Jones, Mason, and Rosenfeld (1984). Fons (1994) and Sarig and Warga (1989) found that yield spreads for certain types of bonds are flat or even downward sloping, findings that are inconsistent with what structural models predict.

One of the shortcomings of reduced-form models is that the hazard rate function does not explain the economic reasoning behind default. Instead, it treats default as an exogenous event. In the future, reduced-form models will need to incorporate factors driving defaults into the specification for the intensity rate and loss rate.

CREDIT RISK MANAGEMENT TOOLS

There are three important variables when considering credit risk from a portfolio perspective: (1) the probability of default for each obligor, (2) the loss given default, and (3) the default correlations (i.e., the degree to which the default rates of obligors are related). Banks and software vendors have designed risk management systems taking these variables into consideration. The output of these systems provide a measure of credit risk, the valued of defaultable obligations, and, in the case of regulated entities, the amount of the capital charges for credit risk.

Fostered by the Basel Committee on Bank Supervision, the measure of credit risk estimated by these models is Value-at-Risk (VaR), referred to as *credit VaR*. This measure is similar to VaR for market risk described in the previous chapter and seeks to capture "specific risk" that includes concentration risk, downgrade risk, and credit spread risk.

The major industry-sponsored analytic tools for credit risk management are CreditMetrics, KMV, CreditRisk⁺, and CreditPortfolioView. There are several review articles in the literature that explain the attributes of these systems. Hence, we will not review them here in any detail.[11] We also describe another credit risk management system, Cognity. In the last section of this chapter, we illustrate this system in more detail because it integrates credit risk and market risk and allows for return distributions that follow a stable distribution.

CreditMetrics

CreditMetrics was developed by JPMorgan to evaluate portfolios of defaultable obligations. This analytical methodology has as its foundation a transition rating system developed either internally or as given by a major rating agency. Portfolio value changes over a given risk horizon due exclusively to credit risk result from credit migrations of the underlying obligors. A recovery rate or loss given default is taken from historical averages depending on seniority in order to compute a bond's residual value in the event of default. The objective of the approach is to

---

[11] See, for example, Crouhy, Galai, and Mark (2000) and D'Souza and Racheva-Jotova (2003).

estimate the loss distribution for the portfolio value outcomes and to compute the credit VaR of the entire portfolio, recognizing diversification benefits from adding credit assets that have less than perfect default correlation among each other. The system's theoretical foundation is the Merton model. A firm's asset returns determine the credit rating for its debt obligations; dependence between credit rating movements of obligors is explained by correlated firm asset return processes, which is proxied by the correlation between firms' equity returns.

CreditMetrics is useful because the transition matrices are readily available information and it recognizes portfolio diversification benefits derived from portfolio choice theory. A drawback with the methodology is the assumption that interest rates are fixed. Making credit events the only source of risk by not taking into account market risk is contrary to empirical evidence.

KMV

In the KMV methodology, information contained in equity prices and balance sheets of firms is used to extract the probability of default of individual obligors.[12] Applying the option pricing theory framework to the valuation of defaultable obligations developed by Merton (1974), KMV derives a probability of default called the *Expected Default Frequency* (EDF) as an alternative to a transition probability matrix. EDF depends on the (1) firm's capital structure, (2) current asset value, and (3) volatility of the asset's return process. The EDF is firm-specific, factoring in a transition probability to other credit classes, and with each EDF having an associated spread curve and an implied rating as defined by the major rating agencies. Instead of being aggregated into rating classes, firms are categorized in the KMV methodology using a "distance-to-default index" measure.

There are three steps involved in computing a firm's EDF in the KVM methodology. First, the market value and volatility of a firm's assets need to be estimated. Second, using option pricing theory applied to the valuation of defaultable obligations, the distance-to-default index measure is computed. Finally, the distance-to-default index measure is combined with a large dataset of actual default rates to compute the probability of default.

There are a number of advantages of the KMV methodology. By utilizing the market value of equity to determine implied asset value and volatility, the default probabilities that are generated contain market information. The distance-to-default index measure that is used to esti-

---

[12] KMV is a risk management software company focusing on credit risk management. It was acquired by Moody's and has merged with Moody's Risk Management Services subsidiary.

mate the EDFs based on historical data on migration and default rates is independent of the distributional assumptions on the firm's asset value process. The chief disadvantage of the KMV methodology is that a firm's value and the expected rate of return and volatility are required as inputs and these inputs are not directly observable. In addition, the riskless rates are assumed to be deterministic.

CreditRisk⁺

CreditRisk⁺, a methodology developed by Credit Suisse Financial Products,[13] applies actuarial science mathematics used in the insurance industry. The approach involves estimating a distribution of credit losses on a portfolio due solely to default. Thus, credit losses due to credit rating changes are not considered. Moreover, a firm's capital structure is not considered and no assumption is made about the causes of default.

There are two advantages of this methodology relative to Credit-Metrics and KMV. First, the methodology permits stochastic interest rates. Second, the methodology provides closed-form expressions for the probability distribution of portfolio credit losses. A limitation of the methodology is that it only considers the possibility of default, ignoring the causes of default. By treating the default process as exogenous, the methodology is similar to the reduced-form modeling approach. As with the other methodologies described above, CreditRisk⁺ assumes no market risk because the term structure of interest rates is nonstochastic. Consequently, no recognition is given as to how changes in interest rates can affect credit exposures over time.

CreditPortfolioView

CreditPortfolioView, a credit risk management system developed by McKinsey, takes into consideration the influence that the state of the economy has on both defaults and migration probabilities. The methodology is a multiperiod and multifactor econometric model that simulates joint conditional distributions of default and migration probabilities for different ratings of firms (classified according to industry and country), conditional on the state of the economy. Macroeconomic variables are used as proxies for the state of the economy and they include growth in gross disposable product, unemployment rate, levels of long-term interest rates, aggregate savings, government expenditures, and foreign exchange rates. The CreditPortfolioView methodology is consistent with the empirical observation that default and migration probabilities vary over time.

---

[13] See Credit Suisse Financial Products, "Credit Risk Management Framework" (October 1997).

Cognity

Developed by Bravo Risk Management Group and now distributed by FinAnalytica, Cognity is a portfolio risk management system that integrates market risk and credit risk. Cognity is based on stable Paretian distributions in order to capture the empirical anomalies observed in credit assets' return distributions discussed in Chapter 11.

Typically, credit returns have distributions that are characterized by skewed returns with heavy downside tails. The heavy-tailed nature of credit returns implies that there is a greater probability for large outlier events to occur than thin-tailed distributions. Defaultable obligations typically have returns that are left skewed. The reason that these returns are left skewed is because the probability of a defaultable obligation realizing substantial price appreciation is relatively small. (The maximum price is the undiscounted value of the coupon payments plus principal.) However, there is a large probability of receiving a small profit through interest payments. The distribution tends to be skewed around a positive value with a very small positive tail reflecting the limited upside potential. Adverse movements in credit quality occur with a small probability, but can have a significant negative impact on the value of the asset. These credit quality migrations have the ability to generate significant losses thus producing skewed distributions with large downside tails. Additionally, these skewed returns with heavy downside tails are characteristic of portfolios of defaultable obligations as well.

For these reasons, the Cognity system is based on the stable Paretian distribution rather than the normal distribution to facilitate simulation techniques that permit users to assess market and credit risk exposure that account for extreme market moves. In the credit risk literature, Brownian motion is assumed to drive a defaultable obligations's return process (see Chapter 10). The discrete time counterpart of Brownian motion is a random walk with Gaussian innovations. However, empirical evidence suggests the distribution of asset returns are non-Gaussian. As discussed in other chapters, many financial asset return processes exhibit heavy tails, skewness, stochastic volatility, and volatility clustering and we have discussed the advantages of using stable distributions in such cases.

The Cognity system is modular with market risk, credit risk, and portfolio optimization modules. Like RiskMetrics, the market risk module provide for computations of Monte Carlo VaR but extended to allow for stable distributions and thus stable Monte Carlo VaR. The market risk system also provides standalone and marginal VaR, conditional VaR estimation, what-if analysis, stress testing, and scenario analysis of changes in market rate/prices, volatilities, correlations and yield curve movements. The credit risk module integrates market risk with credit risk to compute credit VaR, marginal credit VaR, and expected returns and standard deviation of returns.

Cognity uses two main models for credit risk analysis of portfolios containing defaultable obligations. The Asset Value Model is similar to CreditMetrics and the Default Rate Model has similar characteristics of McKinsey's CreditPortfolioView. The choice of model depends on the nature of the portfolio including the availability of data.

AN INTEGRATED MARKET AND CREDIT RISK MANAGEMENT FRAMEWORK BASED ON THE STRUCTURAL APPROACH[14]

In this section, we will explain how to integrate credit risk and market risk. We use the Cognity framework in our illustration.

Most structural models do not admit analytical solutions for the value of the bond and/or the default probability. In these cases, it is common to employ Monte Carlo simulation. The four key steps in the Monte Carlo approach are:

Step 1. Modeling dependence structure: The dependence structure between market risk factors and the credit risk drivers must be modeled.

Step 2. Scenario generation: Each scenario in the Monte Carlo simulation corresponds to a possible "state of the world" at the end of the risk horizon. For our purposes, the "state of the world" is just the credit rating of each of the obligors in the portfolio and the corresponding values of the market risk factors affecting the portfolio.

Step 3. Portfolio valuation: For each scenario, the portfolio should be evaluated to reflect the new credit ratings and the values of the market risk factors. This step offers a large number of possible future portfolio values.

Step 4. Summarize results: From the scenarios generated in the previous steps, an estimate for the distribution of the portfolio value can be obtained. Any number of descriptive statistics for this distribution can be reported.

The general methodology described above is valid for every Monte Carlo approach for structural models. Exhibit 15.1 summarizes the calculation process by showing the data required for each step. The shaded

---

[14] This chapter and the sections that follow draw largely from Racheva-Iotova, Stoyanov, and Rachev (2003) and Cognity (2003).

EXHIBIT 15.1   Summary of the Calculation Process and Data Required for Each Step of the Monte Carlo Simulation for a Structural Model with the Key Components of the Model Shaded

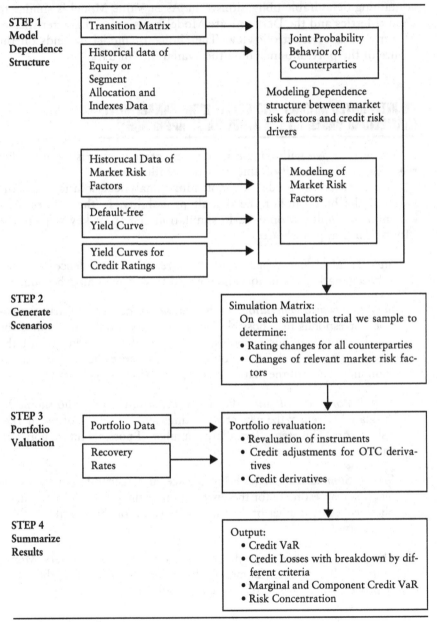

Adapted from Racheva-Iotova, Stoyanov, and Rachev (2003) and Cognity (2003).

boxes in the exhibit identify the key components of the model. In the rest of this section, we describe the key steps outlined above. It is important to emphasize that the following two approaches for integrated risk management describe a way one could proceed and not the way one must proceed.

Step 1. Model Dependence Structure

The general assumption of the model is that the driver of credit events is the asset value of a company. This means one should be able to model the dependence structure between asset values of the counterparties.

As in CreditMetrics, at this point we assume that the dependence structure between asset values of two firms can be approximated by the dependence structure between the stock prices of those firms. This fact offers a very natural solution to the problem: If we are successful in modeling dependence structure between stock prices and all relevant market risk factors (interest rates, exchange rates, etc.), then we accomplish simultaneously two goals:

- We construct dependency between credit risk events of our obligors.
- We model dependency between market risk factors and the credit risk drivers.

If one uses as a measure of dependence the correlation between risk factors (as in CreditMetrics), the above task is trivial—all one needs is to estimate the correlation matrix for the stock prices and the relevant market risk factors. This approach has certain disadvantages, which were explained in Chapter 6. The solution proposed was to estimate copulas. This is extremely important in structural models for credit risk because this property postulates that the asset values of two firms shall have exactly the same copula as the stock prices of these two companies. The latter is true if we consider the stock price of a company as a call option on its assets and if the option pricing function giving the stock price is continuously increasing with respect to the asset values.

Thus, one can model structural dependence using a simplified approach using correlations like a measure for dependency or the copula approach.

What can be done in cases where there is no information about stock prices for a given obligor? The idea of segmentation described in CreditMetrics can be used. The essence of this approach is that the investor determines the percentage of the allocation of obligor volatility among the volatilities of certain market indexes and explains the dependence between obligors by the dependence of the market indexes that drive obligors' volatility.

Step 2. Scenario Generation

Now let us see how to generate scenarios of future credit ratings for the obligors in the portfolio and simultaneously for the changes of the market risk factors. Each set of future credit ratings and values of the market risk factors corresponds to a possible "state of the world" at the end of the planned risk horizon.

The steps to scenario generation are as follows:

1. Establish asset return thresholds for the obligors in the portfolio.
2. Generate scenarios of asset returns and the market risk factors using appropriate distribution—this is an assumption to be imposed.
3. Map the asset return scenarios to credit rating scenarios.

If we are using the multivariate normal distribution as a probability model for the log-returns of asset values and market risk factors, generating scenarios is a simple matter of generating correlated, normally distributed variables.[15]

When using stable distributions the following substeps are required:

1. Estimate the parameters of the stable distribution for each factor (asset values or market risk factor) using historical data. As explained in Chapter 8, while there are several approaches, maximum likelihood estimation provides the most accurate results.
2. This first substep models the marginal distributions of the risk drivers.
3. Employ the dependence structure model in Step 1 and construct a multivariate distribution of the marginals that are stable with estimated parameters from Step 2.
4. Generate scenarios sampled from the multivariate probability model developed in Step 3.

Once we have scenarios for the asset values, credit ratings for each scenario are assigned. This is done by comparing the asset value in each scenario to the rating thresholds.

Step 3. Portfolio Valuation

For nondefault scenarios, the portfolio valuation step consists of applying a valuation model for each particular position within the portfolio over each scenario. The yield curve corresponding to the credit rating of the obligor for this particular scenario should be used.

For default scenarios, the situation is slightly different. There are two approaches dealing with the recovery rate required for default scenarios:

---

[15] There is a well-known algorithm for doing this.

■ Assume constant recovery rates—then the value of a position in case of a default scenario is simply the nominal amount times the assumed recovery rate.

■ Allow the recovery rate to be a random variable.

As discussed in many empirical studies, recovery rates are not deterministic quantities but rather display a large amount of variation. This variation of value in the case of default is a significant contributor to risk. It is popular to model recovery rates by using Beta distributions[16] with a specified mean and standard deviation.

In this case, for each default scenario for a given obligor, we should generate a random recovery rate for each particular transaction with a defaulted obligor. The value of a given position in case a particular default scenario is realized will be different.

Step 4. Summarize Results

From the portfolio value scenarios generated in the previous steps, the distribution of the portfolio values can be estimated. The mean and standard deviation of future portfolio value can be computed from the simulated portfolio values using sample statistics. However, because of the skewed nature of the portfolio distribution, the mean and standard deviation may not be good measures of risk. Because the distribution of values is not normal, percentile levels from the standard deviation cannot be inferred. Given the simulated portfolio values, better measures, for example empirical quantiles or mean shortfall, should be computed.

In addition to statistics describing the portfolio distribution, one can evaluate individual assets and assess how much risk each asset contributes to the portfolio. To this end, marginal statistics can be used. In general, the *marginal statistic* for a particular asset is the difference between that statistic for the entire portfolio and that statistic for the portfolio not including the asset in question.[17] This marginal figure may

---

[16] See Chapter 3 for a discussion of the Beta distribution.

[17] To compute the marginal tenth percentile of the i-th asset in the portfolio, one can take

$$
q_{10}\left[(Q_1,...,Q_i,...Q_n) \begin{bmatrix} I_{1,1} \cdots I_{1,j} \cdots I_{1,m} \\ \cdots \; \cdots \; \cdots \; \cdots \; \cdots \\ I_{i,1} \; \cdots \; I_{i,j} \; \cdots \; I_{i,m} \\ \cdots \; \cdots \; \cdots \; \cdots \; \cdots \\ I_{n,1} \cdots I_{n,j} \cdots I_{n,m} \end{bmatrix} \right] - q_{10}\left[(Q_1,...,0,...Q_n) \begin{bmatrix} I_{1,1} \cdots I_{1,j} \cdots I_{1,m} \\ \cdots \; \cdots \; \cdots \; \cdots \; \cdots \\ I_{i,1} \; \cdots \; I_{i,j} \; \cdots \; I_{i,m} \\ \cdots \; \cdots \; \cdots \; \cdots \; \cdots \\ I_{n,1} \cdots I_{n,j} \cdots I_{n,m} \end{bmatrix} \right]
$$

where Q_i is the amount of i-th position, $I_{i,j}$ is the j-the simulated value for the i-th instrument, and q_{10} represents the tenth percentile of the values in question.

be interpreted as the amount by which we could decrease the risk of our portfolio by removing the i-th position.

AN INTEGRATED MARKET AND CREDIT RISK MANAGEMENT FRAMEWORK BASED ON THE INTENSITY-BASED MODEL

In the Cognity model, there are five key steps in the Monte Carlo approach to credit risk modeling based on stochastic modeling of the default rate:

Step 1. Build econometric models for default rates and for the explanatory variables: An econometric model is evaluated for the default probability of a segment based on explanatory variables (macrofactors, indexes, etc.) using historical data for default frequencies in a given segment and historical time series for the explanatory variables.

Step 2. Generate scenarios: Each scenario corresponds to a possible "state of the world" at the end of the risk horizon. Here, the "state of the world" is a set of values for the market variables and for the explanatory variable defined in Step 1.

Step 3. Estimate default probabilities under each scenario: For each scenario, estimate the default probabilities of the segments using the scenario values of the explanatory variables and the model estimated in Step 1. Simulate subscenarios for the status of each obligor (default/nondefault) based on the estimated default probability.

Step 4. Portfolio valuation: For each scenario, revalue the portfolio to reflect the new credit status of the obligor and the values of the market risk factors. This step generates a large number of possible future portfolio values.

Step 5. Summarize Results: Having the scenarios generated in the previous steps, an estimate for the distribution of portfolio values is obtained and can be used to compute any descriptive statistics for this distribution.

Exhibit 15.2 provides a schema describing the calculation process and the data required for each step. The key components of the model are shaded in the exhibit. Here we provide a description of the key steps outlined in the exhibit.

EXHIBIT 15.2 Summary of the Calculation Process and Data Required for Each Step of the Monte Carlo Simulation for an Intensity-Based Model with the Key Components of the Model Shaded

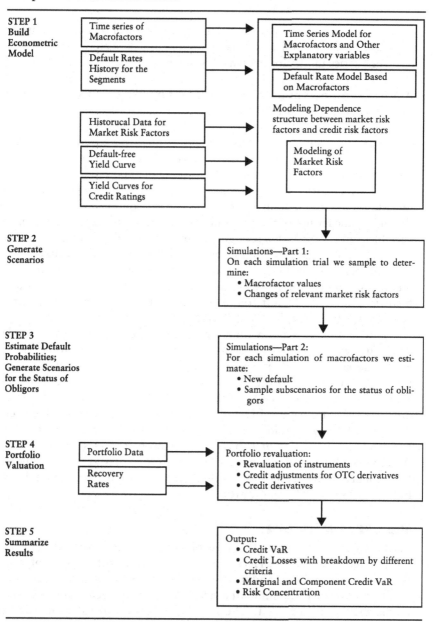

Adapted from Racheva-Iotova, Stoyanov, and Rachev (2003) and Cognity (2003).

Step 1. Build the Econometric Models

This first step is in fact the most challenging and critical task of the model. Two crucial models should be defined and estimated:

- An econometric model for default probability of a segment based on explanatory variables like macro-factors, indexes, etc.
- Time series model for explanatory variables

A brief description of the mathematics for building the two econometric models is described at the end of this chapter.

Default probability models should be evaluated for each segment. The segment definitions can be flexible enough based on credit rating, industry, region, and size of the company, provided the time series of default rates are available for each of the segments.

The explanatory variables that might be suitable to represent the systematic risk of the default rates in the chosen country-industry segments depend on the nature of the portfolio and might be industry indices, macro-variables (gross disposable product, unemployment, dividend growth, inflation rate), and long-term interest rates, exchange rates, and the like.

The first task is to define a model for default probability of a segment based on explanatory variables (macrofactors, indexes, etc.) using historical data for default frequencies in a given segment and historical time series for the explanatory variables.

The second model is a time series model for explanatory variables. The usual way to model dependent variables is to employ some kind of autoregressive moving average model (ARMA (p,q) model) described in Chapter 9. It is important to note that the proper modeling of default rate will depend very much on the proper modeling of dependent variables. For the modeling of macrofactors, a general model—stable vector AR(1)–ARCH–type model described later in this chapter which allows the modeling of the *joint* behavior of macrofactors—is proposed. The ARCH component of the model takes care of volatility clustering and the model's stable residuals result in fatter tails of the residuals and higher variability of default rates.

Step 2. Generate Scenarios

Each scenario corresponds to a possible "state of the world" at the end of the selected risk horizon. Here, the "state of the world" is a set of values for the market variables and for the explanatory variable defined in Step 1.

The scenarios are simulated according to the vector-autoregressive model discussed in Step 1. The important feature of the model is that the macro-factors and market risk factors are modeled by a *joint* probability distribution.[18] The latter means that the realizations of the market risk factors depend on the realizations of the macrofactors.

Step 3. Estimation of the Default Probabilities

In Step 3, the default probabilities are estimated under each scenario for each of the segments using the simulated values of the explanatory variables and the model estimated in Step 1. Then subscenarios for the status of each obligor (default/nondefault) based on the estimated default probability are simulated.

For each scenario set j in Step 2, we estimate the probability of default for each segment based on the model estimated in Step 1:

$$P_{s,j} = f_s(X_{1,j}, ...X_{N,j}) + u_j$$

where $P_{s,j}$ is the default probability for the segment s under the j-th simulation. Now, for each scenario j, independent subscenarios for each counterparty state (default or nondefault) based on its probability of default $P_{s,j}$ are generated as shown in the following schematic:

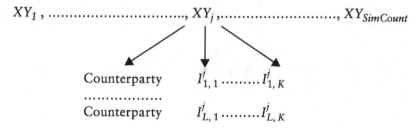

where $I_{L,k}^j$ is the state of the counterparty L under the j-th scenarios set for the k-th sub-scenario and

$$I_{L,k}^j = \begin{cases} 1 = \text{default} \\ 0 = \text{no default, } s \end{cases}$$

$$E(I_{L,k}^j) = P_{s,j} = f(X_{1,j}, ...X_{N,j})$$

where s is the segment of the L-th counterparty.

At this point, the full set of scenarios describing the possible "states of the world" in terms of market risk factor values and obligors' statutes (default or nondefault) is obtained.

---

[18] Relevant market variables (such as interest rates) should also be included in the model.

Step 4. Portfolio Valuation

For each scenario, the portfolio to reflect the new credit status of the obligor and the values of the market risk factors is revalued. The result is a large number of possible future portfolio values.

This step is similar to the corresponding step in the structural model described earlier. The only difference is that in the current model there is a simplification—it considers only default or nondefault status for an obligor.

Step 5. Summarize Results

At this point, a number of possible future portfolio values have been created. The final task is then to synthesize this information into meaningful risk estimates using descriptive statistics.

BUILDING AN ECONOMETRIC MODEL FOR THE INTENSITY-BASED MODEL

As explained in the previous section, two models must be estimated: (1) an econometric model for the default probability of a segment based on explanatory variables and (2) time series model for the explanatory variables.

To define a model for the default probability of a segment based on explanatory variables using historical data for default frequencies in a given segment and historical time series for the explanatory variables, a function f is selected and its parameters selected such that

$$DF_{s,t} = f(X_{1,t}, ...X_{N,t}) + u_t \tag{15.1}$$

where $DF_{s,t}$ is the default frequency in the segment s for the time period t and $X_{i,t}$ is the value of the i-th explanatory variable at time t, $i = 1...N$.

A time series model for explanatory variables is then modeled. Some kind of ARMA (p,q) model is usually employed to model dependent variables. That is the same as assuming that

$$X_t = a_0 + \sum_{i=1}^{p} a_i X_{t-i} + \sum_{j=1}^{q} b_j e_{t-i} + e_t \tag{15.2}$$

where e_t is $N(0,\sigma^2)$,

It is important to note that the proper modeling of default rates will depend very much on the proper modeling of dependent variables. From equations (15.1) and (15.2) we can write

$$DF_{s,t} = f\left(\sum_{i=1}^{p} a_{1,i} X_{1,t-i} + \sum_{j=1}^{q} b_{1,j} e_{1,t-i} + e_{1,t}, ...,\right.$$

$$\left. \sum_{i=1}^{p} a_{n,i} X_{n,t-i} + \sum_{j=1}^{q} b_{n,j} e_{n,t-i} + e_{n,t} \right) + u_t \qquad (15.3)$$

$$= g(X_{1,t-1}, ..., X_{1,t-p_1}, ..., X_{n,t-p_n}, e_{1,t}, ..., e_{1,t-q_1}, ..., e_{n,t-q_n}) + u_t$$

The improper use of normal residuals in equation (15.3) will end up with "incorrect" scenarios (simulations) for the possible default rates.

For the modeling of macro-factors, the more general model—stable vector AR(1)–ARCH–type model—is the suggested model. Under this model $X_t = A_1 X_{t-1} + E_t$, where $X_t = (X_1, ..., X_n)'$ is the vector of explanatory variables, A_1 is n by n-matrix, and $E_t = (e_{1,t}, ..., e_{n,t})'$ is the vector of residuals, which are modeled by multivariate stable ARCH model.

Exhibits 15.3 and 15.4 show the difference between modeling residuals using the traditional normal distribution and using the proposed

EXHIBIT 15.3 Difference Between Modeling Residuals Using the Traditional Normal Distribution and Using Stable Paretian Distribution: Changes in Monthly Inflation Rate from 2/65 to 12/99

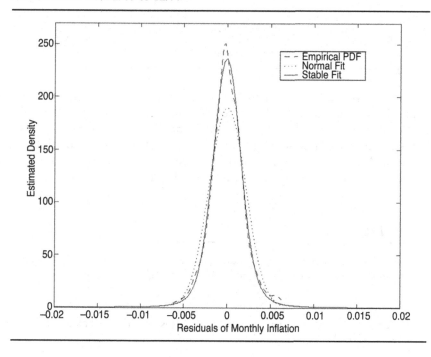

EXHIBIT 15.4 Difference Between Modeling Residuals Using the Traditional Normal Distribution and Using Stable Paretian Distribution: Monthly Change in Dividend Growth

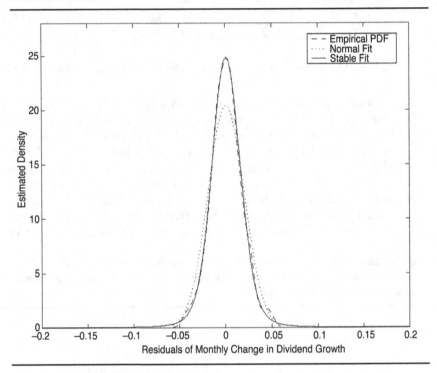

family of stable Paretian distributions on two macro time series, changes in inflation rate and dividend growth rate.[19] Employing stable residuals results in fatter tails of the residuals and higher variability of default rates. The ARCH component of the model takes care of volatility clustering. Moreover, since the model is a vector autoregressive model, one will eventually succeed in modeling joint behavior of macrofactors.

REFERENCES

Anson, J. P., F. J. Fabozzi, M. Choudhry, and R. R. Chen. 2004. *Credit Derivatives: Instruments, Applications, and Pricing*. Hoboken, NJ: John Wiley & Sons.

---

[19] The methodology for calculating the residuals is provided in Tokat, Rachev, and Schwartz (2003).

Artzner, P., and F. Delbaen. 1992. "Credit Risk and Prepayment Option." *Astin Bulletin* 22: 81–96.

Artzner, P., and F. Delbaen. 1994. "Default Risk Insurance and Incomplete Markets." Working paper, Univerité Luis Pasteur et C.N.R.S, Strasbourg.

Black, F., and J. Cox. 1976. "Valuing Corporate Securities: Some Effects of Bond Indenture Provisions." *Journal of Finance* 31: 351–367.

Black, F., and M. Scholes. 1973. "The Pricing of Options and Corporate Liabilities." *Journal of Political Economy* 81 (3): 637–654.

Briys, E., and F. DE Varenne. 1997. "Valuing Risky Fixed Rate Debt: An Extension." *Journal of Financial and Quantitative Analysis* 32 (2): 239–248.

Cognity. 2003. *Integrated Risk Management System.* Technical Documentation of FinAnalytica Inc., www.finanalytica.com.

Cossin, D. 1997. "Credit Risk Pricing: a Literature Survey." *Finanzmarkt und Portfolio Management* 11 (4): 398–412.

Cossin, P., and H. Pirotte. 2001. *Advanced Credit Risk Analysis: Financial Approaches and Mathematical Models to Assess, Price and Manage Credit Risk.* Chichester: John Wiley & Sons.

Crouhy, M., D. Galai, and R. Mark. 2000. "A Comparative Analysis of Current Credit Risk Models." *Journal of Banking and Finance* 24 (1–2): 59–117.

D'Souza, D., and B. Racheva-Jotova. 2003. "Credit Risk Modeling: A Literature Survey." Working paper.

Duffie, D. 1994. "Forward Rate Curves with Default Risk." Working paper, Graduate School of Business, Stanford University.

Duffie, D., and M. Huang. 1996. "Swap Rates and Credit Quality." *Journal of Finance* 51: 921–949.

Duffie, D., M. Schroder, and C. Skiadas. 1996. "Recursive Valuation of Defaultable Securities and the Timing of Resolution of Uncertainty." *Annals of Probability* 6 (4): 1075–1090.

Duffie, D., and K. Singleton. 1997. "An Econometric Model of the Term Structure of Interest Rate Swap Yields." *Journal of Finance* 52 (4): 1287–1322.

Duffie, D., and K. Singleton. 1999. "Modeling Term Structures of Defaultable Bonds." *Review of Financial Studies* 12 (4): 687–720.

Fabozzi, F. J., J. Howe, T. Makabe, and T. Sudo. 1993. "Recent Evidence on the Distribution Patterns in Chapter 11 Reorganizations." *Journal of Fixed Income*, Spring: 6–23.

Flesaker, B., L. Houghston, L. Schreiber, and L. Sprung. 1994. "Taking All the Credit." *Risk Magazine* 7: 105–108.

Fons, J. S. 1994. "Using Default Rates to Model the Term Structures of Defaultable Bonds." *Financial Analysts Journal*, September-October: 25–32.

Franks, J. R. and W. N. Torous. 1989. "An Empirical Investigation of U.S. Firms in Reorganization." *Journal of Finance* 44: 747–769.

Franks, J. R., and W. N. Torous. 1994. "A Comparison of Financial Recontracting in Distressed Exchanges and Chapter 11 Reorganizations." *Journal of Financial Economics* 35: 349–370

Jackson, T.H. 1986. "Of Liquidation, Continuation, and Delay: An Analysis of Bankruptcy Policy and Nonbankruptcy Rules." *American Bankruptcy Law Journal* 60: 399–428.

Jarrow, R. A., D. Lando, and S. M. Turnbull. 1997. "A Markov Model for the Term Structure of Credit Risk Spreads." *Review of Financial Studies* 10: 481–523.

Jarrow, R. A., and S. M. Turnbull. 1995. "Pricing Derivatives on Financial Securities Subject to Credit Risk." *Journal of Finance* 50: 53–85.

Jones, E. P., S. P. Mason, and E. Rosenfeld. 1984. "Contingent Claim Analysis of Corporate Capital Structures: An Empirical Investigation." *Journal of Finance* 39 (3): 611–625.

Kim, J., K. Ramaswamy, and S. Sundaresan. 1993. "Does Default Risk in Coupons Affect the Valuation of Corporate Bonds?: A Contingent Claim Model." *Financial Management* 22 (3): 117–131.

Lando, D. 1994. "Three Essays on Contingent Claims Pricing." PhD. thesis, Graduate School of Management, Cornell University.

Lando, D. 1998. "On Cox Processes and Credit Risky Securities." *Review of Derivatives Research* 2 (2/3): 99–120.

Longstaff, F., and E. Schwartz. 1995. "A Simple Approach to Valuing Fixed and Floating Rate Debt." *Journal of Finance* 50 (3): 789–819.

Madan, D and H. Unal. 1998. "Pricing the Risks of Default." *Review of Derivatives Research* 2 (2/3): 121-160.

Mason, S., and S. Bhattacharya. 1981. "Risky Debt, Jump Processes and Safety Covenants." *Journal of Financial Economics* 9 (33): 281–307.

Meckling, W. H. 1977. "Financial Markets, Default, and Bankruptcy." *Law and Contemporary Problems* 41: 124–177.

Merton, R. 1973. "Theory of Rational Option Pricing." *Bell Journal of Economics,* Spring: 141–183.

Merton, R. 1974. "On the Pricing of Corporate Debt: The Risk Structure of Interest Rates." *Journal of Finance* 29 (2): 449–470.

Miller, M. H. 1977. "The Wealth Transfers of Bankruptcy: Some Illustrative Examples." *Law and Contemporary Problems* 41: 39–46.

Nielsen, L., J. Saà-Requejo, and P. Santa-Clara. 1993. "Default Risk and Interest Rate Risk: the Term Structure of Default Spreads." Working paper, INSEAD.

Racheva-Iotova, B., S. Stoyanov, and S.T. Rachev. 2003. "Stable Non-Gaussian Credit Risk Model: The Cognity Approach." In *Credit Risk: Measurement, Evaluations and Management,* ed. G. Bol, G. Nakhaheizadeh, S.T. Rachev, T. Rieder, and K-H. Vollmer, 179–198. Heidelberg: Physica-Verlag Series: Contributions to Economics: .

Rogers, L. C. G. 1999. "Modeling Credit Risk." Unpublished manuscript.

Sarig, O., and A. Warga. 1989. "Some Empirical Estimates of the Risk Structure of Interest Rates." *Journal of Finance* 44 (5): 1351–1360.

Schönbucher, P. 1999. "A Tree Implementation of a Credit Spread Model for Credit Derivatives." Department of Statistics, Bonn University.

Tokat, Y., S. T. Rachev, and E. Schwartz. 2003. "The Stable Non-Gaussian Asset Allocation: A Comparison with the Classical Gaussian Approach." *Journal of Economic Dynamics and Control* 27: 937–969.

Warner, J. B. 1977. "Bankruptcy, Absolute Priority, and the Pricing of Risky Debt Claims." *Journal of Financial Economics* 4: 239–276.

Weiss, L. A. 1990. "Bankruptcy Resolution: Direct Costs and Violation of Priority of Claims." *Journal of Financial Economics* 17: 285–314.

Wilson, T. 1997a. "Portfolio Credit Risk (1)." *Risk* 10 (9): 111–116.

Wilson, T. 1997b. "Portfolio Credit Risk (2)." *Risk* 10 (10): 56–61.

Zhou, C. 1997. "A Jump-diffusion Approach to Modeling Credit Risk and Valuing Defaultable Securities." Working paper, Federal Reserve Board, Washington, DC.

CHAPTER 16

Operational Risk

A large number of losses borne by financial institutions are attributed to neither market risk nor credit risk. In fact, it is the large magnitude losses that rarely occur (i.e., low frequency, high severity losses) that cause the most serious danger: Recall the dramatic consequences of unauthorized trading, fraud, human errors for Orange County (United States in 1994), Barings (Singapore in 1995), Daiwa (Japan in 1995), among many others.[1] In this chapter, we explain how operational risk is measured and discuss evidence against the statistical distributions suggested by the Basel Committee for Regulatory Supervision for measuring exposure to operational risk.

OPERATIONAL RISK DEFINED

In attempting to define operational risk, Wilson (2000) begins with subcategories of what is typically viewed as operational risk.[2] These include:

- Control risk
- Process risk
- Reputational risk
- Human resources risk
- Legal risk
- Takeover risk

---

[1] Additionally, risks of natural disasters, significant computer failures, and terrorist attacks are other such examples of nonmarket, noncredit risk-related events (for example, the financial consequences of the September 11, 2001 attack).

[2] For an explanation of these operational risk subcategories, see Wilson (2000, 379–383).

- Marketing risk
- Systems risk
- Aging technology
- Tax changes
- Regulatory changes
- Business capacity
- Legal risk
- Project risk
- Security
- Supplier management

Wilson then identifies three approaches to defining operational risk that include all or some of these subcategories of operational risk.

The first is a broad-brush approach which he refers to as "wide definition" and includes all the subcategories of operational risk listed previously. It excludes market risk and credit risk. At the other extreme is the second approach, what Wilson refers to as "narrow risk." This approach limits operational risk to the risks associated with the operations department of a firm. Wilson includes the following subcategories of operational risk as part of this narrow risk definition: control risk, process risk, human resources risk, systems risk, and security risk. The third approach distinguishes between events for which the firm has control and those that are beyond its control. According to this approach, those events for which a firm has control are defined as operational risk while those that are beyond the firm's control are defined as "strategic risk." Strategic risk encompasses all of the operational risk subcategories listed above *except* control risk, process risk, human resources risk, and systems risk.

Crouhy, Galai, and Mark (2000, 343) state that operational risk

> ... refers to various potential failures in the operating of the firm, unrelated to uncertainties with regard to the demand function for the products and services of the firm. These failures can stem from a computer breakdown, a bug in major computer software, an error of a decision make in special situations, etc.

They go on to subdivide operational risk into two categories: operational failure risk and operational strategic risk. The former risk is the potential failure from operating a business caused by the use of people, processes, and technology. Specifically, Crouhy, Galai, and Mark (2000, 344) define operational failure risk as "the risk that exists *within* the business unit caused by the failure of people, process or technology." While one can expect that a certain level of failure may occur, it is the unexpected failures that give rise to the risk. In contrast to operational failure risk, operational strategic risk arises from factors *outside* the firm. This includes a new competitor whose entrance to the market significantly changes the norm for doing business in the industry, new regulations that adversely impact the firm, natural catastrophes, changes in regulations, and changes in the political landscape.

Operational risk is defined in the Basel II Capital Accord (Basel II) as "the risk of loss resulting from inadequate or failed internal processes, people and systems or from external events" (Basel Committee on Banking Supervision, 2001b). Operational risks affect the risk profiles of financial institutions. According to the Basel Committee on Supervisory Regulation (2001b, 1):

> Developments such as the use of more highly automated technology, the growth of e-commerce, large-scale mergers and acquisitions that test the viability of newly integrated systems, the emergence of banks as very large-volume service providers, the increased prevalence of outsourcing and the greater use of financing techniques that reduce credit and market risk, but that create increased operational risk, all suggest that operational risk exposures may be substantial and growing.

The definition adopted in Basel II has been justified due the absence of reliable industry databases on extreme tail operational loss events.[3]

The types of events that the Committee on Banking Supervision have identified as having the potential to result in substantial losses include:

- *Internal fraud.* For example, intentional misreporting of positions, employee theft, and insider trading on an employee's own account.
- *External fraud.* For example, robbery, forgery, cheque kiting, and damage from computer hacking.

---

[3] The ultimate objective of the Committee on Bank Supervision is to develop a more comprehensive measure of operational risk that is more consistent with the purpose of regulatory capital in providing a cushion against unexpected loss. Allen and Bali (2004) propose a first step toward this ultimate goal in their model that calibrates "bottom-up" operational risk models. (In a bottom-up model, the risk factors and costs inherent in the firm's production process are the focus of the analysis; in a top-down model, the calculation of operational risk is based on the overall cost to the firm of operational loss events. See Allen, Boudoukh, and Saunders (2004).) Allen and Bali use equity returns to measure the impact of operational loss events on overall firm value. and thereby as an estimate of operational risk exposure.

- *Employment practices and workplace safety.* For example, workers compensation claims, violation of employee health and safety rules, organised labour activities, discrimination claims, and general liability.
- *Clients, products and business practices.* For example, fiduciary breaches, misuse of confidential customer information, improper trading activities on the bank's account, money laundering, and sale of unauthorised products.
- *Damage to physical assets.* For example, terrorism, vandalism, earthquakes, fires and floods.
- *Business disruption and system failures.* For example, hardware and software failures, telecommunication problems, and utility outages.
- *Execution, delivery and process management.* For example, data entry errors, collateral management failures, incomplete legal documentation, unapproved access given to client accounts, non-client counterparty misperformance, and vendor disputes.

CAPITAL REQUIREMENT FOR OPERATIONAL RISK

The Basel Committee on Banking Regulation suggested five approaches to assess capital charges for the unexpected portion of operational losses (expected operational losses are subject to capital provisions), to be implemented by every bank by the end of 2006 (Basel Committee on Banking Supervision, 2001a). The approaches are: (1) Basic Indicator approach, (2) Standardized approach, (3) Internal Measurement approach, (4) Scorecard approach, and (5) Loss Distribution approach. The latter three are grouped under the Advanced Measurement approaches.

Under Basel II, the capital charge is determined by a fixed factor α multiplied by the gross income of each individual institution. The fixed factor α (usually 12%) is based on the banks' overall allocation of economic capital to operational risks. Under the Standardized approach, the capital charge is the sum of the products of fixed factors β and the exposure indicators across all business lines. β is proportional to the relative weighting of the business line. In the Internal Measurement approach, bank's activities are divided into business lines and risk event types. For each such combination, the capital charge is the product of the expected loss given the event and the internal scaling factor γ that transforms the expected into the unexpected losses and also accounts for the distributional form of the loss frequency and severity.

In the Scorecard approach, the initial capital charge is readjusted over time according to the changes in financial indicators of the bank that serve as proxies for risk. The Loss Distribution approach makes use of the exact distribution of the loss frequency and severity based on the internal loss data of each bank. For every business line and event type combination, the frequency and severity distributions are estimated. Then each capital charge is calculated as the Value-at-Risk at a predetermined confidence level $1 - \alpha$ ($VaR_{1-\alpha}$), and the total capital charge is the sum of $VaR_{1-\alpha}$.

The Basel Committee on Banking Supervision suggests using the lognormal distribution for the severity and Poisson distribution for the frequency of operational losses. These probability distributions are described in Chapter 3.

COMPARISON OF MARKET, CREDIT, AND OPERATIONAL RISK DISTRIBUTIONS

In the market risk models, the oscillations in the market indicators are in general of low magnitude and can take both positive and negative signs. Moreover, the price quotes are always available whenever markets are open, suggesting a continuous-type process for market risk. As a result, diffusion processes with Brownian motion as risk driver are often used to model market risks despite the evidence discussed in previous chapters. On the contrary, empirical evidence suggests that operational losses are highly skewed, nonnegative,[4] and possess heavier tails than what the normal distribution would predict, in that high-scale losses should be given a positive probability. For these reasons it is obvious that the normal distribution is inappropriate for modeling the magnitudes of operational losses. As for the frequency distribution, the nature of the operational losses is discrete and should be accounted for in examining the cumulative loss behavior. This is similar to credit risk modeling in which the frequency of default is of nontrivial concern.

Another issue is created by the timing at which events are recorded. In the market risk models, the market positions are recorded on the daily basis by marking-to-market, whereas time lags are present between the occurrences of the operational loss events and the times of their effective impacts on a bank's earnings. In this chapter, for example, the date on which the state of affairs of an event was "closed" or "assumed closed" is used to model the frequency distribution.

---

[4] In this chapter, losses are assumed to lie on the positive part of the real line.

AGGREGATED STOCHASTIC MODELS FOR OPERATIONAL RISK

The Basel Committee on Banking Supervision suggests using a compound Poisson process for modeling operational losses. Under this model, loss frequencies follow the Poisson law, and the loss amounts are (1) independent from the time when the loss occurs; (2) independent and identically distributed; and can (3) follow an arbitrary probability distribution. The Basel Committee on Banking Supervision suggests the Lognormal distribution. In this section, we present evidence from a study that neither supports the distributional assumption for the loss magnitudes nor the assumption of a constant hazard rate governing the frequency distribution.

As a more flexible model for the occurrence of the losses, one can use a generalized form of Poisson processes, the doubly stochastic Poisson process or a Cox process, discussed in Chapter 10, to model operational losses. The stochastic intensity factor will allow for different forms of the loss arrival distribution. Additionally, the restrictive assumption of lognormally distributed loss magnitudes has to be replaced by a more flexible class of probability distributions, which allows for the explanation of extreme events as observed in reality. As a result, we obtain a compound Cox process as a flexible model for the cumulative loss distribution.

Empirical Evidence from the Basel Committee on Banking Supervision

Two surveys conducted over 1998–2000 and 2001 by the Basel Committee on Banking Supervision revealed diversity in the operational loss frequency and severity distributions across business lines and event types (Basel Committee on Banking Supervision, 2003). Comparison of Exhibits 16.1 and 16.2 indicates the nonuniformity in the frequency and severity of the loss distributions across various event types. Similar patterns have been found to hold for the distributions across various business lines.

It is possible to classify different event type/business line combinations into four groups:

1. Low frequency/low severity
2. Low frequency/high severity
3. High frequency/low severity
4. High frequency/high severity

EXHIBIT 16.1 Percent Severity by Event Type

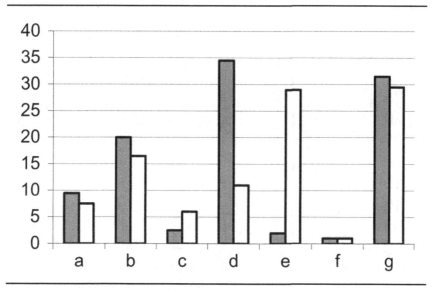

Notes:
1. Gray bars refer to 2001 survey; white bars refer to 2002 survey.
2. The event type classifications are: a = internal fraud; b = external fraud; c = employment practices and workplace safety; d = clients, products and business services; e = damage to physical assets; f = business disruption and system failures; and g = execution, delivery and process management.
Source: Adapted from Figure 1a, Basel Committee on Banking Regulation (2003, 14).

Classification of Compound Processes

For the purpose of operational risk modeling, Chernobai and Rachev (2004) identify four types of compound processes:

Compound Process 1: Both losses and interarrival times thin tailed

Compound Process 2: Heavy-tailed losses, thin tailed interarrival times

Compound Process 3: Thin-tailed losses, heavy-tailed interarrival times

Compound Process 4: Both losses and interarrival times heavy tailed

Depending on the process types, the aggregated loss process would possess different finite sample and limiting properties.

Empirical Evidence from Actual Operational Loss Data

Using frequency and operational loss data from a European bank from 1950–2002, Chernobai and Rachev (2004, 2005) provide empirical evi-

EXHIBIT 16.2   Percent Frequency by Event Type

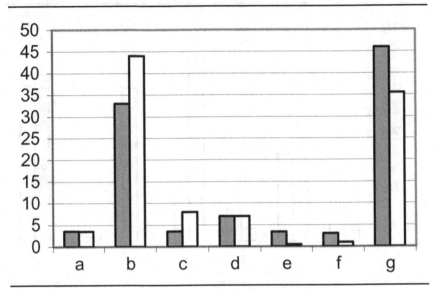

Notes:
1. Gray bars refer to 2001 survey; white bars refer to 2002 survey.
2. The event type classifications are: a = internal fraud; b = external fraud; c = employment practices and workplace safety; d = clients, products and business services; e = damage to physical assets; f = business disruption and system failures; and g = execution, delivery and process management.
Source: Adapted from Figure 1b, Basel Committee on Banking Regulation (2003, 14).

dence on the best distribution to characterize operational risk.[5] The loss severity data are measured in U.S. dollars and the loss frequency data are represented as the number of days between consecutive dates. Only events whose state of affairs were "closed" or "assumed closed" were considered for the analysis.

The total number of data points used for the analysis was 1,727 for the frequency data and 1,802 for the severity. The loss events were classified into six types: (1) relationship, (2) human, (3) legal, (4) processes, (5) technology, and (6) external. The magnitudes of losses were adjusted for inflation. A number of distributions were fit and the maximum likelihood estimates of the parameters were provided for the interarrival times and the loss amounts by Chernobai and Rachev. Their study finds that the symmetric stable distribution provides the best fit for the interarrival times data while the exponential distribution shows a relatively

---

[5] The name of the bank is not disclosed by the authors.

poor fit. For the loss magnitudes, similarly, the symmetric stable distribution shows the best fit.

Chernobai and Rachev also test for the iid assumption. An ARMA (1,1) model was fit to their data after the mean was subtracted. For all except the "External" type excess losses at least one of the AR(1), MA(1) coefficients was significant, indicating the failure of the iid assumption. The coefficients were significant for the "Relationship," "Human," and "External" type interarrival times. Clustering of the volatility was found to be present for the "Relationship," "Human," and "Processes" type interarrival times, as suggested by the ARCH(1) and GARCH(1) coefficients being significantly different from zero. ARCH/GARCH effect was not observed for the loss amounts.

Normal and stable distributions were fit to the standardized residuals from the ARMA(1,1) models. Chernobai and Rachev found that stable distributions showed the best fit for the excess losses in almost all cases, and for the excess interarrival times for all cases.

To summarize, the study by Chernobai and Rachev provides evidence against that uniform use of Lognormal and Poisson distributions for the severity and frequency distributions for operational losses, as initially suggested by the Basel Committee on Banking Supervision. Stable distribution shows the best fit to the frequency and severity data. Furthermore, they find the iid assumption proves to be a serious flaw.

Findings by Allen and Bali (2004) using equity returns to measure operational risk are consistent with the findings by Chernobai and Rachev. Allen and Bali find evidence of both fat tails and skewness.

REFERENCES

Allen, L., and T. Bali. 2004. "Cyclicality in Catastrophic and Operational Risk Measurements." Working paper, Baruch College, CUNY, September.

Allen, L., J. Boudoukh, and A. Saunders. 2004. *Understanding Market, Credit and Operational Risk: The Value at Risk Approach.* Oxford: Blackwell Publishing.

Basel Committee on Banking Supervision. 2001a. "Consultative Document: Operational Risk." www.bis.org. January.

Basel Committee on Banking Supervision. 2001b. "Working Paper on the Regulatory Treatment of Operational Risk." www.bis.org. September.

Basel Committee on Banking Supervision. 2003. "Sound Practices for the Management and Supervision of Operational Risk." www.bis.org. February.

Basel Committee on Banking Supervision. 2003. "The 2002 Loss Data Collection Exercise for Operational Risk: Summary of the Data Collected." www.bis.org. March.

Bening, V. E., and V. Y. Korolev. 2002. *Generalized Poisson Models and Their Applications in Insurance and Finance.* Boston: VSP International Science.

Chernobai, A., and S. T. Rachev, 2004. "Stable Modelling of Operational Risk." (2004). In *Operational Risk Modelling and Analysis,* ed. Marcello Cruz, London: Risk Books: 173–170.

Chernobai, A., and S. T. Rachev. 2005. "Toward Effective Financial Risk Management: Stable Modeling of Operational Risk." Presented at the IFAC World Congress 2005 Prague and to appear in the Proceedings.

Crouchy, M., D. Galai, and B. Mark. 2000. "Operational Risk." In *The Professional's Handbook of Financial Risk Management,* ed. M. Lore and L. Borodovsky, 342–376. London: Butterworth-Heinemann.

Wilson, D. 2000. "Operational Risk." In *The Professional's Handbook of Financial Risk Management,* ed. M. Lore and L. Borodovsky, 377–412. London: Butterworth-Heinemann.

Option Pricing

CHAPTER 17

Introduction to Option Pricing and the Binomial Model

In the three chapters in Part Five, we will look at option pricing and the importance of the return distribution assumption in models used to compute the theoretical value of an option. In this chapter, we begin with the basics of options and option pricing. We then explain and illustrate a discrete option pricing model, the binomial model. We conclude this chapter by showing how the binomial model converges as we increase the number of trading periods between the current date and the option's expiration date. This leads naturally into the topic covered in Chapter 18, the Black-Scholes option pricing model and the assumptions underlying the model. Some of the assumptions about the stock price process made by the Black-Scholes model are rather restrictive and are not supported by empirical evidence. In Chapter 19, we discuss these limitations and review the more popular generalizations of the Black-Scholes model.

OPTIONS CONTRACTS

There are two parties to an option contract: the *buyer* and the *writer* (also called the *seller*). In an option contract, the writer of the option grants the buyer of the option the right, but not the obligation, to purchase from or sell to the writer underlying asset at a specified price within a specified period of time (or at a specified date). The writer grants this right to the buyer in exchange for a certain sum of money, which is called the *option price* or *option premium*. The price at which the underlying asset may be bought or sold is called the *exercise price* or *strike price.* The date after which an option is void is called the *expiration date* or *maturity date.*

When an option grants the buyer the right to purchase the underlying asset from the writer (seller), it is referred to as a *call option*, or simply, a *call.* When the option buyer has the right to sell the underlying asset to the writer, the option is called a *put option*, or simply, a *put.*

The timing of the possible exercise of an option is an important characteristic of the contract. There are options that may be exercised at any time up to and including the expiration date. Such options are referred to as *American options.* Other options may be exercised only at the expiration date; these are called *European options.*

The maximum amount that an option buyer can lose is the option price. The maximum profit that the option writer (seller) can realize is the option price. The option buyer has substantial upside return potential, while the option writer has substantial downside risk.

Options may be traded either on an organized exchange or in the over-the-counter (OTC) market. Exchange-traded options have three advantages. The first is standardization of the exercise price, the quantity of the underlying asset, and the expiration date of the contract. Second, the direct link between buyer and seller is severed after the order is executed because of the interchangeability of exchange-traded options. The clearinghouse associated with the exchange where the option trades performs the guarantee function. Finally, the transactions costs are lower for exchange-traded options than for OTC options.

The higher cost of an OTC option reflects the cost of customizing the option for the common situation where an institutional investor needs to have a tailor-made option because the standardized exchange-traded option does not satisfy its investment objectives. Investment banking firms and commercial banks act as principals as well as brokers in the OTC options market. Most institutional investors are not concerned that an OTC option is less liquid than an exchange-traded option because they use OTC options as part of an asset/liability strategy in which they intend to hold them to expiration. OTC options can be customized in any manner sought by an institutional investor. Basically, if a dealer can reasonably hedge the risk associated with the opposite side of the option sought, it will create the option desired by a customer. OTC options are not limited to European or American types. An option can be created in which the option can be exercised at several specified dates as well as the expiration date of the option. Such options are referred to as *limited exercise options, Bermuda options*, and *Atlantic options.*

BASIC COMPONENTS OF THE OPTION PRICE

The option price is a reflection of the option's intrinsic value and any additional amount over its intrinsic value. The premium over intrinsic value is often referred to as the time value or time premium.

Intrinsic Value

The *intrinsic value* of an option is the economic value of the option if it is exercised immediately, except that if there is no positive economic value that will result from exercising immediately then the intrinsic value is zero.

The intrinsic value of a call option is the difference between the current price of the underlying asset and the strike price if positive; it is otherwise zero. For example, if the strike price for a call option is $100 and the current asset price is $105, the intrinsic value is $5. That is, an option buyer exercising the option and simultaneously selling the underlying asset would realize $105 from the sale of the asset, which would be covered by acquiring the asset from the option writer for $100, thereby netting a $5 gain.

When an option has intrinsic value, it is said to be "in the money." When the strike price of a call option exceeds the current asset price, the call option is said to be "out of the money"; it has no intrinsic value. An option for which the strike price is equal to the current asset price is said to be "at the money." Both at-the-money and out-of-the-money options have an intrinsic value of zero because it is not profitable to exercise the option. Our hypothetical call option with a strike price of $100 would be: (1) in the money when the current asset price is greater than $100; (2) out of the money when the current asset price is less than $100; and (3) at the money when the current asset price is equal to $100.

For a put option, the intrinsic value is equal to the amount by which the current asset price is below the strike price. For example, if the strike price of a put option is $100 and the current asset price is $92, the intrinsic value is $8. That is, the buyer of the put option who exercises it and simultaneously sells the underlying asset will net $8 by exercising. The asset will be sold to the writer for $100 and purchased in the market for $92. For our hypothetical put option with a strike price of $100, the option would be: (1) in the money when the asset price is less than $100; (2) out of the money when the current asset price exceeds $100; and (3) at the money when the strike price is equal to $100.

Time Value

The time value of an option is the amount by which the option price exceeds its intrinsic value. The option buyer hopes that, at some time prior to expiration, changes in the market price of the underlying asset will increase the value of the rights conveyed by the option. For this prospect, the option buyer is willing to pay a premium above the intrinsic value. For example, if the price of a call option with a strike price of $100 is $9 when the current asset price is $105, the time value of this option is $4 ($9 minus its intrinsic value of $5). Had the current asset price been $90 instead of $105, then the time value of this option would be the entire $9 because the option has no intrinsic value.

There are two ways in which an option buyer may realize the value of a position taken in the option. First is to exercise the option. The second is by selling the call option for $9. In the first example above, selling the call is preferable because the exercise of an option will realize a gain of only $5—it will cause the immediate loss of any time value. There are circumstances under which an option may be exercised prior to the expiration date; they depend on whether the total proceeds at the expiration date would be greater by holding the option or exercising and reinvesting any cash proceeds received until the expiration date.

BOUNDARY CONDITIONS FOR THE PRICE OF AN OPTION

Theoretical boundary conditions for the price of an option also can be derived using arbitrage arguments. For example, let us assume the underlying asset is a stock. It can be shown that the minimum price for an American call option is its intrinsic value; that is,

Call option price ≥ Max [0, (Price of stock − Strike price)]

This expression says that the call option price will be greater than or equal to the difference between the price of the underlying stock and the strike price (intrinsic value), or zero, whichever is higher.

The boundary conditions can be "tightened" by using arbitrage arguments. The idea is to build two portfolios which lead to the same payoff after one year. Assume the holdings of the two portfolios are as follows:

Portfolio A holdings: One European call option that expires in one year and a 1-year investment equal to the present value of the strike price for the call option invested at the risk-free rate. (The present value is computed using the risk-free rate and the investment matures on the expiration date of the option.)

Portfolio B holdings: One share of the underlying stock and a short position in the European put option with the same characteristics as the European call option (i.e., same underlying stock, strike, and expiration date).

Let us compare the payoffs of these two portfolios at the end of one year. There are two possible scenarios for the price of the stock one year from now:

Scenario 1—Terminal stock price is higher than the strike price for both options: Consider first Portfolio A. The call option will be exercised. The investment matures and has a value equal to the strike price. The proceeds to exercise the call option are obtained from the matured investment. Therefore, the value of Portfolio A is equal to the price of the stock one year from now. In Portfolio B, the put option is worthless because the price of the stock is greater than the strike price. The only asset of value in Portfolio B is the stock. Consequently, the value of Portfolio B is equal to the price of the stock one year from now. In summary we can see that the value of the two portfolios coincide at the expiration date of the two European options.

Scenario 2—Terminal stock price is less than or equal to the strike price of both options: Consider first Portfolio A. The call option will be worthless. The investment matures and will have a value equal to the strike price of the call option. For Portfolio B, the put option will be excised and therefore the one share of stock will be lost due to the exercise. Portfolio B receives the strike price when the put option is exercised and therefore that is the value of Portfolio B. Consequently, Portfolio A and Portfolio B have the same value.

Since in both scenarios the two portfolios have the same outcome, they must be priced the same. If not, market participants could make riskless profits by buying the cheaper portfolio and selling the more expensive one. Thus we know today that:

Value of Portfolio A = European call price + Present value of the strike price

Value of Portfolio B = Price of stock − European put price

(there is a minus sign before the European put price because it is a short position) and since

Value of Portfolio A = Value of Portfolio B

European call price + Present value of the strike price
= Price of stock − European put price

We then have the following boundary condition,

European call price
= Price of stock − Present value of the strike price − European put price

The above relationship is referred to as *put-call parity.*
The value of the call option cannot be negative. Therefore,

European call price = Max (Price of stock − Present value of the strike price
                                          − European put price, 0)

Since the European put price cannot be negative, we can rewrite the above as

> European call price
> ≥ Max (Price of stock − Present value of the strike price, 0)

DISCRETE-TIME OPTION PRICING: BINOMIAL MODEL

The extreme case is an option pricing model that uses a set of assumptions to derive a single theoretical price, rather than a range. Several models have been developed to determine the theoretical value of an option. The most popular one was developed by Black and Scholes (1973) for valuing European call options.

Basically, the idea behind the arbitrage argument in deriving these option pricing models is that if the payoff from owning a call option can be replicated by (1) purchasing the stock underlying the call option; and (2) borrowing funds, then the price of the option will be (at most) the cost of creating the replicating strategy.

In this section, we provide a short review of discrete-time option pricing model, specifically the binomial model. The discrete-time option pricing model motives the Black-Scholes model, a continuous-time model discussed in the next chapter, by considering the situation where asset price movements are described by a multiplicative binomial process over discrete time.[1] In Chapter 19, we discuss various extensions of the Black-Scholes model among them models assuming the return for the underlying asset follows a stable Paretian distribution.

---

[1] This "binomial" approach to option pricing seems to have been proposed independently by Sharpe (1978), Cox, Ross, and Rubinstein (1979), and Rendleman and Barter (1979).

To derive a one-period binomial option pricing model for a call option, we begin by constructing a portfolio consisting of: (1) a long position in a certain amount of the stock; and (2) a short call position in this underlying stock. The amount of the underlying stock purchased is such that the position will be hedged against any change in the price of the stock at the expiration date of the option. That is, the portfolio consisting of the long position in the stock and the short position in the call option is riskless and will produce a return that equals the risk-free interest rate. A portfolio constructed in this way is called a *hedged portfolio*.

We can show how this process works with an extended illustration. Let us first assume that there is a stock that has a current market price of $80 and that only two possible future states can occur one year from now. Each state is associated with one of only two possible values for the stock, and they can be summarized in this way:

State	Price
1	$100
2	70

We assume further that there is a call option on this stock with a strike price of $80 (the same as the current market price) that expires in one year. Let us suppose an investor forms a hedged portfolio by acquiring ⅔ of a unit of the stock and selling one call option. The ⅔ of a unit of the stock is the so-called *hedge ratio*, the amount of the stock purchased per call sold (how we derive the hedge ratio will be explained later). Let us consider the outcomes for this hedged portfolio corresponding to the two possible outcomes for the stock.

If the price of the stock one year from now is $100, the buyer of the call option will exercise it. This means that the investor will have to deliver one unit of the stock in exchange for the strike price, $80. As the investor has only ⅔ unit of the stock, he has to buy ⅓ at a cost of $33⅓ (the market price of $100 times ⅓). Consequently, the outcome will equal the strike price of $80 received, minus the $33⅓ cost to acquire the ⅓ unit of the stock to deliver, plus whatever price the investor initially sold the call option for. That is, the outcome will be

$$\$80 - \$33\tfrac{1}{3} + \text{Call option price} = \$46\tfrac{2}{3} + \text{Call option price}$$

If, instead, the price of the stock one year from now is $70, the buyer of the call option will not exercise it. Consequently, the investor will own ⅔ of a unit of the stock. At a price of $70, the value of ⅔ of a unit is $46⅔. The outcome in this case is then the value of the stock plus whatever price the investor received when he initially sold the call option. That is, the outcome will be

$$\$46\tfrac{2}{3} + \text{Call option price}$$

It is apparent that, given the possible stock prices, the portfolio consisting of a short position in the call option and $\tfrac{2}{3}$ of a unit of the stock will generate an outcome that hedges changes in the price of the stock; hence, the hedged portfolio is riskless. Furthermore, this holds regardless of the price of the call, which affects only the magnitude of the outcome.

Deriving the Hedge Ratio

To show how the hedge ratio can be calculated, we will use the following notation:

S = current stock price

u = 1 plus the percentage change in the stock's price if the price goes up in the next period

d = 1 plus the percentage change in the stock's price if the price goes down in the next period

r = a risk-free one-period interest rate (the risk-free rate until the expiration date)

C = current price of a call option

C_u = intrinsic value of the call option if the stock price goes up

C_d = intrinsic value of the call option if the stock price goes down

E = strike price of the call option

H = hedge ratio, that is, the amount of the stock purchased per call sold

For reasons that will become clear later, we will assume that the inequality $0 < d < 1 + r < u$ is fulfilled.

In our illustration, u, d, and H are

$$u = \$100/\$80 = 1.250$$

$$d = \$70/\$80 = 0.875$$

$$H = \tfrac{2}{3}$$

Further, State 1 in our illustration means that the stock's price goes up; and State 2 means that the stock's price goes down.

The investment made in the hedged portfolio is equal to the cost of buying H amount of the stock minus the price received from selling the call option. Therefore, because

$$\text{Amount invested in the stock} = HS$$

then

$$\text{Cost of the hedged portfolio} = HS - C$$

The payoff of the hedged portfolio at the end of one period is equal to the value of the H amount of the stock purchased minus the call option price. The payoffs of the hedged portfolio for the two possible states are defined in this way:

State 1, if the stock's price goes up: $uHS - C_u$

State 2, if the stock's price goes down: $dHS - C_d$

In our illustration, we have these payoffs:

If the stock's price goes up: $1.250\ H\ \$80 - C_u$ or $\$100\ H - C_u$

If the stock's price goes down: $0.875\ H\ \$80 - C_d$ or $\$70\ H - C_d$

If the hedge is riskless, the payoffs must be the same. Thus,

$$uHS - C_u = dHS - C_d \qquad (17.1)$$

Solving equation (17.1) for the hedge ratio, H, we have[2]

$$H = \frac{C_u - C_d}{(u - d)S} \qquad (17.2)$$

To determine the value of the hedge ratio, H, we must know C_u and C_d. These two values are equal to the difference between the price of the stock and the strike price in the two possible states. Of course, the min-

---

[2] The mathematically skilled reader will recognize that this expression is similar to a discrete approximation of the derivative of the call price with respect to the strike price. This is exactly how we will define and use the hedge ratio in the next chapter in the continuous-time setting. The hedge ratio (denoted by Δ in the next chapter) will help us to immunize a portfolio against a change in the value of the underlying.

imum value of the call option, in any state, is zero. Mathematically, the differences can be expressed as follows:

If the stock's price goes up: $C_u = max[0, (uS - E)]$

If the stock's price goes down: $C_d = max[0, (dS - E)]$

As the strike price in our illustration is $80, uS is $100, and dS is $70. Then,

If the stock's price goes up: $C_u = max[0, (\$100 - \$80)] = \$20$

If the stock's price goes down: $C_d = max[0, (\$70 - \$80)] = \$0$

To continue with our illustration, we substitute the values of u, d, S, C_u, and C_d into equation (17.2) to obtain the hedge ratio's value:

$$H = \frac{\$20 - \$0}{(1.25 - 0.875)\$80} = \tfrac{2}{3}$$

This value for H agrees with the amount of the stock purchased when we introduced this illustration.

Now we can derive a formula for the call option price. Exhibit 17.1 diagrams the situation. The top left half of the exhibit shows the current price of the stock for the current period and at the expiration date. The lower left-hand portion of the exhibit does the same thing using the notation above. The upper right-hand side of the exhibit gives the current price of the call option and the value of the call option at the expiration date; the lower right-hand side does the same thing using our notation. Exhibit 17.2 uses the values in our illustration to construct the outcomes for the stock and the call option.

Deriving the Price of a Call Option

To derive the price of a call option, we can rely on the basic principle that the hedged portfolio, being riskless, must have a return equal to the risk-free rate of interest. Given that the amount invested in the hedged portfolio is $HS - C$, the amount that should be generated one period from now is

$$(1 + r)(HS - C) \tag{17.3}$$

EXHIBIT 17.1   One-Period Option Pricing Model

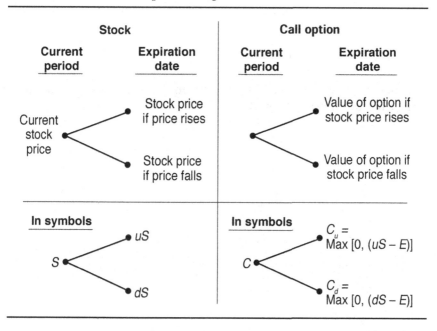

EXHIBIT 17.2   One-Period Option Pricing Model Illustration

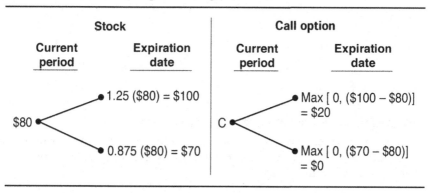

We also know what the payoff will be for the hedged portfolio if the stock's price goes up or down. Because the payoff of the hedged portfolio will be the same whether the stock's price rises or falls, we can use the payoff if it goes up, which is

$$uHS - C_u$$

The payoff of the hedged portfolio given above should be the same as the initial cost of the portfolio given by equation (17.3). Equating the two, we have

$$(1 + r)(HS - C) = uHS - C_u \qquad (17.4)$$

Substituting equation (17.2) for H in equation (17.4), and solving for the call option price, C, we find

$$C = \left(\frac{1 + r - d}{u - d}\right)\left(\frac{C_u}{1 + r}\right) + \left(\frac{u - 1 - r}{u - d}\right)\left(\frac{C_d}{1 + r}\right) \qquad (17.5)$$

Equation (17.5) is the formula for the one-period binomial option pricing model. We would have derived the same formula if we had used the payoff for a decline in the price of the underlying stock.

Applying equation (17.5) to our illustration where

u = 1.250
d = 0.875
r = 0.10
C_u = $20
C_d = $0

we get

$$C = \left(\frac{1 + 0.10 - 0.875}{1.25 - 0.875}\right)\left(\frac{\$20}{1 + 0.10}\right) + \left(\frac{1.25 - 1 - 0.10}{1.25 - 0.875}\right)\left(\frac{\$0}{1 + 0.10}\right)$$

$$= \$10.90$$

Probabilistic Interpretation of the Binomial Formula

Looking more closely at equation (17.5) we recognize that this valuation formula has a natural interpretation in terms of probability theory. First, the two quantities

$$q = \frac{1 + r - d}{u - d}$$

and

$$\tilde{q} = \frac{u - 1 - r}{u - d}$$

have the following properties:

■ $q, \tilde{q}$ add up to unity:

$$q + \tilde{q} = \frac{1 + r - d + u - 1 - r}{u - d} = \frac{u - d}{u - d} = 1$$

■ Positivity: $q, \tilde{q} > 0$

Consequently, we can interpret q as an implicitly defined probability for the event that the stock price goes up and $\tilde{q} = 1 - q$ as the probability for the opposite event that the stock price goes down. In this light, the call price given in formula (17.5) equals the discounted expected payoff of holding a call option. This interpretation is rather intuitive: When you are asked what price you are willing to pay to participate in a game with a stochastic outcome (= the call option), then you will calculate the expected payoff of this game (= $C_u \cdot q + C_d \cdot (1 - q)$). But because you receive the payoff not today but at the expiration date of the option, you discount the expected payoff to obtain its presented value:

$$C = \frac{1}{1 + r}(C_u \cdot q + C_d(1 - q)) = \frac{1}{1 + r} E_Q(C_1)$$

where C_1 denotes the random payoff of the call option at expiration date $t = 1$ and $E_Q(C_1)$ is the expected value of the one-period payoff. This formula is equal to equation (17.5).

There is one important issue related to this interpretation: The probabilities used for valuing the option are not exogenously given, they are implicitly derived from the model. We will denote this probability distribution as the "risk-neutral distribution". The reason is that under this probability measure, the stock has an expected growth rate equal to the risk-free interest rate r:

$$\begin{aligned}
E_Q(S_1) &= uS \cdot q + dS \cdot (1 - q) \\
&= \frac{1 + r - d}{u - d} uS + \frac{u - 1 - r}{u - d} dS \\
&= \left(\frac{u + ru - du}{u - d} + \frac{(u - d)(1 + r)}{u - d} \right) S \\
&= \frac{(u - d)(1 + r)}{u - d} S \\
&= S(1 + r)
\end{aligned}$$

We meet this risk-neutral measure again in the next chapter, where we introduce the Black-Scholes option pricing model.

The approach we presented for pricing options may seem oversimplified, given that we assume only two possible future states for the price of the underlying stock. In fact, we can extend the procedure by making the periods smaller and smaller, and in that way calculate a fair value for an option. It is important to note that extended and comprehensive versions of the binomial pricing model are in wide use throughout the world of finance. Moreover, the other popular option pricing model, the Black-Scholes model discussed in the next chapter, is in reality the mathematical equivalent of the binomial approach as the intervals become very small. Therefore, the approach we have described in detail here provides the conceptual framework for much of the analysis of option pricing that today's financial market participants regularly perform.

Extension to Two-Period Model

By dividing the time to expiration into two periods, we can represent price changes within the time period to expiration of the option and add more realism to our model. The extension to two intermediate periods requires that we introduce more notation. To help understand the notation, look at Exhibit 17.3. The left panel of the exhibit shows, for the stock, the initial price, the price one period from now if the price goes up or goes down, and the price at the expiration date (two periods from now) if the price in the previous period goes up or goes down. The right panel of Exhibit 17.3 shows the value of the call option at the expiration date and the value one period prior to the expiration date.

EXHIBIT 17.3   Two-Period Option Pricing Model

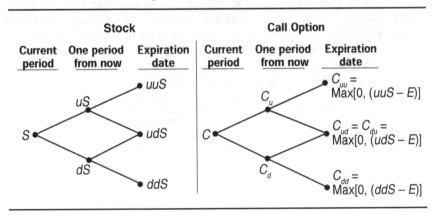

The new notation has to do with the value of the call option at the expiration date. We now use two subscripts. Specifically, C_{uu} is the call value if the stock's price went up in both periods, C_{dd} is the call value if the stock's price went down in both periods, and C_{ud} (which is equal to C_{du}) is the call value if the stock's price went down in one period and up in one period.

We solve for the call option price, C, by starting at the expiration date to determine the value of C_u and C_d. This can be done by using equation (17.5) because that equation gives the price of a one-period call option. Specifically,

$$C_u = \left(\frac{1+r-d}{u-d}\right)\left(\frac{C_{uu}}{1+r}\right) + \left(\frac{u-1-r}{u-d}\right)\left(\frac{C_{ud}}{1+r}\right) \qquad (17.6)$$

and

$$C_d = \left(\frac{1+r-d}{u-d}\right)\left(\frac{C_{du}}{1+r}\right) + \left(\frac{u-1-r}{u-d}\right)\left(\frac{C_{dd}}{1+r}\right) \qquad (17.7)$$

Once C_u and C_d are known, we can solve for C using equation (17.5).

Expressing equations (17.6) and (17.7) with the help of the risk-neutral probabilities, we obtain:

$$C_u = \frac{1}{1+r}(q \cdot C_{uu} + C_{ud} \cdot (1-q))$$

and

$$C_d = \frac{1}{1+r}(q \cdot C_{ud} + C_{dd} \cdot (1-q))$$

Using this in the formula for the current call option price given by equation (17.5), we obtain after some calculus:

$$C = \frac{1}{1+r}(C_{uu} \cdot q^2 + 2C_{ud} \cdot q(1-q) + C_{dd} \cdot (1-q)^2)$$

$$= \frac{1}{1+r}E_Q(C_2)$$

where C_2 denotes the random payoff of the call option at expiration date $t = 2$ and $E_Q(C_2)$ is the expected value of the two-period payoff.

We can recognize that the probabilities occurring in the above formula are the same as for a binomial distribution with parameters 2 and q.

To make this more concrete, let us use numbers. We assume that the stock's price can go up by 11.8% per period or down by 6.46% per period. That is,

$$u = 1.118 \quad \text{and} \quad d = 0.9354$$

Then, as shown in the top left panel of Exhibit 17.4, the stock can have three possible prices at the end of two periods:

Price goes up both periods: $uuS = (1.118)(1.118)\$80 = \$100$

Price goes down both periods: $ddS = (0.9354)(0.9354)\$80 = \$70$

Price goes up one period and down the other:

$udS = (1.118)(0.9354)\$80 = duS = (0.9354)(1.118)\$80 = \$83.66$

Notice that the first two prices are the same as in the illustration of the one-period binomial model. By breaking the length of time until expiration to two periods rather than one, and adjusting the change in the stock price accordingly, we now have three possible outcomes. If we

EXHIBIT 17.4   Two-Period Option Pricing Model Illustration

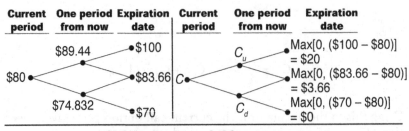

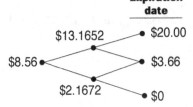

breakdown the length of time to expiration into more periods, the number of possible outcomes that the stock price may take on at the expiration date will increase. Consequently, what seemed like an unrealistic assumption about two possible outcomes for each period becomes more realistic with respect to the number of possible outcomes that the stock price may take at the expiration date.

Now we can use the values in the top right panel of Exhibit 17.4 to calculate C. In our example we assumed a risk-free interest rate of 10%. When we divide our holding period in two, the risk-free interest rate for one period is now 4.88% because when compounded this rate will produce an interest rate of 10% from now to the expiration date (two periods from now). First, consider the calculation of C_u using equation (17.6). From Exhibit 17.4 we see that

$$C_{uu} = \$20 \quad \text{and} \quad C_{ud} = \$3.66$$

therefore,

$$C_u = \left(\frac{1+0.0488-0.9354}{1.118-0.9354}\right)\left(\frac{\$20}{1+0.0488}\right) + \left(\frac{1.118-1-0.0488}{1.118-0.9354}\right)\left(\frac{\$3.66}{1+0.0488}\right)$$
$$= \$13.1652$$

From Exhibit 17.4,

$$C_{dd} = \$0 \quad \text{and} \quad C_{du} = \$3.66$$

therefore,

$$C_u = \left(\frac{1+0.0488-0.9354}{1.118-0.9354}\right)\left(\frac{\$3.66}{1+0.0488}\right) + \left(\frac{1.118-1-0.0488}{1.118-0.9354}\right)\left(\frac{\$0}{1+0.0488}\right)$$
$$= \$2.1672$$

We have inserted the values for C_u and C_d in the bottom panel of Exhibit 17.4 and can now calculate C by using equation (17.5) as follows

$$C_u = \left(\frac{1+0.0488-0.9354}{1.118-0.9354}\right)\left(\frac{\$13.1652}{1+0.0488}\right) + \left(\frac{1.118-1-0.0488}{1.118-0.9354}\right)\left(\frac{\$2.1672}{1+0.0488}\right)$$
$$= \$8.58$$

Considering Dividends

Dividends can be incorporated into the binomial pricing model by using the dividend amount at each point for the value of the stock. So, if the dividend one period from now is expected to be $1, then S_u and S_d in the left panel of Exhibit 17.3 would be $S_u + \$1$ and $S_d + \$1$, respectively. In Exhibit 17.4, this means that in the top left panel, the value for the stock one period from now would be $90.44 and $75.832, instead of $89.44 and $74.832.

CONVERGENCE OF THE BINOMIAL MODEL

The binomial model in its present form seems not to be an appropriate tool for determining the prices of real-world options. One has the impression that it is like a toy model for explaining the main ideas. Nevertheless, the binomial model is frequently used by practitioners for valuing so called "path dependent options." In order to understand the modeling power of the binomial model, we must look at what happens if we increase the number of trading periods between the current date and the expiration date.

Let us choose for reasons of simplicity the current date t_0 equal to zero and the expiration date t_1 equal to one. If there is no possibility to trade between t_0 and t_1, then we have the one-period model described above. In the second stage, we insert one new trading date between $t_0 = 0$ and $t_1 = 1$ at $t = \frac{1}{2}$. The resulting model is equal the two-period model of the previous section. Continuing this procedure we end up with a model which on the n-th stage offers $n + 1$ trading dates

$$t_k = \frac{k}{n}$$

$k = 0, ..., n$ and $n + 1$ possible values for the asset S at expiration date $t_1 = 1$. These values are given by

$$S_1^{(n)} = \{u^k d^{n-k} S_0 \big| (k = 0, ..., n)\}$$

where $S_0 = S$ denotes the current value of the stock. Exhibit 17.5 visualizes the model on the n-th stage of iteration.

We can generalize our pricing formula for a European call option with strike price X and expiration date $t = 1$ to

EXHIBIT 17.5   Refining the Binomial Model (The stock price process on the n-th stage of iteration)

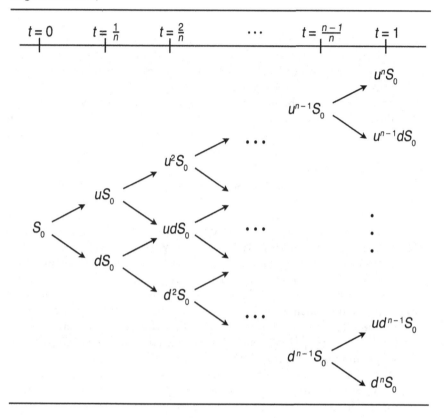

$$C = \frac{1}{(1+r)^n} E_Q(\max(S_1 - X, 0))$$

$$= \frac{1}{(1+r)^n} \sum_{k=0}^{n} \max(u^k d^{n-k} S_0 - X, 0) \cdot Q(S_1 = u^k d^{n-k} S_0)$$

$$= \frac{1}{(1+r)^n} \sum_{k=0}^{n} \max(u^k d^{n-k} S_0 - X, 0) \cdot \binom{n}{k} q^k (1-q)^{n-k}$$

where again

$$q = \frac{1 + r - d}{u - d}$$

equals the risk-neutral probability for an up-movement of the stock. We can see that the probability distribution which occurs in the above equation equals the binomial distribution with parameters n and q, which explains the name of the model.

There is one problem with our iteration procedure which prevents the above model from being realistic: If we keep the values of the parameters r, u, and d independent of n, then the model will "explode" if we increase n. One reason is that the value at date $t = 1$ of a portfolio that invests all the money in the bank account equals $(1 + r)^n$, which becomes bigger and bigger for increasing n. This is certainly not realistic and thus we should define a rate of interest $r^{(n)}$ for the small trading intervals, which depends on the current stage of iteration. $r^{(n)}$ should be chosen such that the interest rate for the total time interval under consideration $[t_0, t_1]$ remains unchanged. We consequently chose $r^{(n)} = (1 + r)^{1/n} - 1$.

A similar problem occurs with the stock price process. If the jump sizes u and d are chosen to be independent from the stage of iteration, then we are faced with possibly very large values for the stock price at the option expiration date which are unrealistic. We should chose a similar approach as for the interest rate; thus we impose that the expected relative growth rate $\mu^{(n)} = \mathrm{Elog}(S_1^{(n)}/S_0)$ as well as the variance $\sigma^{2(n)} = \mathrm{Vlog}(S_1^{(n)}/S_0)$ converge to finite limits μ and σ^2.

Now we can ask a natural question: What happens if we increase the number of trading dates between today and the date of expiration to infinity? The answer is not so easy and the general treatment of this question is beyond the scope of this chapter.[3] Intuitively, there are two possibilities: Either the probability for a jump goes to zero and we obtain something like a piecewise constant jump process or the jump sizes go to zero and we end up with a continuous limit process. This is the way, we present it below. Cox-Ross-Rubinstein (1979) have shown that for the special choice

$$u^{(n)} = e^{\sqrt{\frac{\sigma^2}{n}}} \text{ and } d^{(n)} = e^{-\sqrt{\frac{\sigma^2}{n}}}$$

the following limit distribution for the final stock price S_1 is obtained:

---

[3] A complete description of discrete binomial models and their possible limits is discused in Rachev and Rüschendorf (1994) and Rachev and Mittnik (2000).

$$\log S_1^{\infty} - \log S_0 \sim N\!\left(r^{\infty} - \frac{1}{2}\sigma^2, \sigma^2\right)$$

where

$$r^{\infty} = \log(1 + r)$$

denotes the continuously compounded risk-free rate of return from the current date $t = 0$ to the expiration date $t = 1$. This result is obtained by an application of the Central Limit Theorem.

The convergence of the binomial distribution to the normal distribution and the convergence of the corresponding stock price distribution to the lognormal distribution is visualized in Exhibit 17.6. The previous equation shows that in the limit the expected continuously

EXHIBIT 17.6 Probability Distribution of S for Different Stages of Iteration and the Limit Distribution (In the current example we have $S_0 = 100$, $\sigma = 20\%$, and $r = 5\%$.)

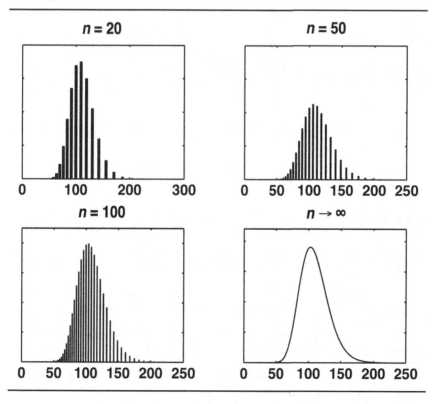

compounded rate of return of the stock equals the risk-free rate of return r^∞. This is an important result which we will meet again in the context of the Black-Scholes formula in the next chapter.

The value of a European call option with strike price X and expiration date $t = 1$ can now be obtained by calculating the following expected value:

$$C = e^{-r^\infty} E_Q(\max(S_1 - X, 0))$$

$$= e^{-r^\infty} \int\limits_{-\infty}^{\infty} \max(S_0 e^{r^\infty - 0.5\sigma^2 + \sigma z} - K, 0)\varphi(z)dz$$

where φ is the density function of a standard normal random variable. This expected value can be explicitly calculated and we obtain a special case of the famous Black-Scholes formula:

$$C = S_0 \Phi(d_1) - e^{-r^\infty} X\Phi(d_2)$$

where

$$d_1 = \frac{\log(S/K) + r^\infty + 0.5\sigma^2}{\sigma}$$

$$d_2 = d_1 - \sigma$$

and Φ denotes the cumulative distribution function of the standard normal distribution.

In the next chapter we discuss the Black-Scholes Option Pricing Model.

REFERENCES

Black, F., and M. Scholes. 1973. "The Pricing of Corporate Liabilities." *Journal of Political Economy*, May–June: 637–659.

Cox, J. C., and S. A. Ross. 1976. "The Valuation of Options for Alternative Stochastic Processes." *Journal of Financial Economics* 3 (March): 145–166.

Cox, J. C., S. A. Ross, and M. Rubinstein. 1979. "Option Pricing: A Simplified Approach." *Journal of Financial Economics* 7: 229–263.

Merton, R. 1973. "The Theory of Rational Option Pricing." *Bell Journal of Economics and Management Science* 4 (Spring): 141–183.

Rachev, S. T., and S. Mittnik. 2000. *Stable Paretian Models in Finance.* Chichester: John Wiley & Sons.

Rachev, S. T., and L. Rüschendorf. 1994. "On the Cox, Ross and Rubinstein Model for Option Pricing." *Theory of Probability and Its Applications* 39: 150–190.

Rendleman, R. J., and B. J. Bartter. 1979. "Two-State Option Pricing." *Journal of Finance* 34: 1092-1100.

Sharpe, W. F. 1978. *Investment.* Englewood Cliffs, NJ: Prentice Hall.

CHAPTER 18

Black-Scholes Option Pricing Model

In the previous chapter we have seen how one can obtain a continuous-time stock price process by iteratively refining the binomial model. This chapter introduces the most popular continuous-time model for option valuation based on the Black-Scholes theory. We start with a motivation for the results presented in this chapter. The main task will be to find an appropriate stochastic model for the potential evolution of a stock price.

MOTIVATION

Let us assume that the price of a certain stock in June of Year 0 ($t = 0$) is given to be $S_0 = \$100$. We want to value an option with strike price $X = \$110$ maturing in June of Year 1 ($t = T$). As additional information we are given the continuously compounded one year risk-free interest rate $r = 5\%$. Exhibit 18.1 visualizes potential paths of the stock between $t = 0$ and $t = T$. How can we define a reasonable model for the stock price evolution?

It is clear that the daily changes or the change between the current and the next quotes cannot be predicted and can consequently be seen as realizations of random variables. On the other hand, we know that if we are investing in stocks then we can *expect* a rate of return in the long run which is higher than the risk-free rate. Let us denote that unknown expected rate of return as μ. Here and in the rest of this chapter, we assume that the stock pays no dividend.

EXHIBIT 18.1 Possible Paths of the Stock Price Evolution over One Year with $S_0 =$ $100 and $X = $110

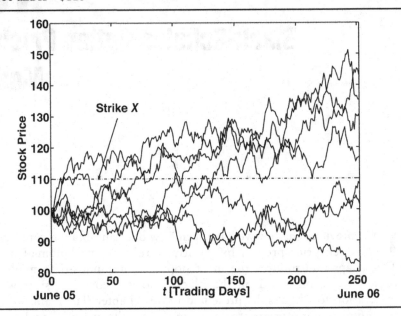

Furthermore, we know that stock returns exhibit random fluctuations—called volatility. Let σ denote the unknown daily rate of volatility. Here and below we have implicitly assumed that the expected return and the volatility of the stock are time independent. This assumption might be violated in practice. Formalizing our ideas about the stock price we come up with the following equation for the return of the stock in a small time interval of length Δt:

$$\underbrace{\frac{S_{t+\Delta t} - S_t}{S_t}}_{\substack{= \text{ Return in} \\ \text{period } [t, t+\Delta t]}} = \mu \cdot \Delta t + \underbrace{\sigma \cdot \varepsilon_t^{\Delta t}}_{\text{"Stochastic noise"}}$$

The stochastic noise $\sigma \cdot \varepsilon_t^{\Delta t}$ should have the following properties:

- No systematic influence: $E(\varepsilon_t^{\Delta t}) = 0$
- No dependence between the noise of different dates: The random variables ε_t and ε_s are independent for $s \neq t$.
- The variance of the noise is proportional to the length of the time interval Δt.

One possible model for the noise process is provided by a stochastic process called *Brownian motion*, which we discussed in Chapter 10. We can just define

$$\varepsilon_t^{\Delta t} = W_{t+\Delta t} - W_t$$

and obtain a noise process which fulfills all of the above requirements. We know from Chapter 10 that the increments of the Brownian motion are independent and that the variance of the increments is proportional to the length of the considered time interval. Additionally, the expectation of the increments is zero.

With this definition, it is possible to write the equation for the return process in the following form:

$$\frac{S_{t+\Delta t} - S_t}{S_t} = \mu\Delta t + \sigma(W_{t+\Delta t} - W_t)$$

If we decrease the length Δt of the time interval over which the increment is considered constant, then we can switch to a "differential type" notation:[1]

$$\frac{dS_t}{S_t} = \mu \cdot dt + \sigma \cdot dW_t, \quad t \geq 0$$

The process defined in the above equation is called *geometric Brownian motion*. In explicit notation the geometric Brownian motion possesses the following form (see Chapter 10):

$$S_t = S_0 e^{\left(\mu - \frac{1}{2}\sigma^2\right)t + \sigma W_t}$$

and S_t is lognormally distributed. This process is used in the Black-Scholes model to describe the stock price dynamic. Additionally, the model assumes the existence of a risk-free asset—called money market account or bond—with the following dynamic:

---

[1] We must admit at this point that a priori such a notation makes no sense, especially as we have noted in Chapter 10 that the paths of the Brownian motion are not differentiable. Nevertheless, there is a theory (the Itô theory) which gives sense to these so-called stochastic differential equations.

$$\frac{dB_t}{B_t} = r \cdot dt, \quad t \geq 0 \Leftrightarrow B_t = B_0 e^{rt}, t \geq 0 \qquad (18.1)$$

BLACK-SCHOLES FORMULA

Black and Scholes (1973) have shown that it is possible—under some assumptions discussed in this section—to duplicate the payoff of a European call option with a continuously rebalanced portfolio consisting of the two assets S and B. This means that the price of the call option equals the initial costs for starting the hedging strategy.

The *Black-Scholes option pricing model* computes the fair (or theoretical) price of a European call option on a nondividend-paying stock with the following formula:

$$C = S\Phi(d_1) - Xe^{-rT} \Phi(d_2) \qquad (18.2)$$

where

$$d_1 = \frac{\ln(S/X) + (r + 0.5\sigma^2 T)}{\sigma\sqrt{t}} \qquad (18.3)$$

$$d_2 = d_1 - \sigma\sqrt{T} \qquad (18.4)$$

$\ln(\cdot)$ = natural logarithm
C = call option price
S = current stock price
X = strike price
r = short-term risk-free interest rate
e ≈ 2.718 (natural antilog of 1)
T = time remaining to the expiration date (measured as a fraction of a year)
σ = expected return volatility for the stock (standard deviation of the stock's return)
$\Phi(\cdot)$ = the cumulative distribution function of a standard normal distribution

The option price derived from the Black-Scholes option pricing model is "fair" in the sense that if any other price existed in a market where all the assumptions of the Black-Scholes model are fulfilled, it would be possible to earn riskless arbitrage profits by taking an offsetting position in the underlying stock. That is, if the price of the call option in the market is higher than that derived from the Black-Scholes option pricing model, an investor could sell the call option and buy a certain number of shares in the underlying stock. If the reverse is true, that is, the market price of the call option is less than the "fair" price derived from the model, the investor could buy the call option and sell short a certain number of shares in the underlying stock. This process of hedging by taking a position in the underlying stock allows the investor to lock in the riskless arbitrage profit. The number of shares necessary to hedge the position changes as the factors that affect the option price change, so the hedged position must be changed constantly.

COMPUTING A CALL OPTION PRICE

To illustrate the Black-Scholes option pricing formula, assume the following values:

Strike price = $45
Time remaining to expiration = 183 days
Current stock price = $47
Expected return volatility = Standard deviation = 25%
Risk-free rate = 10%

In terms of the values in the formula:

S = 47
X = 45
T = 0.5 (183 days/365, rounded)
σ = 0.25
r = 0.10

Substituting these values into equations (18.3) and (18.4):

$$d_1 = \frac{\ln(47/45) + (0.10 + 0.5[0.25]^2)0.5}{0.25\sqrt{0.5}} = 0.6172$$

$$d_2 = 0.6172 - 0.25\sqrt{0.5} = 0.440443$$

From a normal distribution table,

$$\Phi(0.6172) = 0.7315 \quad \text{and} \quad \Phi(0.4404) = 0.6702$$

Then

$$C = 47(0.7315) - 45(e^{-(0.10)(0.5)})(0.6702) = \$5.69$$

Exhibit 18.2 shows the option value as calculated from the Black-Scholes option pricing model for different assumptions concerning (1) the standard deviation for the stock's return (i.e., expected return volatility); (2) the risk-free rate; and (3) the time remaining to expiration. Notice that the option price varies directly with three variables: expected return volatility, the risk-free rate, and time remaining to expiration. That is: (1) the lower (higher) the expected volatility, the lower (higher) the option price; (2) the lower (higher) the risk-free rate, the lower (higher) the option price; and (3) the shorter (longer) the time remaining to expiration, the lower (higher) the option price.

EXHIBIT 18.2   Comparison of Black-Scholes Call Option Price Varying One Factor at a Time

Base Case
Call option:
Strike price = $45
Time remaining to expiration = 183 days
Current stock price = $47
Expected return volatility = standard deviation of a stock's return = 25%
Risk-free rate = 10%

Holding All Factors Constant except Expected Return Volatility

Expected Price Volatility	Call Option Price
15%	4.69
20	5.17
25 (base case)	5.59
30	6.26
35	6.84
40	7.42

EXHIBIT 18.2 (Continued)

Holding All Factors Constant Except the Risk-Free Rate

Risk-Free Interest Rate	Call Option Price
7%	5.27
8	5.41
9	5.50
10 (base case)	5.69
11	5.84
12	5.99
13	6.13

Holding All Factors Constant except Time Remaining to Expiration

Time Remaining to Expiration	Call Option Price
30 days	2.85
60	3.52
91	4.15
183 (base case)	5.69
273	6.99

SENSITIVITY OF OPTION PRICE TO A CHANGE IN FACTORS: THE GREEKS

In employing options in investment strategies, an asset manager or trader would like to know how sensitive the price of an option is to a change in any one of the factors that affect its price. Sensitivity measures for assessing the impact of a change in factors on the price of an option are referred to as the "the Greeks." In this section, we will explain these measures for the factors in the Black-Scholes model. Specifically, we discuss measures of the sensitivity of a call option's price to changes in the price of the underlying stock, the time to expiration, expected volatility, and interest rate. Exhibit 18.3 gives an overview and lists the sensitivities of the option price with respect to all parameters of the Black and Scholes model.

EXHIBIT 18.3 Sensitivities of the Option Price with Respect to Each Parameter of the Black-Scholes Model

Parameter	Corresponding Greek	Analytic Expression
Stock price S	Delta	$$\Delta = \frac{\partial C}{\partial S} = \Phi(d_1)$$
Stock price S (convexity adjustment)	Gamma	$$\Gamma = \frac{\partial^2 C}{\partial S^2} = \frac{\varphi(d_1)}{S\sigma\sqrt{T}}$$
Volatility σ	Vega	$$\upsilon = \frac{\partial C}{\partial \sigma} = S \cdot \varphi(d_1) \cdot T$$
Time to maturity T	Theta	$$\Theta = \frac{\partial C}{\partial T} = -\frac{S\varphi(d_1)\sigma}{2\sqrt{T}} - rXe^{-rT}\Phi(d_2)$$
Interest rate r	Rho	$$\rho = \frac{\partial C}{\partial r} = X \cdot T \cdot e^{-rT} \cdot \Phi(d_2)$$

Price of a Call Option Price and Price of the Underlying: Delta and Gamma

In developing an option-pricing model, we have seen the importance of understanding the relationship between the option price and the price of the underlying stock. Moreover, an asset manager employing options for risk management wants to know how the option position will change as the price of the underlying changes.

One way to do so is to determine the derivative of the call option price with respect to the spot price of the underlying stock:

$$\Delta = \frac{\partial C}{\partial S} = \Phi(d_1) \tag{18.5}$$

This quantity is called the "delta" of the option. and can be used in the following way to determine the expected price change in the option if the stock increases by about \$1:

$$\Delta C = C(S + \$1) - C(S) \approx \frac{\partial C}{\partial S}\Delta S = \$\Phi(d_1) \tag{18.6}$$

The relation given by (18.6) holds true for small changes in the price of the underlying. For large changes the assumed linear relationship between call and option price is not valid and we must make a so-called convexity adjustment:

$$\Delta C = C(S + \$x) - C(S) \approx \frac{\partial C}{\partial S}\Delta S + \frac{1}{2} \cdot \underbrace{\frac{\partial^2 C}{\partial S^2}}_{= \Gamma} (\Delta S)^2$$

Here Γ denotes the "options gamma" which measures the curvature of the option price as a function of the price of the underlying stock.

Exhibit 18.4 visualizes this effect. We see that for small variations in the stock price the "true price" and both approximations nearly coincide. But for medium-sized variations, only the convexity-adjusted approximation is still accurate. For large variations in the underlying stock price both approximations fail.

EXHIBIT 18.4   Accuracy of Simple Delta Approximation and Convexity-Adjusted Delta-Gamma Approximation

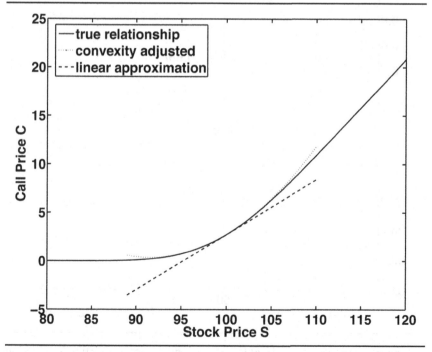

Note: The example is calculated for a one month option with strike $X = \$100$ and current stock price $S = \$100$ with an interest of 10% p.a. and a volatility of 20% p.a.

The impact of the parameters stock price, interest rate, time to maturity, and volatility on the option's delta is visualized in Exhibit 18.5. We can recognize that the influence of a change in the underlying on the option value measured by the option's delta increases with increasing stock price. Intuitively, this is clear as for large values of the underlying stock the option behaves like the stock itself, whereas for values of the underlying stock near zero, the option is virtually worthless. Also, we can see that if the option is at the money, the impact of a change in the value of the underlying stock increases with increasing time to maturity and with increasing interest rate, which is not as obvious. The delta of the option that is at the money decreases with increasing volatility. The reason is as follows. Imagine that you possess an option on an underlying which is virtually nonrandom. In this case, the value of the option equals its intrinsic value and therefore a change in the underlying stock price has a large impact on the value of the option

EXHIBIT 18.5   Delta as a Function of the Parameters

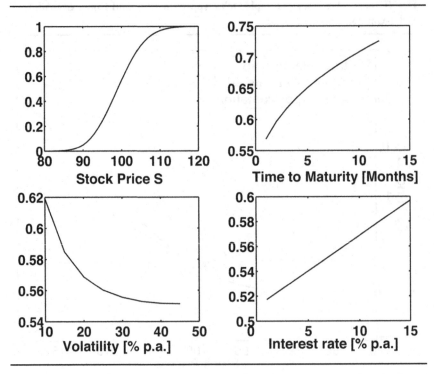

Note: The example is calculated for a one month option with strike $X = \$100$ and current stock price $S = \$100$ with an interest of 10% p.a. and a volatility of 20% p.a.

provided that the current stock price is above the strike. In a stochastic environment (i.e., nonzero volatilty), every movement of the stock can be immediately followed by a movement in the opposite direction. This is why the option price is not as sensitive to stock price movements when volatility is high (i.e., delta decreases with increasing volatility).

For gamma, it is clear that the impact of a change in the price of the underlying is the highest if the option is at the money. If the option is far out or far in the money, we have $C \approx 0$ or $C \approx S$ and, therefore, the second derivative with respect to S will vanish.

Below we will give a brief overview of the remaining sensitivity measures called theta, vega, and rho. Exhibit 18.6 visualizes the effect of the current stock price on the Greeks gamma, theta, rho, and vega.

The Call Option Price and Time to Expiration: Theta

All other factors constant, the longer the time to expiration, the greater the option price. Since each day the option moves closer to the expira-

EXHIBIT 18.6   Variation of the Greeks with Respect to the Current Price of the Underlying Stock

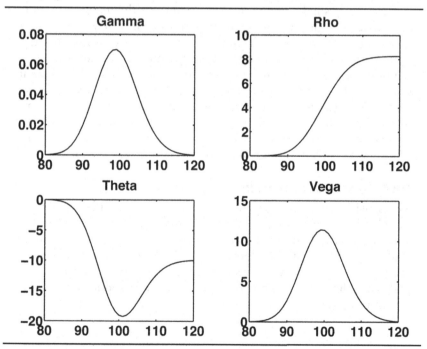

Note: The example is calculated for a one month option with strike $X = \$100$ and spot price $S = \$100$ with an interest of 10% p.a. and a volatility of 20% p.a.

tion date, the time to expiration decreases. The theta of an option measures the change in the option price as the time to expiration decreases, or equivalently, it is a measure of time decay.

Assuming that the price of the underlying stock does not change (which means that the intrinsic value of the option does not change), theta measures how quickly the time value of the option changes as the option moves toward expiration.

Buyers of options prefer a low theta so that the option price does not decline quickly as it moves toward the expiration date. An option writer benefits from an option that has a high theta.

Option Price and Expected Volatility: Vega

All other factors constant, a change in the expected volatility will change the option price. The vega[2] (also called "kappa") of an option measures the dollar price change in the price of the option for a 1% change in the expected price volatility. The option price is most sensitive with respect to a change in volatility when the option is at or near the money. This can be easily understood as follows. Imagine the option is very deep out of the money (i.e., the option is virtually worthless). In this case, any small change in the volatility of the underlying will have no impact on the option price. It will still be nearly zero. The same holds true if the option is far in the money (i.e., it is nearly sure that the option will end in the money and the price of the option equals nearly the price of the stock). In this case, the impact of a small change in the volatility of the stock is negligible as well and, therefore, vega will be small. The situation is different if the option ranges near at the money. In this case, the option is very sensitive to volatility changes as they change the probability of ending in or out of the money dramatically. That is why we have a high vega for an option near the money.

Call Option Price and Interest Rate: Rho

The sensitivity of the option price to a change in the interest rate is called "rho." The option's rho is the least popular among the Greeks. Nevertheless, it is of practical value as it can be used to immunize a trader's position against interest-rate risk. An equivalent concept which might be familiar to some readers is the duration of a bond. For our purposes, rho plays a minor role and we have introduced it for the sake of completeness.

---

[2] Vega is not a Greek letter. Vega is used to denote *v*olatility, just as theta is used for *t*ime and rho is used for interest *r*ate.

The Greeks and Portfolio Applications

In practical applications, the Greeks are used to hedge portfolios with respect to certain risk exposures. Because a portfolio is a linear combination of assets and as the derivative of a linear combination of functions equals the linear combination of the derivatives, we can simply calculate the Greek of a portfolio of options or other assets as the linear combination of the individual Greeks. When we seek to build a portfolio in a way that one or several of the Greeks equal zero, then the portfolio is said to be hedged with respect to the respective risk factor. A zero-delta portfolio, for example, is insensitive with respect to small changes in the value of S, and similarly for the other factors.

COMPUTING A PUT OPTION PRICE

We have focused our attention on call options. How do we value put options? This is done by using the following *put-call parity relationship* which gives the relationship among the price of the common stock, the call option price, and the put option price. For a nondividend-paying stock, we derived this relationship in the previous chapter. For a dividend-paying stock, it can be shown that the relationship is equal to:

European call price = Price of stock – Present value of the strike price
– European put price – Present value of dividends

If we can calculate the fair value of a call option, the fair value of a put with the same strike price and expiration on the same stock can be calculated from the put-call parity relationship.

ASSUMPTIONS UNDERLYING THE BLACK-SCHOLES MODEL AND BASIC EXTENSIONS

The Black-Scholes model is based on several restrictive assumptions. These assumptions were necessary to develop the hedge to realize riskless arbitrage profits if the market price of the call option deviates from the price obtained from the model. Here, we will look at these assumptions and mention some basic extensions of the model that make pricing more realistic. In this next chapter, we will discuss extensions of the basic model.

Taxes and Transactions Costs

The Black-Scholes model ignores taxes and transactions costs. The model can be modified to account for taxes, but the problem is that there is not one unique tax rate. Transactions costs include both commissions and the bid-ask spreads for the stock and the option, as well as other costs associated with trading options. This assumption, together with the next two, is the most important for the validity of the Black-Scholes model. The derivation of the price depends mainly on the existence of a replicating portfolio. When transaction costs exist, even if they are negligibly small, then the hedge portfolio can no longer be built and the argument leading to the uniqueness of the price fails.

Trading in Continuous Time, Short Selling, and Trading Arbitrary Fractions of Assets

One crucial assumption underlying the Black-Scholes model is the opportunity to (1) perform trades in continuous time; (2) to buy a negative number of all traded assets (short selling); and (3) to buy and sell arbitrary fractions of all traded assets. Only these more or less unrealistic assumptions together with the previously discussed absence of transaction costs and taxes allow the derivation of the unique call option price by the hedging argument. The portfolio, consisting of certain fractions of the bond and the underlying stock, needs an ongoing rebalancing that is only possible in a market that allows continuous-time trading. Additionally, the number of stocks and bonds needed in the portfolio to replicate the option can be an arbitrary real number, possibly negative.

Variance of the Stock's Return

The Black-Scholes model assumes that the variance of the stock's return is (1) constant over the life of the option and (2) known with certainty. If (1) does not hold, an option pricing model can be developed that allows the variance to change. The violation of (2), however, is more serious. As the Black-Scholes model depends on the riskless hedge argument and, in turn, the variance must be known to construct the proper hedge, if the variance is not known, the hedge will not be riskless.

Stochastic Process Generating Stock Prices

To derive an option pricing model, an assumption is needed about the way stock prices move. The Black-Scholes model is based on the assumption that stock prices are generated by a geometric Brownian motion. As explained in Chapter 10, the geometric Brownian motion is a stochastic process with continuous paths. In reality, one can sometimes observe that the market exhibits large fluctuations that cannot be explained by a continuous-time process with constant volatility as the Brownian motion. In theory, there are two possibilities to overcome this problem. Either one introduces the previously mentioned stochastic volatility or one allows for jumps in the stock price. Merton (1973) and Cox and Ross (1976) have developed option pricing models assuming a jump process.

Risk-Free Interest Rate

In deriving the Black-Scholes model, two assumptions were made about the risk-free interest rate. First, it was assumed that the interest rates for borrowing and lending were the same. Second, it was assumed that the interest rate was constant and known over the life of the option. The first assumption is unlikely to hold because borrowing rates are higher than lending rates. The effect on the Black-Scholes model is that the option price will be bound between the call price derived from the model using the two interest rates. The model can handle the second assumption by replacing the risk-free rate over the life of the option by the geometric average of the period returns expected over the life of the option.[3]

Dividends

The original Black-Scholes model is for a nondividend-paying stock. In the case of a dividend-paying stock, it may be advantageous for the holder of the call option to exercise the option early. To understand why, suppose that a stock pays a dividend such that, if the call option is exercised, dividends would be received prior to the option's expiration date. If the dividends plus the accrued interest earned from investing the dividends from the time they are received until the expiration date are greater than the time premium of the option (i.e., the excess of the option price over its intrinsic value), then it would be optimal to exercise the option. In the case where dividends are not known with certainty, it will not be possible to develop a model using the riskless arbitrage argument.

In the case of known dividends, a shortcut to adjust the Black-Scholes model is to reduce the stock price by the present value of the dividends. Black (1975) has suggested an approximation technique to value a call option for a dividend-paying stock.[4] A more accurate model

---

[3] Returns on short-term Treasury bills cannot be known with certainty over the long term. Only the expected return is known, and there is a variance around it. The effects of variable interest rates are considered in Merton (1973).

[4] The approach requires that the investor at the time of purchase of the call option and for every subsequent period specify the exact date the option will be exercised.

for pricing call options in the case of known dividends has been developed by Roll (1977), Geske (1979, 1981), and Whaley (1981).

The Option Is a European Option

The Black-Scholes model assumes that the call option is a European call option. Because the Black-Scholes model is on a nondividend-paying stock, early exercise of a call option will not be economic because, by selling rather than exercising the call option, the option holder can recoup the time value. The binomial option pricing model can easily handle American call options.

BLACK-SCHOLES MODEL APPLIED TO THE PRICING OF OPTIONS ON BONDS: IMPORTANCE OF ASSUMPTIONS

While the Black-Scholes option pricing model was developed for non-dividend paying stocks, it has been applied to options on bonds. We conclude this chapter by demonstrating the limitations of applying the model to valuing options on bonds. This allows us to appreciate the importance of the assumptions on option pricing. To do so, let us look at the values that would be derived in a couple of examples.

We know that there are coupon-paying bonds and zero-coupon bonds. In our illustration we will use a zero-coupon bond. The reason is that the original Black-Scholes model was for common stock that did not pay a dividend and so a zero-coupon bond would be the equivalent type of instrument. Specifically, we look at how the Black-Scholes option pricing model would value a zero-coupon bond with three years to maturity assuming the following:

Strike price = $88.00
Time remaining to expiration = 2 years
Current bond price = $83.96
Expected return volatility = standard deviation = 10%
Risk-free rate = 6%

The Black-Scholes model would give an option value of $8.116. There is no reason to suspect that this value generated by the model is incorrect. However, let us change the problem slightly. Instead of a strike price of $88, let us make the strike price $100.25. The Black-Scholes option pricing model would give a fair value of $2.79. Is there any reason to believe this is incorrect? Well, consider that this is a call option on a zero-coupon bond that will never have a value greater than its maturity value of $100. Consequently, a call option with a strike price of $100.25 must have a value of zero. Yet, the Black-Scholes option pricing model tells us that the value is $2.79! In fact, if we assume a higher expected volatility, the Black-Scholes model would give an even greater value for the call option.

Why is the Black-Scholes model off by so much in our illustration? The answer is that there are three assumptions underlying the Black-Scholes model that limit its use in pricing options on fixed-income instruments.

The first assumption is that the probability distribution for the underlying asset's prices assumed by the Black-Scholes model permits some probability—no matter how small—that the price can take on any positive value. But in the case of a zero-coupon bond, the price cannot take on a value above $100. In the case of a coupon bond, we know that the price cannot exceed the sum of the coupon payments plus the maturity value. For example, for a five-year 10% coupon bond with a maturity value of $100, the price cannot be greater than $150 (five coupon payments of $10 plus the maturity value of $100). Thus, unlike stock prices, bond prices have a maximum value. The only way that a bond's price can exceed the maximum value is if negative interest rates are permitted. While there have been instances where negative interest rates have occurred outside the United States, users of option pricing models assume that this outcome cannot occur. Consequently, any probability distribution for prices assumed by an option pricing model that permits bond prices to be higher than the maximum bond value could generate nonsensical option prices. The Black-Scholes model does allow bond prices to exceed the maximum bond value (or, equivalently, assumes that interest rates can be negative).

The second assumption of the Black-Scholes model is that the short-term interest rate is constant over the life of the option. Yet the price of an interest rate option will change as interest rates change. A change in the short-term interest rate changes the rates along the yield curve. Therefore, for interest rate options it is clearly inappropriate to assume that the short-term rate will be constant.

The third assumption is that the variance of returns is constant over the life of the option. As a bond moves closer to maturity, its price volatility declines and therefore its return volatility declines. Therefore, the assumption that variance of returns is constant over the life of the option is inappropriate.

REFERENCES

Black, F. 1975. "Fact and Fantasy in the Use of Options." *Financial Analysts Journal,* July–August: 36–41, 61–72.

Black, F., and M. Scholes. 1973. "The Pricing of Corporate Liabilities." *Journal of Political Economy,* May–June: 637–659.

Cox, J. C., and S. A. Ross. 1976. "The Valuation of Options for Alternative Stochastic Processes." *Journal of Financial Economics* 3: 145–166.

Geske, R. 1979. "A Note on an Analytical Formula for Unprotected American Call Options on Stocks with Known Dividends." *Journal of Financial Economics* 6: 375–380.

Geske, R. 1981. "Comment on Whaley's Note." *Journal of Financial Economics* 8: 213–215.

Merton, R. 1973. "The Theory of Rational Option Pricing." *Bell Journal of Economics and Management Science* 4 (Spring): 141–183.

Whaley, R. 1981. "On the Valuation of American Call Options on Stocks with Known Dividends." *Journal of Financial Economics* 8: 207–211.

CHAPTER 19

Extension of the Black-Scholes Model and Alternative Approaches

In the previous two chapters we introduced the classical option pricing theory which was developed in the 1970s mainly by Black, Scholes, and Merton. It did not take a long time until the first attacks on the validity of the theory were identified in the literature. The problem is, that some of the assumptions on the stock price process made by the Black and Scholes model are rather restrictive and some of them contradict empirical evidence.[1] In this chapter, we provide a short overview of the most popular generalizations of the classical Black-Scholes model. We begin with a description of a well-known observation regarding option prices that is not explained by the Black-Scholes model, the "smile effect."

THE "SMILE EFFECT"

One famous effect which cannot be explained in the Black-Scholes model is the so-called "smile effect." The smile effect describes the phenomenon that the graph of implied volatilities of a cross-section of European call options against their strike prices exhibits a U-shape. The implied volatility $\sigma_I(X)$ of a European call option with strike X and time to maturity T and market price $C(X)$ is defined as the volatility which makes the Black-Scholes price equal to the market price. It is called

---

[1] For a comprehensive discussion of the biases in the Black-Scholes model, see Chapter 17 in Hull (1998).

"implied volatility," as it is obtained by making the theoretical price as given by the Black-Scholes model equal to the market price. Considering the implied volatility for options with the same maturity T, but different strikes, we observe patterns as illustrated exemplarily in Exhibit 19.1. The left graph shows the "classical volatility smile" as it is observed in foreign exchange and interest rate markets whereas the right panel visualizes the asymmetric smile which is typical for equity markets.[2] But the implied volatility depends not only on the strike price of options with a fixed maturity but it differs also among options with the same strike but different maturities. And third, the implied volatility of a specific option with a fixed strike price and fixed maturity does not remain constant through time but evolves dynamically.

In summary, we have that the implied volatility for a fixed point in time is given by a surface depending on the strike price and the time to maturity. This implied volatility surface is not constant through time but evolves through time. For every specific underlying, the Black-Scholes model offers only one constant volatility parameter σ. As an obvious consequence, the Black-Scholes model is not able to describe or to explain the observed market patterns.

EXHIBIT 19.1   Possible Implied Volatility Graphs

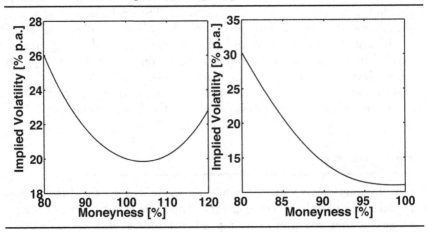

Note: The left plot shows a typical implied volatility graph. The right plot shows an asymmetric volatility smile (sometimes denoted as "smirk" or "skew") typical for stock options. The implied volatility is plotted against moneyness which is nothing but the strike price expressed in percentage of the current price of the underlying stock.

---

[2] The significant asymmetry is typical for the time after the October 1987 equity market crash in the United States. Before the crash, the smile for equity options was similar to the other markets. For an overview of "typical smile patterns," see Thompkins (2001).

This fits very well to our findings in Chapter 11, where we have already stated that asset returns exhibit phenomena such as volatility clustering, skewness, and heavy tails. There have been suggestions as to how to overcome the deficiencies of the Black-Scholes model and in the next section we explain the main ideas of the different approaches. We have divided the chapter in two parts where the first deals with generalizations of the Black-Scholes model in continuous time, whereas the second part treats possible variants of the Black-Scholes model in discrete time.

CONTINUOUS-TIME MODELS

Continuous-time generalizations of the geometric Brownian motion for option pricing purposes can be divided into several subclasses. *Stochastic volatility models* going back to the Hull-White model (1987)[3] try to provide a more realistic stochastic process for the underlying by introducing a second stochastic process for the volatility (i.e., not only the stock price itself but also the variance of the stock price is random). Second, there are the so-called *local volatility models* which are based on the insight that every empirically observed option price structure may be generated by a unique diffusion process. To face the criticism that stock price variation cannot be explain by a stochastic process with continuous paths, several researchers have introduced *pure jump models* or combinations of jump and diffusion processes.

A popular representative of the latter class is the jump diffusion model by Merton (1976). Another possibility to explain the large variation in stock prices is the use of Lévy processes. We will briefly discuss the method of subordination, as, for example, examined in Rachev and Rüschendorf (1994) and Hurst, Platen, and Rachev (1999),[4] and the finite moment log stable process introduced by Carr (2003).

Stochastic Volatility Models

As just mentioned, one of the first stochastic volatility models has been suggested by Hull and White. The underlying stock price is modeled by the following process:

$$dS_t = S_t r dt + S_t \sqrt{V_t} d W_t^{(1)}$$

---

[3] Independently, Scott (1987) and Wiggins (1987) have suggested stochastic volatility models.

[4] See also Rachev and Mittnik (2000) and the references therein.

where r denotes the risk-free rate of return and the local variance V_t follows a stochastic process itself given by:

$$dV_t = a(b - V_t)dt + V_t^\alpha \xi dW_t^{(2)}$$

where a, b, α, and ξ are real constants and $W^{(1)}$, $W^{(2)}$ denote two possibly correlated Brownian motions.

Hull and White show that if the two Brownian motions are independent, the price of a European call option can still be calculated by using the Black-Scholes formula for the time-varying volatility. The only difference is that one has to take the average of Black-Scholes formula generated prices over all possible paths of the volatility. Hedging becomes more difficult in the stochastic volatility setting as it is no longer possible to generate a risk-free portfolio consisting of the European call option and a fraction of the underlying stock. The reason is that we are faced with two different risk drivers: the random volatility and the noise in the stock price itself. Thus we need three assets depending on the same risk drivers to eliminate both risk drivers completely. One can demonstrate, for example, that given two options on the same stock with different strike prices and/or different maturities, we are able to build a risk-free portfolio consisting of fractions of these two options and a certain portion of the underlying stock.

Stochastic volatility models are difficult to handle and it took a while until efficient parameter estimation and calibration to the current market prices of stochastic volatility models became possible thanks to the papers by Stein and Stein (1991) and Heston (1993). These authors showed that for a special class of stochastic volatility models, the risk neutral distribution of the underlying at maturity can be explicitly derived in terms of its Fourier transform and then the price of a European call option can efficiently be evaluated by a special inversion formula.[5] This approach founded the popularity of stochastic volatility models as it overcame their main disadvantage: A model estimation based on classical concepts such as maximum-likelihood estimation is difficult or even impossible as the volatility is not observable in the market. In addition, every set of stock prices which is available for the estimation consists of a discrete sampling from the continuous-process specification which means that paths properties are not observable as

---

[5] Other models in this framework have been suggested. An attempt for a unified framework in the class of stochastic volatility models has been made by Lewis (2000) and Duffie, Pan, and Singleton (2000) who have proposed the class of affine jump diffusions containing the stochastic volatility models as a special case.

well. The inversion approach, in contrast, allows for a parameter estimation by calibrating the model to the observed option prices which means that the model parameters are determined by minimizing the distance between the model prices and the market prices. As a consequence, the calibrated model will more or less reflect the current market situation and the model can be used to determine the prices of instruments which are currently not traded at the market or whose prices are not reliable. This approach is referred to as "smile consistent pricing." At a first glance, this fact seems appealing but nevertheless there is a caveat: The calibration approach does not explain the observed prices. This means that even if the prices of plain vanilla instruments such as European call options are nearly perfectly replicated by the model, then it might still be that the prices of exotic instruments obtained by the model are wrong. In other words: There might be several models reproducing the liquid prices which strongly differ in the prices suggested for illiquid instruments.[6]

Local Volatility Models

Another class of "smile-consistent" option pricing models which is connected to but nevertheless quite different from the stochastic volatility models are the so-called "local volatility models." In contrast to the previously discussed stochastic volatility models, the local volatility models keep the appealing property of market completeness known from the Black-Scholes model. Still, it will be possible—at least theoretically—to hedge a long position in a European call by selling a certain number of shares of the underlying stock. In the case of local volatility models, the fit to the observed market prices is achieved by allowing for a locally deterministic volatility.

What does this mean? The volatility of tomorrow will still not be known today and is therefore random, but we know today, that the volatility of tomorrow can be described as a function of tomorrow's stock level S_t and the time t. This is achieved as follows. Imagine that we are given a complete set of prices for a European call option with maturity T, i.e., for every strike $X > 0$. Let $C(X)$ denote the corresponding option price. We know from Breeden and Litzenberger (1978) that it is possible to derive the risk-neutral density function f of the underlying stock price from these option prices by

$$f(X) = \frac{\partial^2}{\partial X^2} C(X)$$

---

[6] For further information about the theory and the empirical performance of stochastic volatility models, see Bakshi, Cao, and Chen (1997).

That is, the risk-neutral density function equals the second derivative of the call prices with respect to the strike.

Now we could ask the following question: Is there a volatility function $\sigma(t,S_t)$ such that the stochastic process defined by

$$\frac{dS_t}{S_t} = rdt + \sigma(t, S_t)dW_t$$

and starting in S_0 is generating exactly the terminal risk-neutral density function f defined by the market prices? Dupire (1994), Rubinstein (1994), and Derman and Kani (1994) gave the answer and showed that the local volatility $\sigma(t,S_t)$ can be obtained as a function of the strikes and the derivative of the market call prices with respect to the maturity and the second derivative with respect to the strike. The local volatility can be seen as an average over all instantaneous volatilities in a stochastic volatility framework.

Local volatility models allow for an easy calibration to market prices and prices of liquid options can be reproduced. In addition, the local volatility models define a complete market which means that a perfect hedge of all derivatives is possible—at least theoretically. Difficulties in the application of local volatility models can occur when the user has to decide which option prices to use for the calibration. In practice, a complete set of option prices, that is, an option price for every strike price and every maturity is never observable and additionally not all observable prices are reliable. A second issue is the choice of the functional form for the local volatility function. The concrete specification of the local volatility function as, for example, linear in S or linear in t or perhaps a polynomial in S and t or some other parametric function in S and t might strongly influence the result of the calibration procedure and as a consequence all derived quantities like hedge ratios or prices of exotic instruments. Last but not least, one disadvantage which was already mentioned before is the market prices are not explained but the model is simply calibrated to the market prices. Therefore, it might be that the model needs very frequent recalibration.[7]

Models with Jumps

The first popular jump model was suggested by Merton (1976) and imposes the following dynamic for the evolution of the underlying stock price:

---

[7] For a detailed analysis of the empirical performance of local volatility models, see Whaley, Fleming, and Dumas (1998) where the stability of the local volatility function through time is tested.

$$dS_t = S_{t-}((\mu - \lambda k)dt + \sigma dW_t + q dN_t)$$

where N denotes a Poisson process with intensity λ independent of the Brownian motion W and the jump size q is normally distributed with mean k and variance δ^2. S_{t-} denotes the left-side limit of S at time t.

The interpretation of the above equation is the following. Imagine that the current stock price is S_t and we are interested in the distribution S_{t+dt} where dt denotes a very small time step. Then the equation says that the return of the stock consists of a deterministic drift, a normally distributed noise, and a probability of λdt that a jump of mean size k will occur. The argument for these jumps is the fact that some fluctuations of stock markets cannot be explained by a Brownian motion which allows only for small variation in small time intervals.

Typically in the jump diffusion framework it is assumed that the risk associated with the jumps is idiosyncratic risk (i.e., no risk premium is paid for jump risk). Under this assumption, a pricing equation for European call options can be derived in the Merton model. Other popular jump diffusion processes have been suggested by Bakshi and Chen (1997a, 1997b) and Andersen and Andreasen (2001). These models are related or even belong to the already mentioned class of affine models as described in Duffie, Pan, and Singleton (2000).

The advantage of the jump diffusion is the greater variability in describing the evolution of a stock's price. The disadvantage concern again the fact that parameter estimation based on historical observations is difficult or not feasible. Therefore, the parameters which are obtained from a calibration procedure to market prices of liquid options can not be examined for internal consistency. It is not guaranteed that the process is able to capture the statistical patterns of the underlying stock, nor it is guaranteed that the model will lead to reliable prices for illiquid instruments. In this case, the same problems might arise as described in the previous two sections.

Models with Heavy-Tailed Returns

In trying to capture the empirically observed heavy-tailed and possibly skewed return distributions, some researchers and practitioners have tried to overcome the unrealistic assumption of a geometric Brownian motion underlying the Black-Scholes model by directly replacing the risk driver with a process exhibiting heavy-tailed increments. Theoretically there are two related possibilities to proceed. The first is provided by a concept called *subordination* and the second models the risk driver by a Lévy-process. As many Lévy processes may be represented as a subordinated Brownian motion and many subordinated processes turn out to be equivalent to the well-known Lévy processes, the distinction between the two approaches is not sharp and more a question of the underlying motivation.

The idea underlying of subordination is that one keeps the assumption of Brownian motion as the risk driver but replaces the physical clock by an artificial and random clock which reflects market activity. When market activity is high, the clock runs faster which compresses the path of the Brownian motion resulting in a more volatile pattern and when market activity is low the time scale is stretched, which decreases the volatility. This idea of a random clock is realized by means of a stochastic subordinator $(T_t)_{t \geq 0}$, i.e. a stochastic process with increasing paths. The risk driver $(Z_t)_{t \geq 0}$ is then defined as

$$Z_t = W_{t(t)} \quad t \geq 0$$

where $(W_t)_{t \geq 0}$ is a standard Brownian motion. Subordinated stock price models have been considered among many others by Mandelbrot and Taylor (1967), Rachev and Rüschendorf (1994), Madan and Seneta (1990), Janicki, Popova, Ritchken, and Woyczynski (1997), and Hurst, Platen, and Rachev (1999). A complete treatment of many variants of subordinated stock price models can be found in Rachev and Mittnik (2000).

It has been understood, that for special choices of the subordinator $(T_t)_{t \geq 0}$, the resulting process $(Z_t)_{t \geq 0}$ might turn out to be a well-known Lévy process. As an example, we mention the case where $(T_t)_{t \geq 0}$ is a maximally right skewed[8] stable motion with index of stability $\alpha/2$. In this case, the resulting process $(Z_t)_{t \geq 0}$ will be an α-stable Lévy motion. Therefore, the concept of subordination is related to the direct use of Lévy processes as risk drivers. There have been many suggestions as to which Lévy process is the most appropriate one to model the risk driver in stock price models. For example, Eberlein, Keller, and Prause (1998) have proposed the hyperbolic model and Carr and Wu (2000) the finite moment log-stable process. Carr and Wu (2004) have applied the concept of subordination to Lévy processes and have worked with time-changed Lévy processes.

An immediate advantage of these models is their capability of capturing the statistical properties of return distributions such as the frequently mentioned heavy tails and skewness. Disadvantages are difficult to state in general, but they include the Markovian structure of the processes which means that volatility clustering cannot be explained. Similar criticism as for the affine models apply also for the Lévy models as the parameter estimation is based on calibration to model prices and finally some models suffer from "too heavy tails" which means that second or higher

---

[8] In this context "maximally right skewed" means that the skewness parameter of the stable distribution equals one. Additionally, we assume that the index of stability $\alpha/2$ is less than one. These two facts imply that the support of this probability distribution is restricted to the positive half line.

moments or option prices might be infinite. The latter holds true for models based on α-stable Lévy motion and was overcome by Carr and Wu (2000) by using a finite moment log-stable process. The idea is to use a maximally left-skewed risk driver for the log-returns which in turn will generate finite exponential moments and finite option prices.

DISCRETE-TIME MODELS

When dealing with generalizations or variants of the Black-Scholes model in discrete time, we have to further distinguish the following two cases: (1) the state space (i.e., the set of possible values for the underlying stock) is finite or countable and (2) the state space is uncountable infinite. The former case includes the binomial model as its most prominent representative and further variants such as the trinomial model. In this section, we will focus on the latter case where the distribution of the underlying is continuous whereas the time scale, that is, the set of trading dates, is discrete.

Generally speaking, such models for the underlying are denoted as "time series models." The earliest representative of this class of models used for the pricing of options was examined by Rubinstein (1976) and Brennan (1979). They demonstrated that under certain assumptions regarding investor's preferences (i.e., on investor's utility functions) that the Black-Scholes formula still holds when the geometric Brownian motion is replaced by its discrete counterpart:

$$\log S_t - \log S_{t-1} = \mu - \frac{1}{2}\sigma^2 + \sigma\varepsilon_t, \quad \varepsilon_t \overset{iid}{\sim} N(0, 1) \qquad (19.1)$$

The left side of equation (19.1) equals the continuously-compounded return of the underlying stock over one time unit (e.g., trading days, weeks or year). Equation (19.1) tells us that this return consists of a deterministic component which equals $\mu - 0.5\sigma^2$ plus a noise component which is normally distributed with zero mean and variance σ^2. The parameters μ and σ^2 have the same meaning as in the continuous-time Black-Scholes model (i.e., they represent the expected rate of return of the stock price process and the rate of variance of the return process).[9]

---

[9] This can be seen by calculating

$$E_t \frac{S_t}{S_{t-1}} = e^\mu \text{ and } V(\log S_t - \log S_{t-1}) = \sigma^2$$

The advantage of the process given by equation (19.1) over a continuous-time specifications is the fact that the available data are always discrete. Consequently, the estimation of discrete-time processes is easier. Unfortunately, the discrete model in its present form is open to the same criticism as the Black-Scholes model: The model given by equation (19.1) cannot explain volatility clustering, heavy-tailed returns, and volatility smile. Therefore, we will present below three possible generalizations of the Rubinstein/Brennan framework and which are motivated by econometric arguments.

Econometric modeling of financial data means to provide the highest possible accuracy to the empirical observations or in other words to meet the statistical characteristics of financial data. The statistical characteristic of financial data such as stock returns mainly include the following features: Heavy tails, skewed and heavy-tailed residuals, volatility clustering, and possibly long-range dependence in the volatility and or the returns. Market consistent option pricing, on the other hand, means that the model reproduces the prices of the liquid market derivatives. Obviously both aspects are important for any investor depending on the current objectives: For risk management issues such as Value-at-Risk determination, the accurate statistical description of the data generating process is important whereas for pricing of illiquid instruments the reliability of the model prices plays the major role. The problem with both tasks is that the existing models focus either on the first or on the second task.

Duan Model

Duan (1995) proposed enhancing the modeling power of the discrete Black-Scholes model by incorporating a time-varying volatility. This can be done by assuming that the return volatility is governed by a GARCH process:

$$\log S_t - \log S_{t-1} = \mu_t - \frac{1}{2}\sigma_t^2 + \sigma_t\varepsilon_t, \quad \varepsilon_t \overset{iid}{\sim} N(0, 1)$$

(19.2)

$$\sigma_t^2 = \alpha_0 + \sum_{i=1}^{p} \alpha_i\sigma_{t-i}^2\varepsilon_{t-i}^2 + \sum_{i=1}^{q} \beta_i\sigma_{t-i}^2$$

Duan shows that under some assumptions on investors' preferences, which are related to those obtained previously by Brennan and Rubinstein, option prices are uniquely defined through the dynamics of the underlying stock price. The condition on investors' preferences involves a parameter λ—which can be denoted as market price of risk—and which allows the following decomposition of the expected rate of return:

$$\mu_t = r + \lambda \sigma_t$$

The risk-neutral process dynamic which must be used for determining option prices has the following form:

$$\log S_t - \log S_{t-1} = r - \frac{1}{2}\sigma_t^2 + \sigma_t \varepsilon_t, \quad \varepsilon_t \overset{iid}{\sim} N(0, 1)$$

$$\sigma_t^2 = \alpha_0 + \sum_{i=1}^{p} \alpha_i \sigma_{t-i}^2 (\varepsilon_{t-i} - \lambda)^2 + \sum_{i=1}^{q} \beta_i \sigma_{t-i}^2$$

The risk-neutral dynamic price of a European call option with strike X and time to maturity T is given by the following expression:

$$C = e^{-rT} E_Q \max(S_T - X, 0)$$

This expectation has to be calculated numerically.

Duan's option pricing model has the advantage that the process for the underlying stock price is significantly more realistic than its Black-Scholes counterpart. The GARCH process allows for the explanation of volatility clustering as well as for the explanation of symmetric volatility smiles. Nevertheless, the process dynamic of the Duan model cannot capture the fundamental pattern of return distributions such as the leverage effect and the left-skewed and heavy-tailed residuals.

Heston-Nandi Model

Heston and Nandi (2000) have proposed a GARCH option pricing model which—in contrast to the previously discussed model of Duan—has a quasi-closed-form solution for the option price. This property is a fundamental advantage if the model parameters are determined through calibration of model prices to market prices.

The main difference between the Heston-Nandi model and the Duan model is that it allows for correlation between the variance and the stock returns which helps explain the leverage effect. Another attractive feature of the Heston-Nandi model is the explicit recursion formula for the generating function of the terminal stock price. This representation can be used to efficiently determine option prices through a Fourier inversion formula.

All these properties are major advantages of the Heston-Nandi model but nevertheless the model does not significantly improve the statistical fit to the observed realizations under the objective measure. More concrete, even if the model allows for the efficient calibration to observed option prices it is not able to explain the observed prices.

GARMAX Model with STS-Distributed Innovations

Menn and Rachev (2004) suggest a time series model which exhibits satisfactory statistical fit to historic data and at the same time seems flexible enough to explain the market prices of liquid instruments. The process is designed to meet the needs of stock return or index return modeling and possesses the following form:

$$\log S_t - \log S_{t-1} = r_t - d_t + \lambda\sigma_t - \log g(\sigma_t) + \sigma_t \varepsilon_t, \; \varepsilon_t \sim P$$

(19.3)

$$\sigma_t^2 = \alpha_0 + \sum_{i=1}^{p} \alpha_i \sigma_{t-i}^2 \varepsilon_{t-i}^2 + \sum_{i=1}^{q} \beta_i \sigma_{t-i}^2$$

where r_t denotes the risk free rate of return, d_t the dividend rate, λ the market price of risk, and g the moment generating function of the distribution of ε^2.[10]

The model is very similar to the one of Duan (1995) and the main difference lays in the type of distribution for the innovation process. Instead of using the normal distribution, the model proposed by Menn and Rachev allows for skewness and heavy-tailed residuals by applying the class of STS distributions described in Chapter 4. As we know from our discussion of no-arbitrage pricing, the valuation of derivatives must be effected under the risk-neutral measure where the return on investment of all assets is equal to the risk-free rate. The following equation presents a risk-neutral dynamic of the time series model given by equation (19.3):

$$\log S_t - \log S_{t-1} = r_t - d_t - \log g(\sigma_t) + \sigma_t \varepsilon_t$$

(19.4)

$$\sigma_t^2 = \alpha_0 + \sum_{i=1}^{p} \alpha_i \sigma_{t-i}^2 (\varepsilon_t - \lambda)^2 + \sum_{i=1}^{q} \beta_i \sigma_{t-i}^2$$

---

[10] For the description of the model and the understanding of the sequel it is not necessary to know exactly the meaning of "moment generating function." The basic idea of this concept is similar to the one of a "characteristic function," and it is, besides the density function and the distribution function, another method to describe a probability distribution.

EXHIBIT 19.2 Example of a Implied Volatility Surface Generated with the STS-GARCH Model

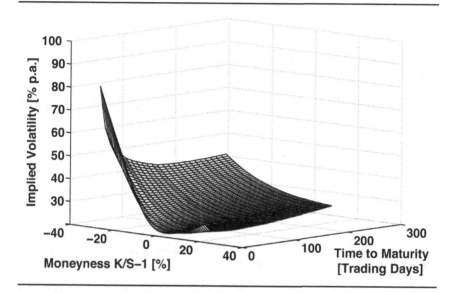

The STS-GARCH-model is able to produce volatility surfaces that are very similar to their market counterparts. An example of such a volatility surface is provided in Exhibit 19.2.

The presented methodology possesses one main advantage: The process dynamic is reliable in "both worlds"—the risk neutral world that is important for pricing purposes and under the objective measure, which is interesting for risk management and forecasting problems. Although these examples raise the hope that the model overcomes some significant disadvantages of the previously discussed models, its superior performance remains to be proven through a large-scaled empirical study.

REFERENCES

Andersen, L., and J. Andreasen. 2001. "Jump-Diffusion Processes: Volatility Smile Fitting and Numerical Methods for Option Pricing." *Review of Derivatives Research* 4: 231–262.

Bakshi, G. S., C. Q. Cao, and Z. Chen. 1997. "Empirical Performance of Alternative Option Pricing Models." *Journal of Finance* 52: 2003–2049.

Bakshi, G. S., and Z. Chen. 1997a. "An Alternative Valuation Model for Contingent Claims." *Journal of Financial Economics* 44: 799–826.

Bakshi, G. S., and Z. Chen. 1997b. "Equilibrium Valuation of Foreign Exchange Claims," *Journal of Finance* 52: 799–826.

Black, F. 1975. "Fact and Fantasy in the Use of Options." *Financial Analysts Journal,* July–August: 36–41, 61–72.

Black, F., and M. Scholes. 1973. "The Pricing of Corporate Liabilities." *Journal of Political Economy,* May–June: 637–659.

Black F. 1976. "Studies of Stock Price Volatility Changes." In *Proceedings of the 1976 Meetings of the American Statistical Association, Business and Economic Statistics Section:* S.177–181

Breeden, D., and R. Litzenberger. 1978. "Prices of State Contingent Claims Implicit in Option Prices." *Journal of Business* 51: 621–651.

Carr, P., and D. B. Madan. 1999. "Option Valuation using the Fast Fourier Transform." *Journal of Computational Finance* 2: 61–73.

Carr, P., and L. Wu. 2003. "The Finite Moment Log Stable Process and Option Pricing." *Journal of Finance* 58: 753–778.

Carr, P., and L. Wu. 2004. "Time-Changed Lévy Processes and Option Pricing." *Journal of Financial Economics* 71: 113–141.

Cox, J. C., and M. Rubinstein. 1985. *Option Markets.* Englewood Cliffs, NJ: Prentice-Hall.

Cox, J. C., and S. A. Ross. 1976. "The Valuation of Options for Alternative Stochastic Processes." *Journal of Financial Economics,* 3 (March): 145–166.

Cox, J. C., S. A. Ross, and M. Rubinstein. 1979. "Option Pricing: A Simplified Approach." *Journal of Financial Economics* 7: 229–263.

Derman, E., and I. Kani. 1994. "Riding on a Smile." *Risk* 7: 32–39.

Duan, J-C. 1995. "The GARCH Option Pricing Model." *Mathematical Finance* 5: 13–32.

Duffie, D., J. Pan, and K. J. Singleton. 2000. "Transform Analysis and Asset Pricing for Affine Jump Diffusions." *Econometrica* 68: 1343–1376.

Dupire, B. 1994. "Pricing with a Smile." *Risk* 7: 18–20.

Eberlein, E., U. Keller, and K. Prause. 1998. "New Insights into Smile, Mispricing, and Value at Risk: The Hyperbolic Model." *Journal of Business* 71: 371–406.

Fleming, J., B. Dumas, and R. E. Whaley. 1998. "Implied Volatility Functions: Empirical Tests." *Journal of Finance* 53: 2059–2106

Geske, R. 1979. "A Note on an Analytical Formula for Unprotected American Call Options on Stocks with Known Dividends." *Journal of Financial Economics*, December: 375–380.

Geske, R. 1981. "Comment on Whaley's Note." *Journal of Financial Economics*, June: 213–215.

Gultekin, N., R. Rogalski, and S. Tinic. 1982. "Option Pricing Model Estimates: Some Empirical Results." *Financial Management* 11: 58–69.

Heston, S. L. 1993. "A Closed Form Solution for Options with Stochastic Volatility with Applications to Bond and Currency Options." *Review of Financial Studies* 6: 327–343.

Heston, S. L., and S. Nandi. 2000. "A Closed-Form GARCH Option Valuation Model." *Review of Financial Studies* 13: 585–625.

Hull, J. C. 1998. *Introduction to Futures and Options Markets: Third Edition.* Upper Saddle River, NJ: Prentice Hall.

Hull, J. C., and A. White. 1987. "The Pricing of Options on Assets with Stochastic Volatilities." *Journal of Finance* 42: 281–300.

Hurst, S. R., E. Platen, and T.S. Rachev. 1999. "Option Pricing for a Logstable Asset Price Model." *Mathematical and Computer Modelling* 29: 105–119.

Janicki, A. W., I. Popova, P. H. Ritchken, and W. A. Woyczynski. 1997. "Option Pricing Bounds in an α-Stable Security Market." *Communication in Statistics-Stochastic Models* 13: 817–839.

Lewis, A. L. 2000. *Option Valuation under Stochastic Volatility.* North Beach, CA: Finance Press.

Madan, D. B. and E. Seneta. 1990. "The Variance Gamma (V.G.) Model for Share Market Returns." *Journal of Business* 63: 511-524.

Madan, D. B., P. Carr, and E. C. Chang. 1998. "The Variance Gamma Process and Option Pricing." *European Finance Review* 2: 79–105.

Mandelbrot, B. B., and M. Taylor. 1967. "On the Distribution of Stock Price Differences." *Operations Research* 15: 1057–1062.

Menn, C. and S. T. Rachev. 2005. "Smoothly Truncated Stable Distributions, GARCH-Models and Option Pricing." Technical Report, University of California at Santa Barbara.

Merton, R. 1973. "The Theory of Rational Option Pricing." *Bell Journal of Economics and Management Science* 4 (Spring): 141–183.

Popova, I., and P. H. Ritchken. 1998. "On Bounding Option Prices in Paretian Stable Markets." *Journal of Derivatives*, Summer: 32–43.

Rachev, S. T., and S. Mittnik. 2000. *Stable Paretian Models in Finance*, Chichester: John Wiley & Sons.

Rachev, S. T., and L. Rüschendorf. 1994. "Models for Option Prices." *Theory of Probability and Its Applications* 39: 120–152.

Rendleman, R. J. and B. J. Bartter. 1979. "Two-State Option Pricing." *Journal of Finance* 34: 1092–1100.

Roll, R. 1977. "An Analytic Formula for Unprotected American Call Options on Stocks with Known Dividends." *Journal of Financial Economics*, November: 251–258.

Rubinstein, M. 1985. "Nonparametric Tests of Alternative Option Pricing Models Using All Reported Trades and Quotes on the 30 Most Active CBOE Option Classes from August 23, 1976 through August 31, 1978." *Journal of Finance* 40: 455–480.

Rubinstein, Mark. 1994. "Implied Binomial Trees." *Journal of Finance* 49: 771–818.

Scott, Louis O. 1987. "Option Pricing when the Variance Changes Randomly: Theory, Estimation, and an Application." *Journal of Financial and Quantitative Analysis* 22: 419–438.

Sharpe, W. F. 1978. *Investments*. Englewood Cliffs, NJ: Prentice Hall.

Stein, E. M., and J. C. Stein. 1991. "Stock Price Distributions with Stochastic Volatility." *Review of Financial Studies* 4: 727–752.

Tompkins, R. G. 2001. "Implied Volatility Surfaces: Uncovering Regularities for Options on Financial Futures." *European Journal of Finance* 7: 198–230.

Whaley, R. 1981. "On the Valuation of American Call Options on Stocks with Known Dividends." *Journal of Financial Economics*, June: 207–211.

Wiggins, James B. 1987. "Option Values Under Stochastic Volatility: Theory and Empirical Estimates." *Journal of Financial Economics* 19: 351–377.

Index

3-tuple. *See* Triple

Absolute distance, minimization, 48
Absolute priority rule, deviations, 259
Accrued interest, recovery, 262
ACF. *See* Autocorrelation function
AD distance. *See* Anderson-Darling distance
AD statistic. *See* Anderson-Darling statistic
Advanced measurement approach, 286
Aggregated stochastic models. *See* Operational risk
Aging effect, 35
Aging technology, 284
Akgiray, A., 8
Allen, L., 285, 291
Alpha quantile (α quantile), 105
    obtaining, 50
Alpha stable (α-stable) Lévy processes, 344–345
Alpha stable (α-stable) random variables, 87
Alpha stable (α-stable) sub-Gaussian distribution, 188
Alpha stable distributions, 81
American options, 296
Andersen, L., 349
Anderson-Darling distance (AD distance), 115–116
Anderson-Darling statistic (AD statistic), 116, 164
Andreasen, J., 349
Anson, J.P., 256, 278
AR. *See* Autoregressive
ARCH. *See* Autoregressive conditional heteroskedasticity
Arithmetic Brownian motion, 153
ARMA. *See* Autoregressive moving average
ARMAX processes, 129, 184
    linearity, 130
    stochastic structure, 129
ARMAX-GARCH process, 131
Arthur, WB, 2, 8
Artzner, P., 194, 243, 246, 262, 279
Asset returns, 82

distributional anomalies, 200
distributions, 4
process, volatility, 264
scenarios, mapping, 270
Asset/liability strategy, 296
Assets
    arbitrary fractions, trading, 332
    current value, 264
    decomposition. *See* Portfolio
    prices
        dependence structure, 72
        obtaining, 224
    pricing models, 223
    put option, 257
    risk, 186
Asset-specific scheme, 226
Assumptions, importance, 334–335
Asymmetry, 48
Asymptotic mean dispersion (MQ) approach, 188
Atlantic options, 296
Autocorrelation, 134–136
Autocorrelation function (ACF), 125. *See also* Autoregressive processes; Partial ACF
    estimation, shape, 135
Autoregressive (AR) path, 128
Autoregressive (AR) processes, 122–126
    ACF, 130
Autoregressive (AR) time series model, 125
Autoregressive conditional heteroskedasticity (ARCH), 6
    component, 278
    models, 130–133, 226, 277
Autoregressive moving average (ARMA), 6, 122–129
    ARMA-GARCH
        example, 133–140
        framework, 133
        models/processes, 164–166, 175–176
        model, 274–276